THE **EMPOWERED** UNIVERSITY

THE
EMPOWERED
UNIVERSITY

SHARED
LEADERSHIP

CULTURE
CHANGE

AND
ACADEMIC
SUCCESS

FREEMAN A. HRABOWSKI III
WITH PHILIP J. ROUS AND PETER H. HENDERSON

Johns Hopkins University Press | Baltimore

Johns Hopkins University Press
2715 North Charles Street
Baltimore, Maryland 21218-4363
www.press.jhu.edu

Library of Congress Cataloging-in-Publication Data

Names: Hrabowski, Freeman A., author. | Rous, Philip J., 1961– author. | Henderson, Peter H., author.
Title: The empowered university : shared leadership, culture change, and academic success / Freeman A. Hrabowski III. With Philip J. Rous and Peter H. Henderson.
Description: Baltimore : Johns Hopkins University Press, 2019. | Includes bibliographical references and index.
Identifiers: LCCN 2019005188 | ISBN 9781421432915 (hardcover : acid-free paper) | ISBN 9781421432922 (electronic) | ISBN 1421432919 (hardcover : acid-free paper) | ISBN 1421432927 (electronic)
Subjects: LCSH: University of Maryland, Baltimore County. | Educational Leadership—Maryland—Baltimore County. | Educational Change—Maryland—Baltimore County. | Community and College—Maryland—Baltimore County. | Universities and colleges—United States—Administration.
Classification: LCC LD3231.M6954 H73 2019 | DDC 378.752/71—dc23
LC record available at https://lccn.loc.gov/2019005188

A catalog record for this book is available from the British Library.

Special discounts are available for bulk purchases of this book. For more information, please contact Special Sales at 410-516-6936 or specialsales@press.jhu.edu.

Johns Hopkins University Press uses environmentally friendly book materials, including recycled text paper that is composed of at least 30 percent post-consumer waste, whenever possible.

To our UMBC colleagues

Contents

Preface

It's about Us

"It's not about me. It's about us."

When outsiders comment on the successes or failures of a university, they often focus on the institution's president, who tends to get the attention, the accolades, or the blame. This view of a university and its progress is misguided, because it takes a community of colleagues working together to make a university thrive for its students and faculty. This book is about advancing a university and supporting academic success by empowering talented colleagues through a deliberate strategy of cultivating shared leadership and culture.

Higher education matters. It absolutely does, and now more than ever, for our students, our society, and our economy. It matters to families that want to see their children and loved ones succeed in a dynamic economy; it matters to students who want to learn about the world and what it means to be human; it matters to employers who seek applicants with technical skills, an aptitude for critical thinking, and the ability to work in teams; it matters to our democracy, which thrives when its citizens are well educated; it matters to the health of our society as it grows increasingly complex and diverse. Student success is important to all of these. It requires individual and social investments. It requires all of us to ensure that our colleges and universities are healthy and work effectively to support students in the classroom, in college, and in life. When this happens, we all benefit.

It is within this context that the culture of our campuses also matters now more than ever, because the values, attitudes, goals, and behaviors that compose a culture limit or encourage what is possible. And so we must each ask of our campuses, "Have we created a shared culture that enables us as a community to work toward and achieve our goals?"

In *The Geography of Bliss*, Eric Weiner discusses how we perceive and relate to our culture: "Where we are is vital to who we are. By 'where,' I'm speaking not only of our physical environment but also of our cultural environment. Culture is the sea we swim in—so pervasive, so all-consuming, that we fail to notice its existence until we step out of it."[1] We must step out of it and think critically about the culture we "swim in." It is challenging to perceive and understand fully the culture of an institution, although perhaps the best place to start is from the perspective of our universities as communities. It is even more challenging to change that culture, intentionally or otherwise. Yet, this is a practice we must adopt and be mindful of as we lead and administer in both the short and the long term at our institutions.

At the University of Maryland, Baltimore County (UMBC), we see the "sea" that is our culture reflected in our commonly held values, norms, mission, goals, and actions. We live this culture in the questions we ask, the achievements we measure and applaud, and the initiatives we support. We enact this culture as a community as we empower administrators, staff, faculty, and students so that anyone can be a leader in identifying and implementing the work we need to do. We build this culture through the "values" we hold in common. We put people first. We emphasize and live shared governance. We embrace and incentivize innovation and risk-taking. We work tirelessly to improve the academic success of students and faculty in a way that supports all students—something we call inclusive excellence.

Culture change is difficult. It does not happen overnight. When we first invested ourselves in work we considered critical for supporting student learning and achievement at UMBC, we hoped to make a difference in the success of our students. We also hoped to change our campus culture, at least a little bit. What we found, though, has been a fascinating, and perhaps unanticipated, transformation—one that has empowered all members of our community to make a difference in the lives of our students. With each programmatic success that sought to alter student outcomes, more and more members of our community began to look at our values, goals, and work in a different way. It was imperceptible at times, but our culture slowly changed. And then, one day, we realized that our campus had changed, the paradigm had shifted, the culture had evolved into something different—with an attitude that saw innovation in teaching and learning as a constant aspiration and with an ethos that embraced and valued inclusivity.

Changing the culture takes hard work, dedication, and commitment—what we call "grit"—over a long period. As we have developed a campus culture that embraces innovation, what has mattered most is a "habit of mind" that is intensely reflective, one that prompts us to always look hard in the mirror. As we do so, we note our strengths and weaknesses, assess our opportunities and challenges, ask what we are doing and why, and encourage ourselves to think about how we can do our work better. We bring objective quantitative and qualitative data to this analysis. We have inclusive, sometimes difficult conversations, to create a shared understanding of problems, opportunities, options for action, uncertainties, and risks. In performing these tasks, we create a shared narrative of where we have been, where we are, and where we are going.

In a sense, this book is a story about how we created a narrative that is both powerful and empowering, one that enables change and sustains it. This narrative and its themes will necessarily change over time. For example, early in my presidency I emphasized that "it is cool to be smart." As our work evolved, though, we collectively shifted our emphasis, and today my colleagues and I talk about the importance of "grit." We now emphasize how, with hard work over time, we—administrators, staff, faculty, and students—can succeed. We also remind ourselves constantly that "success is never final." We must always do better and be better, because the world of which we, as a public university, are a part is also constantly evolving and the rate of change is accelerating. The needs of our dynamic society and the demands of a changing economy require that we respond, adapt, and address new opportunities and challenges as we prepare our students, engage our community, and conduct the research, scholarship, and creative work that enrich us all.

At its core, the empowered university has both shared culture and shared leadership. The latter of these requires emphasizing and living out the notion of shared governance. But it is also more than that. Senior leadership on campus must develop a vision, using an inclusive process, and then encourage deep engagement from those who will be responsible for whether that vision is realized and sustained—our colleagues, including administrators, staff, faculty, and students.

When people talk about UMBC and leadership, I respond by saying that the progress we have made as a campus is because of the dedicated, innovative work of many people over a long period of time. The president and other senior administrators, staff, and faculty play a critical role. They must cultivate allies and champions in our work. Beyond this, they must also empower others to take the initiative and to be the leaders in place—whether that means challenging and working with the administration to take action or conceiving and implementing a new initiative or program.

Leadership can and does come from many sources:

- Women scientists who challenged us to work with them to increase the success of women in our STEM faculty.
- Faculty who have redesigned their courses to improve teaching, learning, and student success.
- A biochemist on our faculty who is one of the nation's most successful mentors of underrepresented minority students in his field.
- Staff who have kept our institution on the leading edge of information technology and data analytics.
- Students who thirty years ago demanded we address and improve our racial climate, and students who just recently challenged us to be a national model for preventing sexual

assault and creating a fair, thorough, and transparent Title IX process.

This book is written in my voice, the voice of Freeman Hrabowski. However, it is the combined work of three authors, our provost Philip Rous, my senior advisor Peter Henderson, and me. We created this writing partnership so that the book would be richer in both detail and perspective. But we also intended this partnership to symbolically make an important point about the work we describe here: Successful, sustained change is never about the work or ideas of just one person. It takes a campus to create a university culture that embraces inclusive excellence and innovation and a campus to support success for all students.

It takes a campus to write about it, too. In researching this book, we listened widely to faculty, staff, and students about their experiences so we could include their voices as well. These conversations not only provided information and perspective to our immediate work but also produced another dimension to the notion that "success is never final." Some of the successful initiatives are even now facing ongoing challenges, new issues, and occasional backsliding, and we were also alerted to additional or developing issues that we, as an institution and a community of learners, must tackle.

This book consists of two parts. In the first part, we discuss what it means to be an empowered university and how that has made a difference at our institution, UMBC. In the second part, we discuss key chapters in our history, covering topics from racial climate to student success, course redesign to service learning, and data analytics to faculty diversity. These are tough topics and tough issues to tackle at any institution. In some areas we have become a national model; in other areas, we are still striving to achieve our goals.

UMBC is unique in many ways, but our story offers lessons for any institution of higher education. The state of Maryland established us at a critical moment, for our society and for higher education. Authorized in 1963 and opened in 1966, we launched just as the baby boom came of age and as Congress enacted the Higher Education Act of 1965 and the Civil Rights Act of 1964. We evolved in parallel with American higher education just as it underwent a major transformation over a dramatic fifty-year period. Other institutions founded at about the same time—for instance, George Mason University, the University of Texas at Dallas, the University of California San Diego, and the University of Alabama at Birmingham—also grew into mature institutions during this period, following a variety of paths. However, university innovation can flourish on any campus, including older ones that have dynamic leaders who articulate a clear vision. For example, we admire the terrific work at such institutions as Arizona State and Georgia State, where Michael Crow and Mark Becker have led their colleagues in institutional transformation, reshaping the higher education enterprise, and enabling many more students to succeed.

One of the challenges in looking back over fifty years at the evolution of a university is that memories will vary about what happened and interpretations will have changed because of other experiences. It helps to have different eyes—people with different experiences and perspectives—examining the facts of the events involved. They ask the hard questions that can clarify what was happening at any given point in time, what the context was, and how decisions were made and implemented.

We would like to thank our colleagues who participated in conversations that informed this book: Vivian Armor, Raji Baradwaj, Taryn Bayles, Bev Bickel, Lee Boot, Stephen Bradley, Lamar Davis, Michael Dillon, David Fink, Eric Ford, Amy Froide, Tiffany Gierasch, David Gleason, Keith Harmon, Ellen Hemmerly, David Hoffman, Kathleen Hoffman, Bobbie Hoye, Tracy Irish, Anupam Joshi, George Karabatis, Tyson King-Meadows, William LaCourse, Diane Lee, Jeff Leips, Sarah Leupen, Jason Loviglio, John Martello, Gib Mason, Patrice McDermott, Yvette Mozie-Ross, Eileen O'Brien, Kathy O'Dell, Marc Olano, Timothy Phin, Autumn Reed, Penny Rheingans, Phyllis Robinson, Julie Ross, Philip Rous, Anne Rubin, Janet Rutledge,

Lynne Schafer, Rehana Shafi, Sally Shivnan, Greg Simmons, Anne Spence, Jack Suess, Joby Taylor, Renetta Tull, Michele Wolff, Nancy Young, and Marc Zupan. Connie Pierson, associate vice provost in institutional research, also promptly responded to our many requests for data. It does take a campus.

Several colleagues also read background materials or specific chapters and offered invaluable suggestions. Greg Simmons, Jack Suess, David Hoffman, and Patrice McDermott read and suggested edits for several chapters. Autumn Reed was especially helpful in providing in-depth review and editing for our chapters on the ADVANCE program and faculty diversity. Greg, Jack, David, Pat, and Autumn deserve credit for substantially improving the manuscript. Any errors of fact or interpretation, however, are ours.

We have also benefited from the writings of our colleagues who have documented their innovative work at UMBC, including William LaCourse and his colleagues, who are documenting their innovative work in teaching and learning in the natural sciences; Kenneth Maton and colleagues, who have researched and written extensively about the Meyerhoff Scholars Program; Michael Summers and colleagues, who are actively documenting their work in adapting the Meyerhoff program at other campuses; Linda Hodges, director of our Faculty Development Center, who has recently written a book on improving teaching in the sciences; and Jack Suess and John Fritz, who have authored pieces on our pioneering work in information technology and data analytics. We are particularly indebted to George LaNoue, professor emeritus of political science and public policy, whose book *Improbable Excellence: The Saga of UMBC* arrived just in time for our institution's fiftieth anniversary and also just in time to provide us with the larger context of the history of UMBC.

It really is about "us" as a campus. One person does not, and cannot, accomplish alone everything we have achieved at UMBC over the past thirty years. I have had the privilege of serving as president with terrific provosts, including Arthur Johnson, Elliot Hirshman, and Philip Rous. I would like to thank all of my colleagues who have served over the years as vice presidents, vice provosts, and deans during my time as president, including my current group of vice presidents: Lynne Schaefer (finance and administration), Nancy Young (student affairs), Jack Suess (information technology), Greg Simmons (institutional advancement), and Karl Steiner (research). Similarly, I would like to thank the staff in the Office of the President, including Doug Pear, Tot Wolston, Lisa Akchin, Peter Henderson, Elyse Ashburn, Candace Dodson-Reed, Anthony Lane, Karen Wensch, Teresa Lupinek, Dawn Stoute, and Bethany Walter, who have been terrific colleagues and have worked with me to advance the university. UMBC has also enjoyed the support of the University System of Maryland leadership.

Lastly, Peter, Philip, and I would like to thank our wives, Laura, Sabrina, and Jackie, respectively, for all of their support in our work at UMBC. They have understood how important this work is to each of us and to our colleagues and students. For that support, we will always be grateful.

Freeman A. Hrabowski III

Note: During UMBC's early years, the campus leader was referred to as "chancellor." During Michael Hooker's term, the state of Maryland reorganized its higher education system and the campus leader assumed the title of "president." In this book we will refer to the first four leaders—Kuhn, Lee, Dorsey, and Hooker—as chancellor and Hrabowski as president.

Part I

1

And Then We Did It

The basketball game tipped off on Friday, March 16, 2018, at 9:35 p.m. Last game of the evening.

At 9:36 p.m, just one minute into the game, Seth Davis, a television commentator on men's basketball, tweeted, "Virginia. Sharpie."[1] For those who don't follow basketball, this means that Seth was already writing off UMBC and writing the University of Virginia (UVA) into the next round of his tournament bracket. For him, it was "game over." The UMBC men's basketball team, Virginia's sixteenth-seed opponent, was already history.

But as we now know, that dismissive prediction turned out to be premature. The underdog Retrievers were not going quietly, and something remarkable was about to happen.

At halftime, the score was Virginia 21, UMBC 21. At 10:46 p.m., just after halftime, @bleachrpreachr tweeted, "RT if you had to Google what UMBC stands for tonight."[2]

Ten minutes later, when UMBC had achieved a commanding lead it would not surrender, Jon Heyman, another sports commentator, tweeted, "UMBC is beating Virginia by 14. UMBC looks fantastic! BTW, anyone know what UMBC is?"[3] @UMBCAthletics tweeted back, "University of Maryland Baltimore County, who are you?"[4]

When it was over, we had made history. Our 74–54 upset win over Virginia was the first time a sixteenth seed had beaten a first seed in the first round of the National Collegiate Athletic Association (NCAA) men's basketball tournament. Former CBS News anchor Dan Rather tweeted, "Do they make glass slippers this big? UMBC carved their program on the Mt. Rushmore of Cinderella stories. I've never seen this much shock and awe on the hardwood. I watched every minute."[5]

But then Rather ended his tweet with an insight that spoke not only about a basketball game but also about the character of our university. He said, *"Whenever you hear, 'we can't,' tell them 'UMBC.'"*

America's Team

For a weekend, we were "Cinderella" and "America's Team." Our bookstore sold more swag overnight than it typically did in a year. And people across the country did google "Who is UMBC?" Many found their way to our website, which, for a time during the second half of the game, crashed under the heavy traffic.

Visitors to our website found more than our success in athletics. They discovered our commitment to and our success in making a difference in the lives of our students. We did not have to invent a narrative to impress those who came to see who we were; we already had an authentic story about academic excellence, inclusivity, and innovation over three decades waiting for people to discover it.

They found that the *US News & World Report* ranks UMBC among the top ten national universities for innovation and for undergraduate teaching.[6]

They found that UMBC ranks in the top ten among research universities in undergraduate computing degrees, along with Carnegie Mellon, University of Washington, Pennsylvania State University, and George Mason, and ahead of Georgia Tech and the Massachusetts Institute of Technology.[7] They would see that we have programs to increase the number of women in computer science and people of all backgrounds in cybersecurity,[8] and that we also have an initiative to educate students who will become strong science and mathematics teachers in under-resourced, urban schools.[9]

They might have found that 40 percent of our graduates in the natural sciences eventually go on to graduate school, and that we support workforce development nationally as a major feeder for employment at the National Security Agency, the US Navy, Northrop Grumman, and other major corporations and government agencies.[10] Our alumni include the president of Clemson, the director of the Johns Hopkins Applied Physic Laboratory, the chair of neurosurgery at Vanderbilt, and the US surgeon general.

They found that UMBC educates more African Americans who go on to earn an MD-PhD than any other institution in the nation,[11] and that we also produce more African Americans who go on to earn a PhD in the natural sciences and engineering than any institution that is not classified as a historically black college and university (HBCU).[12] Our graduates are tenured faculty at the most prestigious universities in the nation, from Harvard to Duke.

They found that our chess team has been national champions several times over the past decade,[13] and that UMBC's "Cyber-Dawgs" are the 2017 National Cyber Defense Champions.[14]

They might have even noted that our men's soccer team had recently made it to the Final Four of the NCAA men's soccer tournament in 2014, where we were knocked out by UVA, a fate we had just avenged.[15] (At that time we also heard the question, "Who is UMBC?" The answer was often, "A team from somewhere in Maryland, I think.")[16]

After the game, the text messages, calls, and interviews were endless and overwhelming, taking hours to work through them all. I did not go to bed until 6:00 a.m. on Saturday, March 17, and even then I was able to sleep for just a few hours.

As we woke up later on Saturday, my colleagues and I found ourselves in a media whirlwind, working enthusiastically to make sure the important stories about UMBC as an academic community were not lost amid the excitement surrounding the basketball team. While fielding further inquiries throughout the day, I worked with my chief of staff, Elyse Ashburn, to write an article for the *Atlantic*, which we titled "The Secret behind the Greatest Upset in College Basketball History" and subtitled "UMBC's big win wasn't a miracle; it was a well-executed plan."[17] Through this article we attempted to get out ahead of events and, instead of merely reacting to the media, present our own authentic narrative about UMBC, the significance of the upset, and the core values we shared within our campus community.

Our primary message in the *Atlantic* focused on how we had set a bold goal for the academic success of our students and had accomplished it despite the skepticism and challenges we had faced:

> We've defied the odds before. Three decades ago, nobody believed you could close the achievement gap between white and underrepresented minority students, who were disproportionately likely to be lower-income and to be less academically prepared, without adjusting academic standards. But UMBC and the philanthropist Robert Meyerhoff didn't believe it had to be that way. We believed you could set high expectations and, with appropriate support, not only help minority students succeed but also excel in some of the toughest fields. We started the Meyerhoff Scholars Program to support, challenge, and mentor underrepresented minority students in the sciences, technology, engineering, and math (STEM). Today, the university is a top producer of African American graduates who go on to earn Ph.D.s in the sciences, and is the leading producer of ones who go on to earn MD-Ph.D.s. . . . *Everybody thought it couldn't be done because it hadn't been done before. And then we did it.*

Our second message emphasized how important it is for UMBC to be a model of inclusivity for our twenty-first-century American society:

> What we saw Friday night reflected inclusive excellence, people of diverse backgrounds, races, and economic classes working together. It's clear from commenters in the media, on social media, and in other

venues, that many people were impressed by the rich diversity of our community, not only on the court, but in the band, on the dance team and cheer squad, and in the audience of alumni, faculty, staff, and students. *We encourage broad participation and interaction among all groups— and in so doing, we are reflecting what we hope America will become.*"[18]

In these divisive times, we are what America hopes to be.

As I reflected further on the sudden and unanticipated national interest in our story, I was struck by how much America loves an underdog. Deep down in our collective psyche we hold to a fundamental belief that in America *anyone* who works hard can win. This is the core of the American dream, that by working hard and playing by the rules you can and will create a better life for yourself and your family.

This notion also lies at the core of what we are about at UMBC. No matter what your background, if you are serious about the work, you can succeed at UMBC, and the UMBC community will also work hard to ensure that you do. Within this context, it is perhaps not surprising that UMBC's mascot is "True Grit." At some institutions they say at freshmen convocation, "Look to your left, look to your right; only two of you will make it." At UMBC, we say, "Look to your left, look to your right; all of you will succeed and if you don't, we haven't done our job."

Of course, the odds were against us in the basketball game, just as one might have thought the odds were against us thirty years ago when we aspired as an institution to improve the academic experiences and outcomes of our students. And yet, UMBC has continued to "punch above its weight," not just in men's basketball but also in the difference we make in the lives of our students and the academic program we provide them. So there was a third important message that I wanted to communicate, one that I told the *New York Times* after the game: "When I think about who we are as an institution and what happened last night, it represents what we tell our students: *If you work hard, there can be these special moments where you're moving towards greatness.*"[19]

Unapologetically Aspirational

Just before March Madness began, I had participated in an event with a panel moderated by Jeff Selingo, former editor at the *Chronicle of Higher Education* and now senior advisor and professor of the practice at Arizona State, entitled "Public Higher Education at the Crossroads." My fellow panelists included presidents Michael Crow of Arizona State, Gordon Gee of West Virginia, Angel Cabrera of George Mason, and Terry Sullivan of UVA. We had a terrific conversation about public perceptions of our universities, state support for public higher education, the mission of public universities, and the kinds of innovations our campuses can implement to better support student success.

It was a coincidence that President Sullivan and I were there together at that time. We took the opportunity to tease each other, all in good fun, with the prospect of the first-round NCAA basketball game between UVA and UMBC looming later in the week. There was something of a point I wanted to make in my good-natured banter, though. Here we were, UMBC, just fifty years old and still working on raising our first $100 million in endowment, going up against one of the finest universities in America, an institution founded more than two hundred years ago by Thomas Jefferson and with almost $9 billion in the bank. My point was that while we might be seen as David going up against Goliath, nonetheless it is critical—for America and for Americans—that all public institutions of higher education, regardless of their pedigree, should be strong.

In fact, earlier that day, UMBC was in the spotlight at another forum, and it was an opportunity to discuss how we had become a strong public university. At the Marriott Marquis Hotel in Washington, DC, Ted Mitchell, president of the American Council on Education (ACE), called me to the stage during the plenary session at the organization's annual meeting to present me with the ACE Lifetime Achievement Award. "Hrabowski has led UMBC since 1992, transforming it into an institution that redefines excellence in higher education through an inclusive culture that connects innovative teaching and learning, research across disciplines, and civic engagement," the ACE announcement had said. Now, up on the stage, Ted added, "President Hrabowski has built UMBC into a powerhouse engine of social mobility and academic excellence, particularly in the area of expanding the number of minority students pursuing degrees in the fields of science and technology."[20]

I accepted the award on behalf of the university and my colleagues. The presentation of the award focused on me, of course, because the attention is so often focused on the leader of an institution. However, the body of work ACE was celebrating with the award was a communal achievement over many years: the accomplishment of our faculty, staff, and students. What was so wonderful was that the entire President's Council, along with others from UMBC, had made the trip from Baltimore to Washington for the awards luncheon. So, after thanking Ted for the award, the first thing I did was acknowledge my colleagues. One person does not, and cannot, accomplish alone everything we have achieved at UMBC over the past thirty years.

Our faculty and staff have appreciated that we used the public visibility and interest arising from our success in basketball to shine a light on the strength of our academic programs and our shared values as a community. It takes a community and its many stakeholders—including and especially our faculty and staff—to produce excellence at an institution like UMBC. The members of our community are called to this important work because it reflects their values and commitment to student success, and we encourage participation through difficult conversations, by asking challenging questions of ourselves, and by being open to different points of view. We recognize that we can agree to disagree with civility by understanding that we share the same core values and then come together to support that which moves us forward. Within this collaborative culture we create the commitment and buy-in that lead to and support innovation. So, I wanted the award to honor the careers of the many people on campus who have transformed the lives of thousands of students. As the saying goes, *It takes a village.*"

We received extensive, substantive coverage in the media over the weekend following our upset victory, and it brought attention to who we are academically. "For so long, it was up to Hrabowski to tell the story as frequently and eloquently as he could. He did it well, but there were still many who missed the message. Then the basketball team made history, and the nation has never been more curious about the House of Grit," wrote the *Washington Post* on the morning of March 17 about UMBC.[21]

The March 17 headline in the *Baltimore Sun* was "Never Heard of UMBC? MIT Has. And Cal Tech. And Harvard. And Stanford," the point being that many of our well-prepared students, including underrepresented minorities in the natural sciences and engineering, routinely move on to institutions like these to earn the PhD or MD-PhD.[22] The *Sun* wrote that we are "something of a nerd factory (and proud of it) that churns out future research scientists, computer scientists, engineers and MD-PhDs at an astonishing rate."

Similarly, the headline in the *New York Times* was "Cinderella Story? It's True for UMBC in Academics, Too." The *Times* wrote that our victory had

> catapulted a school whose competitive claim to fame had long been chess into sports history. But the U.M.B.C. Cinderella story transcends athletics and has been decades in the making. The university, founded in 1966, is better known for producing the most African-American students who go on to complete combined M.D.-Ph.D. programs than it is for turning out professional athletes. Before its 20-point win over the nation's top-ranked basketball team, it was the reigning National Collegiate Cyber Defense Competition champion. A statue of the school's mascot, a Chesapeake Bay retriever named True Grit, has a shiny nose from the tradition of students' rubbing it for good luck before finals, rather than before big games.[23]

UMBC's commitment to academic quality and rigor is real. It's no coincidence that two of the strongest players on the basketball team, Jairus Lyles and Joe Sherburne, earned 4.0 grade point averages in the fall semester before the game or that Joe was named a First-Team Academic All-American. On March 17, the *Washington Post*, which published three articles about us that day—about the game, our social media, and the university—highlighted how "the basketball team exemplifies the spirit of UMBC, which is *unapologetically aspirational.*"[24]

We often read a quote from Nelson Mandela at our commencements: "It always seems impossible until it is done." Indeed, everybody thought a sixteenth seed couldn't win in the first round, because it hadn't been done before. Everybody thought an institutional effort to support underrepresented minority students in STEM could not succeed, because they had not seen it.

But then we did it. As a campus, we are a community, we are inclusive, we are unapologetically aspirational, we aim high and encourage our students to do so, we work hard to get there, and we punch above our weight. We aim to be what America wants to be.

Why? Because higher education matters for our students and for America.

2

Higher Education Matters

Higher education matters. It absolutely does.

The American Council on Education, when presenting me (and therefore UMBC) with a Lifetime Achievement Award, asked me to speak at their annual meeting on the question "Does Higher Education Matter?" My answer was, "Does higher education matter? Does college matter?" I looked out at the lunchtime audience and said, "Just look around. Where would any of us be without the education we have received?" I then asked those who were first in their family or first generation to go to college to stand, and much of the audience stood. "When people ask me 'Does higher education matter?' I say, 'Absolutely!'"

Higher education matters for our students and for America. Many have challenged this notion over the past decade or more, asking for our "value statement," questioning public support for our institutions and wondering aloud, "Is college worth it?" And many of us, defensively, have responded almost apologetically, perhaps with a rather narrow focus on the way we help students acquire the "skills" for a job.

We must tell our stories about how education has made a difference for each of us, for our students, for our communities, for our society. We must stop apologizing. We must speak openly about the many ways that higher education and our institutions of higher learning help students and America thrive. The development of skills for meaningful employment is, of course, an important aspect of what we do. However, if we focus only on that singular dimension of our work, we run the risk of suggesting that the benefits of higher education are principally a private good, whereas the greatest contribution of higher education is the public good that benefits our society in so many ways.

In a dynamic, technologically driven, global economy, higher education is more important than ever to the economic success of both individuals and our society. In a complex, information-heavy society, higher education is more important than ever to a robust and productive civic life in which citizens participate with the capacity to think critically about the problems and opportunities of our local communities, states, nation, and world.

Every year, more families want their children to come to our campuses to learn and prepare for our changing world. At public institutions like UMBC, these are middle- and working-class families by and large. Yet they are diverse in every other respect—race, ethnicity, religion, political affiliation, and more. At convocation the day before our fall semester begins, I routinely ask students to stand if one or both of their parents were born in another country. Remarkably, more than one-third stand. For them, attending our university is a step toward the American dream. They know that higher education matters, now more than ever.

We aim to be what America wants to be. In the long run, the success of our nation depends on how we manage our higher education enterprise in a twenty-first century that demands informed, educated, engaged, and thoughtful citizens, as well as a skilled and knowledgeable workforce that can drive our economy.

Progress requires us, as campus leaders, to ensure both access and success for Americans of all backgrounds and to provide a high-quality education for those who come to our campuses. It also requires us to support student persistence and degree completion. We must also be attentive to the stories that are told, both explicitly and implicitly, about the relevance of higher education to our society and our economy. Individually and collectively, we must shape the narratives about the role of our institutions and the work that we do for students and our communities. The narratives that are told—by us and by others—profoundly affect our political culture and, in turn, the policy choices that influence the trajectory of higher education at the state and federal levels.

A Fifty-Year Experiment

Most people today are surprised when they learn that in 1940, on the brink of World War II, just 5 percent of white Americans and only 1 percent of black Americans had earned a college degree. Even by the 1960s, just 10 percent of Americans over age 25 had earned a bachelor's degree, representing 11 percent of whites and 4 percent of blacks. Most families did not imagine that their children would attend college, an opportunity mostly reserved for the wealthy. With a high school degree and a job in the manufacturing or service industries, many were able to support a middle-class lifestyle and provide the American dream for themselves and their families.

The role of college in American life changed after World War II. Amid postwar prosperity, we saw dramatic growth in college enrollment. That surge was driven by the changing needs of our economy, demand from an expanding middle class that saw higher education as a path to social mobility at a time when tuition was a relatively small percentage of family income, and a baby boom generation graduating from high school that saw college as an important life experience.[1]

What unfolded over the next fifty years was, in essence, a great American experiment facilitated by the federal government, which, with bipartisan support, played a prominent role in promoting this growth in college access and attainment. Our nation and its leaders recognized that this investment not only was good for the lives of individual citizens but also benefited society as a whole. The GI Bill of 1944, signed into law by President Franklin Delano Roosevelt, provided the opportunity for many young people—mainly white men at the time—to go to college following World War II and then the Korean War. Following the Soviet launch of *Sputnik*, Congress passed and President Dwight D. Eisenhower signed the National Defense Education Act of 1958, providing federal funding for students in the sciences, area studies, and foreign languages. The Higher Education Act of 1965, enacted as a component of President Lyndon B. Johnson's "Great Society," expanded federal support for both postsecondary institutions and low-income undergraduates. President Richard M. Nixon signed the Higher Education Act Amendments of 1972 that created the Pell Grant program, making available extensive need-based federal student aid.

During the same period, the landmark 1954 US Supreme Court case *Brown v. Board of Education of Topeka* and then the passage of the Civil Rights Act of 1964 created the possibility that this expansion of college opportunity could be inclusive, extending beyond just whites to African Americans and other minorities. The 1972 Higher Education Amendments also included Title IX, prohibiting discrimination based on gender. The agenda of inclusion had been advanced—through desegregation, affirmative action, and gender equity—though the work has been contested, uneven, and unfinished.

With federal higher education and civil rights legislation in place, the proportion of Americans 25 or older who had earned a bachelor's degree increased to 10 percent in the mid-1960s (when UMBC was founded), 15 percent in the mid-1970s, 20 percent in the late 1980s, 25 percent in 2000, and 30 percent around 2010. During the half century from 1965 to 2015, bachelor's degree attainment for whites increased from 10 percent to 36 percent and for blacks from 4 percent to 22 percent. As of 2015, more than half of Asian Americans over 25, about 15 percent of Hispanic Americans, and a similar percentage of Native Americans have earned a college degree. Meanwhile, college attainment for 25- to 29-year-old men increased from 16 to 34 percent, while that for 25- to 29-year-old women increased from 11 to 39 percent.[2]

Our nation's colleges and universities were deeply engaged and involved in this remarkable experiment in education, playing a central role in this story and its success by adapting, evolving, contributing, and innovating. American universities embraced large increases in student enrollments to meet social, economic, and other national needs. The number of enrolled undergraduates doubled during the 1960s to more than 7 million students by 1970 and has since more than doubled again to 17.3 million in 2014. Today, more than 30 percent of Americans age 25 and over have earned a bachelor's degree. As shown in the box below, general indicators of educational attainment have all moved in the right direction.

As Goldin and Katz have argued in *The Race between Education and Technology*, the United States was a global leader in educational attainment in the post–World War II era, and that leadership played a significant role in the economic prosperity of the "American Century": "That the twentieth century was both the American Century *and* the Human Capital Century is no historical accident. Economic growth in the more modern period requires educated workers, managers, entrepreneurs, and citizens. . . . Because the American people were the best educated in the world, they were in the best position to invent, be entrepreneurial, and produce goods and services using advanced technology."[3] And that was because higher education matters—it mattered to those going to college, but it also mattered for the overall prosperity of our country. Our institutions, our students, and our nation thrived. We thrived.

On a parallel track, the federal-university research partnership grew significantly, with federal funding for research also driving our nation's goals for prosperity, health, and security in post–World War II America. Given the stature of our nation's research enterprise today, many would also be surprised to learn that, prior to World War II, the most prestigious research universities in the world were in Europe and that only a "handful" of American col-

Indicators of Educational Attainment

- High school graduation rates have climbed from about 72% in 2002 to 84% in 2014.[1]
- Undergraduate enrollment of 18- to 24-year-olds increased from 25.5% in 1972 to 40% in 2014. During this period, the enrollment of men increased from 30% to 37% and that of women from 21% to 43%.[2]
- The college enrollment rate of recent high school graduates increased from 45% in 1960 to 55% in 1970. Combined with a growing number of high school graduates from the maturing baby boom generation, college enrollment more than doubled in the 1960s.
- In the 1970s, college enrollment as a percentage of recent high school graduates plateaued around 50%. Around 1980, the percentage began to increase steadily, reaching 63% in 1995 and 70% in 2016.[3]
- In absolute terms, undergraduate enrollment has increased from 7.4 million students in 1970 to 17.3 million in 2014.[4]
- The four-year graduation rate for full-time, new freshmen increased from 33.7% for the 1996 starting cohort to 40.6% for the 2010 cohort. The six-year graduation rate increased from 55.4% to 59.4% for these same cohorts.[5]
- The percentage of Americans over age 25 who have earned a bachelor's degree has increased from 9.7% in 1960 to 33.7% in 2017.[6]

Sources: America's Promise, American Academy of Arts and Sciences' Commission on the Future of Undergraduate Education, US Bureau of Labor Statistics, National Center for Education Statistics.

1. www.americaspromise.org/report/2016-building-grad-nation-data-brief; www.americaspromise.org/are-high-school-graduation-gains-real.

2. https://nces.ed.gov/programs/digest/d15/tables/dt15_302.60.asp.

3. www.bls.gov/opub/ted/2017/69-point-7-percent-of-2016-high-school-graduates-enrolled-in-college-in-october-2016.htm.

4. https://nces.ed.gov/programs/digest/d15/tables/dt15_303.70.asp.

5. https://nces.ed.gov/programs/digest/d17/tables/dt17_326.10.asp.

6. https://nces.ed.gov/programs/digest/d17/tables/dt17_104.10.asp.

leges could then be called "research universities." Similarly, before the war, the federal government was not a major funder of research. Most research on American campuses was funded by private philanthropy. But just as college access has grown over the past seventy-five years, so has our nation's research enterprise and the federal-university partnership, funded by the Department of Defense, the Department of Energy, the National Science Foundation, the National Institutes of Health, the National Institute for Standards and Technology, the National Aeronautics and Space Administration, and many other federal agencies. Today, our nation's research universities are regarded as the best in the world. The research and scholarship conducted on our campuses have led to a rapid expansion in our knowledge base and even the creation of new fields of human inquiry that enrich both academic life and our society.[4]

The creation of this research ecosystem is one of our greatest national achievements. Clark Kerr, chancellor at UC Berkeley and then president of the University of California system, wrote, "At the end of World War II, perhaps six American universities could be called research universities, in the sense the research was the dominant faculty activity. . . . By the early 1960s, there were about 20 and they received half of all federal research and development funds going to higher education. In the year 2000, there were at least 100 and many more aspiring to this status."[5]

This is significant change indeed and a great American success story. We—our faculty, staff, and students—have been deeply immersed in work that has expanded our knowledge, opened new areas of inquiry, and led us to engage and navigate the currents that shape our culture, social relations, economic activity, and technology. During the past half century, our campuses have also been the focal point for the understanding of our own humanity and the crucible for such significant phenomena in our society as the free speech and civil rights movements, protests against the Vietnam War, affirmative action, and advances in science and technology, each of which has profoundly shaped our lives. Belying the image of the tradition-bound, ivy-covered college campus, these changes have made our universities among the most dynamic places and communities in our nation and, very often, have been the dynamos for driving societal change.

Our Unfinished Work

The evolution of American higher education is a success story, but one that is unfinished. Our institutions of higher education must continue to evolve because the society in which we are deeply embedded—and which depends on the work we do—also continues to change. Our campuses are not ivory towers, isolated from the world and from the communities that surround us; we live at the center of American life, with all of its accompanying challenges, controversies, conflicts, and opportunities. So, the role of higher education in the economy and in our civic life evolves; changing demographics transform our institutions into multicultural campuses; global competition deepens, with implications for our work; advancing technology shapes the way we work, as well as what and how we teach; shifting fiscal environments challenge us to seek new sources of revenue; and the notion of what it means to be educated in today's world becomes more complex.

The importance of higher education to economic success and social mobility for Americans continues to increase. Over the past fifty years, our nation has shifted from an industrial economy with significant manufacturing employment to a diversified economy with larger segments devoted to information technology, health care, finance, government services, and high-tech manufacturing. As a consequence, a well-educated and highly skilled citizenry has never been more central to the economic prosperity and social strength of our nation. Entrance to the middle class—once attainable with a high school diploma and a manufacturing or service job—can today be secured primarily through postsecondary education.

We can see the growing importance of higher education in recent hiring and job projections. In the aftermath of the Great Recession, 73 percent of new jobs created were filled by individuals with at least a bachelor's degree.[6] A recent report from Georgetown University's Center on Education and the Workforce (CEW) projected that by 2020 almost two-thirds of jobs will require at least some postsecondary education, and half of these will require at least a bachelor's degree.[7]

At UMBC we are responsive to the needs of Maryland's twenty-first-century economy, about which the CEW report stated the following:

> The fastest-growing occupational groups in the state are healthcare (22%), STEM (18%), and community services and arts (17%). Blue-collar jobs are expected to grow the least between 2010 and 2020, at a rate of 9 percent. . . .
>
> By 2020, 66 percent of all jobs in the state will require some post-secondary training, one percentage point above the national average. During the same period, the state will create 960,100 job vacancies both from new jobs and from retirement. There will be 634,700 job vacancies for individuals with post-secondary credentials, in contrast to 325,400 jobs for high school graduates and dropouts.[8]

Postsecondary education is increasingly salient to individuals, society, and the economy. Consequently, we have more families than ever that want to send their children to our colleges and universities. To meet the demand for both education and educated workers, our nation's institutions of higher education must continue to innovate to support access, learning, completion, and careers.

An educated society is not just good for the economy but also increasingly important to sustaining an informed and robust civic life. I often quote Frederick Lawrence, secretary of Phi Beta Kappa, on the importance of college as preparation for citizenship. He notes that US Supreme Court justice Louis D. Brandeis said that the most important position in a democracy is that of "citizen." Lawrence goes on to say that there are three sets of skills needed to perform the duties of the office of citizen, and each is developed by a liberal arts and sciences education. To quote him, "First, a private citizen must be able to turn raw information into knowledge. . . . Second, a private citizen must be able to evaluate arguments. . . . Finally, a private citizen must be able to engage in reasoned debate with others. . . . Presenting one's own rational claims, based on provable truths, as well as being prepared to listen thoughtfully to those of others, is the hallmark of a liberal education."[9] As an educated citizenry engages in thoughtful, evidence-based discourse, it is best informed for making the difficult policy choices our country requires.

Producing that educated citizenry is our responsibility, and it leaves us with several critical questions: What does it mean to be educated in our society, and how is that changing? When postsecondary success is the ticket to opportunity, how do we change the academic experience so that more students can have access to higher education, complete a degree, and depart from our campuses with the knowledge and skills they need to succeed in the workforce or graduate and professional education? How should we change our approaches to teaching and learning to best convey knowledge, ideas, skills, and competencies?

Many have discussed the critical role of student access, affirmative action, and financial support for addressing disparities in higher education participation and completion. In *Equity and Excellence in American Higher Education*, for example, Bowen, Kurzweil, and Tobin focus on college preparedness, affirmative action, admissions, and financial aid—all critically important for getting students to the front gates of our campuses. In *Crossing the Finish Line*, Bowen, Chingos, and McPherson further examine the data around college completion rates.[10] They provide insightful conclusions about who has access to our institutions and how they fare once there.

Beyond access, we must strengthen the student experience by supporting student participation, learning, and completion once students are on campuses. This is what it means to focus intently on student success. The American Academy of Arts and Sciences has recently reported the following:[11]

- Only 40 percent of students complete a bachelor's degree within four years, and only 60 percent graduate from the college at which they started within six years of entry.

- Only 29 percent of students who start a certificate or associate degree at a two-year college earn a credential within 150 percent of the time required to do so.

The unfortunate truth is that in the United States, even as higher education has become more relevant, nearly half of our new, full-time freshmen do not complete a bachelor's degree within six years. This is an unacceptable statistic, especially given that many who do not complete a degree are saddled with significant student debt that they are hard-pressed to pay off with the lower-paying jobs available to those without a college degree. This does not have to be, and it should not be. As Bill Bowen and Mike McPherson put it just a few years ago, "The earnings evidence tells us unequivocally that what matters for students' lives is not starting college but finishing successfully—completing a degree or certificate. It is what students accomplish in college—the skills they master and the knowledge they acquire—that justifies both the social and the private investment that college demands."[12]

As a society, we are deeply affected by the ongoing march of globalization, and this profound change has significant implications for higher education's role in our society. Many before us have already noted that other countries have, over the past few decades, adopted investment in educational attainment as a long-term cultural, social, and economic strategy. While educational attainment in the United States has not declined, our global standing in educational attainment has. We are no longer the global leaders that we were when the United States was also the dominant economic power of the last half of the twentieth century.

To our credit as a nation, we have focused attention on this issue. About a decade ago, in the space of a few months between 2008 and 2009, college completion joined postsecondary access as a major focus of higher education and national economic policy. Just after Goldin and Katz published *The Race between Education and Technology*, demonstrating the role of educational attainment in America's economic preeminence for a half century, several major players in higher education called for change, noting that the US position in educational attainment had since slipped from world leader to a position much further down the pecking order of the Organisation for Economic Co-operation and Development (OECD). The College Board, the Bill and Melinda Gates Foundation, the Lumina Foundation, and President Barack Obama all called in rapid succession for a national effort to increase postsecondary success, with the goal of boosting the percentage of Americans over age 25 with at least an associate's degree from 40 percent to 55 or 60 percent by 2025.[13]

Just as important, as institutions we have also worked on increasing our degree completion rates over the past decade and more. The national six-year graduation rate for public, bachelor-degree-granting institutions has been climbing slowly. The 1991 starting cohort of first-time full-time freshmen had a 49 percent completion rate in 1997; this has climbed to 59 percent for the 2010 cohort in 2016. At UMBC, we had a similar 1991 cohort completion rate of 46 percent, up from 35 percent in the early 1980s, and Arizona State University (ASU), an institution we admire, had a 1991 cohort completion rate of 48 percent. ASU and UMBC have seen similar increases above the national average, to 67 and 64 percent, respectively, for the 2010 cohort in 2016. Georgia State, another institution we admire, saw an increase from 25 to 53 percent for these cohorts over this same period. Moreover, our six-year completion rate of 65 percent at UMBC tells only part of the story. Another 10 percent of our students transferred and completed a degree within six years at another institution, and a further 10 percent are still enrolled.[14]

The American Academy's Commission on the Future of Undergraduate Education, which I served on, has argued that "we now have the potential to provide every American with an undergraduate degree but over the past 30 years the generational compact has weakened, investments have been reduced, and the rate of attainment lags behind our nation's needs."[15] To fulfill our mission as engines of opportunity, we must improve access, affordability, and attainment more broadly, increasing completion rates and reducing achievement gaps.

The nation's demographic shifts shape both our student population and our nation itself. Paul Taylor of the Pew Research Center describes these changes in this way: "Demographic transformations are dramas in slow motion. America is in the midst of two right now. Our population is becoming majority nonwhite at the same time a record share is going gray. Each of these shifts would by itself be the defining demographic story of its era. The fact that both are unfolding simultaneously has generated big generation gaps that will put stress on our politics, families, pocketbooks, entitlement programs and social cohesion."[16] As the nation has become gradually more diverse, racially and ethnically, our campus populations have as well. At UMBC, our student population, once 85 percent white and 15 percent black, is now about half white, one-quarter Asian American, 15 percent African American, 7 percent Hispanic, 3 percent multiple race, and 4 percent international (of any race). About one-third or more of our new students (freshmen and transfer) are international students, are immigrants, or have at least one parent who is an immigrant. This shift requires us to be more attentive than ever to the diversity in traditions, experiences, prior information, and expectations students bring to campus as we work to ensure that they succeed. It also requires us to fully embrace the tremendous assets these students bring to our scholarly communities.

There remain significant differences in bachelor's degree attainment across demographic groups. As of 2017, Asian Americans over age 25 have a six-year graduation rate of 55.4 percent; whites, 38.1 percent; blacks, 24.3 percent; American Indian / Alaska Native, 20.2 percent; and Hispanics, 17.2 percent.[17] For blacks, 24 percent represents a major increase over the 4 percent we saw in the 1960s, but it is still not good enough. It is possible to close these attainment gaps. At UMBC, the attainment rate for blacks is the same as for the undergraduate population overall.

We have significantly increased college attainment, but not for all and especially not for those from the poorest families. If you are born and raised in the lowest income quartile in the United States, your chances today of completing college—about 1 in 8—are about the same as they would have been in the 1960s. In this regard, we have made little progress. My colleague, former University System of Maryland chancellor Brit Kirwan, said it best: "America is the land of opportunity, the upwardly mobile society. We are that no more. It rings hollow."[18] Suzanne Mettler argues further that our policies affect who does and does not succeed in college and that higher education can actively reinforce inequality instead of providing for social mobility when higher education is more important than ever.[19]

Supplementing our work on broadening access to higher education, we must foster a welcoming and supportive campus climate for students and faculty of all backgrounds and create an environment in which students learn how to listen to one another. We must be open to constant innovation and experimentation, redesigning courses and the student experience to enhance teaching and learning, creating communities of learners who support and motivate each other, deploying data and learning analytics that help us identify opportunities to support students in real-time or improve courses, and infusing courses with experiential and community-engaged learning that may include research, entrepreneurship, or civic engagement. All of these innovations and initiatives act in a complementary fashion to support the dual goals of both equity and excellence—or, as we refer to it, inclusive excellence.

A few years ago I gave a keynote address at the annual conference of the American Association of State Colleges and Universities (AASCU) that was later published as an article, "Beyond the Numbers." In that address I discussed why it was important not just to change the numbers on campus—for example, with regard to graduation rates—but also to change the quality of the experience, particularly for students of color:

> I frequently visit campuses that are working not only to increase their racial and ethnic diversity, but also to improve their institutional

climate in relationship to recruiting and retaining students of color. I recently attended a reception before giving a keynote address at a major public research university, and I asked the following questions of campus leaders assembled: "When people of color are considering coming to the institution and are being recruited—whether they are faculty members, students, or administrators—what language do you use to describe the climate of the institution, and to what extent is that language based on your having listened to the voices of people from diverse groups, and having understood what they have experienced?" I was met with silence, largely because most of us are not accustomed to talking about race or other "sticky issues" of the day, such as gender or sexual orientation. Too often, when we begin talking about these issues, we tend to become uncomfortable and defensive and begin pointing fingers at each other.[20]

We have our work cut out for us. The ongoing divisions in our larger society are palpable. We have seen them in everything from protests of police shootings of black men to the recent events in Charlottesville. In the former case, racial protests have occurred on some of our campuses. In the latter case, we witnessed hateful extremists march across the campus of one of our nation's premier universities.

This reminds us what is at stake in our efforts to ensure the success of students of all backgrounds, for themselves and for our society. Campus unrest, often focusing on racial climate, should not come as a surprise at a time when our long history of social division confronts the increasingly critical role of higher education in fundamentally changing the relationship between advantage and privilege and socioeconomic mobility. Higher education plays a role in either reinforcing or overcoming these divisions as it also works to fulfill—or not—our students' potential.

We understand that diversity occurs in many forms: race, ethnicity, gender and gender identity, sexual orientation, political affiliation, veteran status, first generation in college, income, and more. Any way you want to look at it, we have at UMBC, as well as at most public institutions, a "multicultural campus." In this context, we must pay close attention not just to diversity but to an authentic inclusion of people of different identities and diverse perspectives and backgrounds. An academic community searching for truth and insight must be willing to respectfully engage in conversations, albeit often difficult ones, listening as necessary to those who may think differently from ourselves.

I believe that the more we engage in such conversations, the more trust, dignity, and respect we will engender and, as a result, the easier and more productive these conversations will become. This is not the easy path, but it is the right one. At UMBC we believe in engaging in such difficult conversations because, as will be made clear in the discussion of our work that follows, such discussions were central to driving important changes in our campus culture and to improving the success of our students. They have also enabled us to do much better in providing our students with the education and tools they need as citizens in order to navigate the challenges and opportunities of the twenty-first century—deep knowledge in a field, an awareness of the social context in which they work, consciousness of global challenges and opportunities, the ability to communicate and work in teams, critical thinking, the wisdom to keep asking questions, and the ability to continue to learn and engage effectively throughout their lives.

We are experiencing and responding to global economic integration, a revolution in telecommunications that connects us as easily to Beijing as it does to Baltimore, rapid technological change, and advances in science and medicine. We are witnessing and confronting the grave challenges of climate change, population growth and migration, inequality, cybersecurity, and terrorism. We must prepare our students for this work, and we must also reshape our universities to address these real-world issues.

UMBC is often considered a place where talented students come to study in the natural sciences and engineering. It is true that we do have particular strengths in key scientific and engineering fields. For example, we are among the top ten US research universities in awarding bachelor's degrees in computer and information sciences. Despite this perception, at UMBC we place great emphasis on the importance of liberal education as the foundation of engaged citizenship, and this is reflected in the strength of our programs and scholarship in the arts, humanities, and social sciences. We pursue excellence across the disciplines and interdisciplines, because we want all of our graduates, regardless of their major, to understand the challenges and opportunities embedded in the issues they— and our nation—will confront in their work and in their lives. We understand that our future as a nation and our place in the world depend not just on science and technology, but on a deep understanding of the nature of our own humanity and of our society.

Too often, the STEM fields and the arts and humanities are pitted against each other. Even within the STEM fields we see arguments presented about the relative value of the basic and applied sciences. These are false dichotomies. Even the most focused of tech companies understand the importance of having a broadly educated workforce and the need to exploit the intersection between the traditional disciplines. Cathy Davidson recently reported that a study of Google's hiring and personnel practices revealed that STEM expertise came in eighth out of eight among the qualities held by Google's top employees: "The seven top characteristics of success at Google are all soft skills: being a good coach; communicating and listening well; possessing insights into others (including others [sic] different values and points of view); having empathy toward and being supportive of one's colleagues; being a good critical thinker and problem solver; and being able to make connections across complex ideas."[21] All these qualities and skills are picked up in the arts, humanities, and social sciences.

Our Serious Responsibility

Campus leadership has always been a weighty responsibility. Most would agree that today our campuses are increasingly complicated organizations and the challenges and opportunities we face are growing. This book discusses the ways in which leaders can shape campus culture to promote inclusion, to enhance teaching and learning, to foster student success, and to amplify the university as an engaged actor in the community. Along the way, we'll grapple with issues that determine whether we thrive as institutions, students, and Americans.

To be sure, teaching, learning, and student success are at the heart of our enterprise. As campus leaders, we must be attentive to the progress our faculty and staff are making to ensure the success of students who are serious about the work. We can support active and group study, technology-enabled teaching, experiential learning, and skill development with appropriate credentialing. We can support efforts to provide the academic, social, financial, and counseling support that many students need to persist and complete.

We must manage much more, of course, to ensure that our institutions flourish. Bill McRaven, as he departed his job as chancellor of the University of Texas System, said, "The toughest job in the nation is the one of academic- or health-institution president."[22] Indeed, our colleges and universities are among the most complicated organizations in the world.[23] We provide educational experiences for students. We deliver services, including housing, dining, parking, recreation, counseling, and security. Some of us with major athletic programs are also in the entertainment business. Many of our leading larger research universities manage large, complex medical centers. We supervise operating and capital budgets and revenues in uncertain fiscal environments. Higher education appropriations in many states have declined in real dollars per student over the past decade and more. Tuition and fees, which we often increase to offset those declines, must be politically negotiated with boards and elected officials, and substantial increases in the cost of a college education are no longer sustainable. Consequently, university presidents must manage relationships with many critical stakeholders: students, families, faculty, staff, contractors, alumni, boards, elected officials, and donors, as well as community partners that include corporations, nonprofits, and government agencies.[24]

To meet the growing fiscal needs of our institutions, then, we now seek additional sources of revenue from auxiliary services, contracts and grants, and capital campaigns. As president, I am especially driven to spend more and more time fundraising. Sometimes, this involves working with funding agencies and foundations to develop the connections that lead to grant opportunities. Many times, I am working with my colleagues in institutional advancement to develop proposals for donors or partnerships with corporations. When mentoring current and future presidents, I say, "A day without an ask is like a day without sunshine."

We navigate challenging and shifting political environments. In Maryland we find supportive elected officials who want our public institutions to succeed and clearly understand the critical role that higher education plays in driving the economy of the state and the welfare of our citizens. In many states, however, institutions have experienced state budgetary battles and appropriations cuts, while simultaneously dealing with calls for increased accountability and greater cost-effectiveness.

We work to create truly multicultural, inclusive campuses. We embrace students of all races, ethnicities, religions, genders and gender identities, sexual orientations, veteran statuses, citizenships, or political affiliations. But we must take this work one step further, by providing opportunities and incentives for students of different backgrounds to interact. This is part of learning in the global culture we now inhabit. We must, as educators and institutions, do all we can to implement Title IX in a fair and comprehensive manner.

Some leaders must deal with campuses that are roiled by student protest over issues of inclusion and free speech. I argue that a healthy campus that embraces and has a history of difficult but respectful conversations can have both inclusion and academic freedom at the same time. This does not mean that we are always comfortable, but it does mean that we can provide the space for many points of view as we seek the truth together.

Of course, as we have seen on public campuses on both coasts, there are times when outside groups use our campuses to further their political agendas, often by being deliberately provocative, intolerant, and even violent. These are difficult tests for any president, however seasoned and well intentioned. We can learn from these instances and prepare our campuses for future exigencies.

We lead our campuses as we make the most of long-term challenges and opportunities. Globalization, advances in technology, and demographic shifts have each disrupted and reshaped our economy, society, and culture. The changes resulting from these and other forces affect who comes to study and work on our campuses, the way we do business, the topics we research, the scholarship and ideas we create and share, the classes we teach, and the knowledge we convey to a new generation.

This is serious business for us as leaders, executives, managers, administrators, educators, and students. We must struggle with the social and ethical implications of these forces and resolve the tensions that they create: How do we function in a culture and economy that is increasingly global? How do we manage the rapidly evolving human-technology interface? What is the role of big data, data analytics, and social media in our society, culture, and democracy?

For many of us, whether our institutions are research universities or not, we are focusing on how we can support the research, scholarship, and creative activity of our faculty and students. As we have developed as an institution, this work has also become deeply intertwined with entrepreneurship, economic development, and community engagement.

And, lastly, while balancing all the above, we deal with the daily "unexpected." These come in the form of crises, emergencies, or scandals. Today, the disruptions also arrive in the form of reactions to the daily policy upheavals in a changing political landscape. Sometimes, the unexpected even comes as a pleasant surprise, like your basketball team upsetting the top-ranked team in March Madness.

This is quite a lot to manage. Given all these pressures, it's not a surprise that the average tenure of university presidents is becoming shorter. But in every one of these tasks there is opportunity. I have recently had the privilege of being a member of two national commissions—one on the future of the college presidency and another on the future of undergraduate education—that provided me the opportunity to talk with other leaders in higher education.[25] I was very encouraged that my fellow presidents involved in these two efforts were so positive about the future of higher education and the role it plays in the lives of students and our society. To be sure, we do have many challenges. The members of the two commissions—presidents, faculty, foundation leaders, and others —recognized that their optimism is not shared by everyone. We hear criticisms about cost, access, the value of a college degree, and the role of education in inequality and social mobility, while at the same time we also hear concerns about inclusion, diversity of ideas, free speech, the skills and knowledge we teach, and our ability to support economic development. However, these members still envisioned a strong future for higher education, one in which Americans of all backgrounds have access to high-quality education in environments that provide them the support they need to learn and succeed, and one in which higher education can contribute to solving the big problems of mankind.

I have also discussed these challenges and opportunities with many university leaders in a variety of settings over the past decade. As I have traveled around the country, invited to give speeches, I have had the opportunity to talk with leaders and boards at many other institutions. I am privileged to mentor presidents and other senior leaders of a variety of campuses, often providing advice as they deal with faculty-administration tensions, budget difficulties, diversity and inclusion, unrest, and more, and I learn so much myself by helping fellow campus leaders with these problems. For more than a decade, I have also had the experience of teaching a seminar on the academic role of the university president at Harvard's course for new leaders, which allows me to hear firsthand the questions that new presidents ask. These leaders are deeply aware of our challenges but also eager to learn about approaches that will enable them not just to manage the day-to-day tasks but to lead the kind of change necessary to make the most of our opportunities to serve our students and communities.

At UMBC, we have been fortunate to have a very supportive campus community and boards of visitors and regents, as well as interested and helpful elected officials. This has given us time and space to reflect on what has and has not worked well on our campus. Further, as we conducted our research in preparation for writing this book, we invited campus leaders, staff, faculty, and students to join us in conversation about our shared experiences. We did this for two reasons: first, to enrich the book, because our colleagues brought new information and fresh perspectives about our work together, and second, because we wanted to model in our approach to writing this book the way we, as a campus, approach all of our challenges and opportunities—by having deep, sometimes difficult conversations, but nonetheless respectful, transparent, and productive ones.

These conversations about our challenges and opportunities left me with great hope. We recognize the difficulties of the tasks that lie before us. There are issues of direction, resources, willpower, and more. Yet my colleagues bring with them such enthusiasm and commitment for the work, a willingness to roll up their sleeves to tackle the work, and a readiness to execute the work over the long term.

Providing the support that young people need both to imagine what is possible and to develop their own abilities is the challenge we face as educators. It's also a great opportunity. The nation is counting on us.

For many of us, meeting this awesome responsibility means leading institutional culture change.

3

Culture Change Is Hard as Hell

They laughed.

The auditorium was filled to capacity with college presidents, and you could tell they were laughing from deep down inside, with a mixture of amusement and, perhaps, unease. I sensed a nervous laughter that suggested an understanding of the need for change in higher education on the one hand but also an apprehension about the difficulty of making it happen on the other. How can we change values, expectations, attitudes, and behavior as the role, content, and delivery of higher education evolve to meet the needs of our dynamic society?

Onstage with me were panelists who had just spoken about important, far-reaching ideas shaping the future of higher education: using the insights of cognitive psychology about how students learn to reimagine our approaches to teaching and learning, applying technology to create online courses that both increase accessibility and enhance learning outcomes, organizing the university to better align our institutions with social and economic needs, and implementing new approaches to student financial support that improve affordability for students and produce well-prepared graduates for a robust economy.[1]

These innovations benefit our universities, our students, and our nation, helping us all to thrive in the twenty-first century. Yet, as the panelists spoke, I looked into the audience and realized that what I was seeing on the faces of some presidents were looks of incredulity and concern. The panelists spoke with great confidence about their transformational initiatives. They talked about these changes as if we are able to accomplish them with ease, when, in fact, they involve significant resources, serious effort, and substantial buy-in and leadership from many stakeholders. What was not coming through in the discussion was the amount of work required to lead transformational change.

The presidents in the audience were, perhaps, questioning how their universities could seem so different from these transformational institutions. I realized that this was what I needed to address just as the moderator turned to me, saying, "Freeman, part of your work has focused on how you influence the culture of a campus in order to absorb the kinds of change we're talking about and create opportunities to reach the kind of scale [our speakers are] talking about."

"Let me start by saying something every president in the room will appreciate," I replied. "I have been serving as president for more than twenty years and if there's one undeniable truth, it's that changing the culture of an institution is hard as hell. It just is." The audience erupted with laughter and applause, recognizing that I understood their concerns about how expectations and culture can be changed. When the presidents heard me describe culture change at a university as "hard as hell," they knew I got it.

Yet my task on this panel was not to give the presidents an out but rather the opposite. My job was to pull them into the work of implementing change and encouraging innovation. I continued by saying that, nonetheless, "the job we have as presidents is to convince people that the world of tomorrow can be better than the world of today, however comfortable they may feel at present and however uncomfortable they may feel about change. It is our obligation to address the evolving role of our institutions in society and help students succeed."

Organizational Culture and Institutional Change

Jim Duderstadt, former president of the University of Michigan, has observed, "During most periods, change in the university has proceeded in slow, linear, incremental steps. . . . Today, however, we do not have the luxury of continuing at this leisurely pace, nor can we confine the scope of changes underway. We are witnessing a significant paradigm shift in the very nature of the higher education enterprise . . . which will demand substantial rethinking and reworking on the part of our institutions."[2] So, we must continue to grow, evolve, and innovate to meet today's challenges and seize today's opportunities.

Change in higher education will occur whether we want it or not—because of external and internal problems, developments, and stakeholder agendas. For senior leaders, the questions for us are these: When change comes to us and our campuses, how do we manage it and drive it toward the outcomes we seek? When change isn't happening but should be, how can we be catalysts and manage it? How can we bring others into the work or, even better, enable them to be change agents who lead the work? These questions require us to think first about whether our campus cultures enable the far-reaching changes in teaching and learning, inclusion, technology deployment, data analytics, research, community engagement, and more that we now need to see.

Eric Weiner, writing in *The Geography of Bliss*, spoke of culture this way: "Where we are is vital to who we are. By 'where,' I'm speaking not only of our physical environment but also of our cultural environment. Culture is the sea we swim in—so pervasive, so all-consuming, that we fail to notice its existence until we step out of it. It matters more than we think."[3] Organizational culture is like that. We don't notice it until we stop, take a step back, and think about it. It is by no means monolithic, and yet there is an ethos we can sense. The culture of an institution is evident in our values, traditions, tacit rules and permissions, and accepted approaches. It is evident in our daily activities and our habits of mind. It is evident in the questions we ask and those we choose to ignore, in the achievements we record and celebrate and those that go unnoticed, and in the initiatives we choose to support and those we choose not to support.[4]

I start with this because, when it comes to implementing institutional plans and initiatives, "culture eats strategy for breakfast," as Boris Groysberg and colleagues note. They argue, though, that "it doesn't have to be that way. Our work suggests that culture can, in fact, be managed. The first and most important step leaders can take to maximize its value and minimize its risks is to become fully aware of how it works."[5] So, if we aim to undertake new initiatives and institute new programs and encourage people to behave differently as faculty or students, then we must get the culture right before we ask people to change their behavior.

Most experienced presidents know firsthand how difficult it is to lead substantive change in a university. Indeed, most presidents will be the first to tell you that if a proposed change at a university is perceived as top-down, it has a high likelihood of being dead on arrival for the faculty and staff who must implement it. Forcing change, while sometimes expedient, often undermines long-term sustainable impact. And so, academic leaders are often required to foster innovation by facilitating a change in the culture and practices of an institution. The most effective means of doing this is by clearly articulating a vision for the future through a collaborative process with others—faculty staff, administrators, and students—who broadly embrace it and, as positions turn over, selecting or developing new colleagues who align with the culture, mission, and work.

In our society, many tend to think that authority and power rest solely in the hands of one person at the top of an institution. So, if the institution is prospering, people often assume that it must be because of one person's leadership. Conversely, if there are significant problems, people assume that the person at the top is solely responsible for both the problems and the solutions. It is certainly true that the president is ultimately responsible. Unfortunately, sometimes the president finds out about the problem only after it becomes public. While there is an important role for senior leaders —in particular, presidents, provosts, vice presidents, deans, and senior faculty—in effecting change, those colleges and universities that are innovative enable leadership at all levels of the institution. This broad leadership is critical for a dynamic campus. The work, accountability, responsibility, and credit for the outcomes of change must be shared.

So, I urged the presidents in the audience to think about initiating and engaging the process of change on their campuses by creating a climate that encourages asking questions—asking colleagues to define problems, gather and analyze data, listen to focus groups, struggle collaboratively with potential solutions, take the lead, and work together on a shared path forward. It is in these deeper, and sometimes difficult, conversations that innovation is first imagined and brought forth.

Enabling Culture Change

It is challenging to understand fully the culture of an institution. It is even more challenging to effect and enable culture change. At UMBC, we have focused our attention and resources on work that is critical to improving our administrative operations, building our research, and supporting student learning and achievement. We were guided in our work by questions that reflected our shared values:

- Are we putting people first?
- Are we providing students who come to our campus with the best experience possible?
- Are we doing the very best we can in all aspects of institutional operations given our mission and resources?
- Are we then taking that extra step, "above and beyond," to do more, to do things differently, and to do our work better?

When I started at UMBC as vice provost in the late 1980s, our chancellor had just articulated a new vision that asked us to improve our academics, grow our research, and be a more engaged partner with our community. In his history of UMBC, George La-Noue quotes the publisher of the *Warfield's Business Record* to summarize how Michael Hooker, chancellor from 1986 to 1992, injected our institution with new energy and a new vision during this period: "Prior to [Hooker's] arrival, UMBC appeared somewhat somnambulant, its profile so low, it couldn't even muster a negative image. . . . He helped UMBC stake out territories on the graduate level where competition was limited and opportunities plentiful. He saw that through business, academic, and other partnerships, UMBC could be the foundation for social and economic growth. He has left the institution prepared to build on that forward-looking vision."[6] Hooker had set UMBC on a new trajectory toward a new future.

Yet, in my first years at UMBC, if something went wrong, people would often say, "That's UMBC." That's just the way it is, and the way it is just isn't so great. The attitude among some on campus was that UMBC was not a place where you could always expect excellence, but rather a place where—in spite of pockets of excellence—you would expect some areas to be mediocre. This attitude was, in part, an extension of the mentality of being an underfunded offshoot of the larger campus at College Park. During the early years, because of our enthusiasm for all students, we accepted many who were not academically prepared. It is unlikely that an institution with such a negative prevailing attitude could encourage and enable behavior that would lead to sustained excellence. To move toward the vision articulated by our leadership, something had to change. But how?

The larger vision that Hooker articulated was important, yet there was also a new and different feel at a more granular level. We began to take ourselves much more seriously. We created the Meyerhoff program, and it was a success. We became known as a destination for talented students. We built a research park, without which the state would not have taken us seriously as a research university. We evolved rapidly from a commuter school to a residential research university. We upgraded our admissions standards. We looked carefully at our performance on state audits and how to improve our financial and administrative structures. We celebrated as a community our commitment, hard work, and accomplishments (what we now call "grit and greatness").

It is a cliché, but every journey does begin with a single step and a single success that can demonstrate for others what could be. With each success and subsequent success, more and more members of the community began to look at our goals, values, and work in a different way. Culture change can be imperceptible at times, yet at other times one can recognize that the institution has reached a tipping point. One day, you realize that your campus has changed, the paradigm has shifted, the culture is now perceptibly different. It was in this manner that our campus transformed itself from "That's UMBC" to "unabashedly aspirational."

In 2017, our campus was named one of the nation's top academic workplaces in *Great Colleges to Work For* by the *Chronicle of Higher Education* for the ninth year in a row.[7] We were just one of ten four-year institutions with more than 10,000 students featured on an "honor roll" of those with outstanding marks across nearly every measured category. Those categories included the following:

- Collaborative Governance
- Compensation and Benefits
- Confidence in Senior Leadership
- Diversity
- Job Satisfaction
- Professional/Career Development Programs
- Respect and Appreciation
- Teaching Environment
- Work/Life Balance

The *Chronicle* creates this list of "Great Colleges to Work For" through a survey of faculty, staff, and administrators who rate their workplaces on a range of questions. (Incongruously, as a place that is known for inclusive excellence for its students, one measure that some years we do not get high marks for is "diversity." This demonstrates how honest our campus is, because we have not been doing as well as we should when it comes to faculty diversity in particular. This is an issue we are now addressing in a systematic way, and perhaps that is why the campus now includes diversity as a category of excellence for us. We will elaborate on how we are working on this challenge later in the book.)

During this same period, when we went from "that's UMBC" to "great college to work for," our six-year graduation rate also climbed from 35 percent to more than 65 percent (more if you include the 10% who transfer out of UMBC and earn a degree at another institution and the 10% still enrolled after six years). So, how did we get from being perceived by some as mediocre to "unabashedly aspirational"? We'll talk about particular programs and initiatives below. Here it suffices to say that small innovations and initiatives can lead to big changes. Eventually, over a period of time, the organization is transformed.

Serious, sustainable change is hard work. It is often far harder than we would like to think it will be. When the change we want to see involves race, diversity, differences, and inclusion, it can be even more challenging, as these are topics most Americans are not comfortable discussing. But when change is the right thing to do, we must nevertheless engage and persist.

At UMBC, we are hungry for change. The imperative to evolve rapidly arises from our collective commitment to do all we can to better serve our students and their families; support student learning, persistence, and completion; connect our students and faculty to opportunities in the Baltimore-Washington region; and work to address our region's social and economic needs. At just over fifty years of age, we are yet a young, growing institution, and to advance these goals, we must innovate, continually addressing new needs as they arise while simultaneously laying the foundation of a new model of the public university. Our mantra is "success is never final."

As a campus, we are also a healthy community. This quality is expressed in our ability to be reflective; we can look in the mirror and be honest about what we see, good, bad, or challenging. When issues arise, our culture of reflection leads us to collect data that can inform our decision-making and to have respectful conversations that identify problems and possible solutions. We can acknowledge openly both our strengths and weaknesses, recognize the challenges we face and opportunities we can embrace, and understand how a well-considered response can lead to the desired outcomes. We structure our conversations so that they are inclusive and open to differing perspectives, using our shared governance structures or focus groups with stakeholders for a specific issue.

Change requires courage, because it requires us to see things differently from the way they are at present. It requires us to recognize our failures as well as successes. For change to be possible, you first have to see the world and the lens through which you view it. Only then can you observe what could be and understand what the possibilities are. To make progress, you need to ask different and often difficult questions of yourself and others and then set different expectations so that others begin to see the world from a different perspective too.

Change necessitates courage because, so often, it requires a leap of faith and an acceptance of substantial risk—believing that a goal is achievable even if the outcome is, as yet, unseen: "No one believed it could be done, because it hadn't been done before. And then we did it." We understand that doubt is a fellow traveler with faith, that there's always some uncertainty about the way forward and risk associated with any new initiative. While there are the unusual people who thrive on risk, most who choose to innovate will first weigh the potential benefits of success against both the actual costs of the work and the perceived cost of failure. Any institution that can minimize the costs of failure and increase the rewards to risk-taking will significantly increase innovation.

Change requires grit—commitment and resilience—because it does not happen overnight. Change that matters only succeeds because of long, organized, and sometimes expensive commitments. It requires the engagement of many individuals as leaders and change agents in order to persuade others, and that can require, from time to time, difficult conversations. This can be daunting for some.

Innovation consumes time and energy. Many say, "If only I had the time and resources, then I would do it." When you undertake innovation, it often involves tasks performed in addition to regular responsibilities, rather than instead of them. Yet, at UMBC we have some colleagues who innovate anyway. How does that happen? Funding helps. We have a strong history of successful fundraising and grant writing for educational reforms, initiatives, and programs often deployed at the institutional level. Combined with institutional support, this type of funding can help the leader of an initiative focus on the work. For this reason we have made academic innovation a priority in our fundraising.

Surely, incentives can help. As the reader will note in the discussions below about infusing entrepreneurship into classes or supporting course redesign, we have established several small-grants competitions that provide funding for faculty to undertake work they might not otherwise do. University leaders can rarely be successful in simply telling faculty and staff to do something. As one university president has said, however, "if you need to herd cats, tuna fish helps."

But incentives are not always necessary. Passion is one more characteristic that is found in the context of change. What successful change and innovation often require are the people who lead. They take the initiative, they "go the extra mile," they go "above and beyond" their normal work; there are obstacles, but they are passionate enough to move past those obstacles. We have been fortunate that UMBC has had more than its share of passionate and committed people who will roll up their sleeves and do the work. Our community is better for this broad set of leaders. Our students have benefited substantially from their commitment.

This book relates below several stories of UMBC's work to promote student success and inclusive excellence. It begins in the late 1980s, when we were struggling with both student success and a challenging racial climate. This was also a time when, under new leadership, we were evolving from a commuter school into the mid-size research university that the state of Maryland originally envisioned us to be. My colleagues and I made it a priority to strengthen and improve retention and graduation rates; improve the performance of students across disciplines, including STEM fields; and encourage the success of minorities in STEM. How we addressed these is told in the chapters that follow.

To be sure, there was much improvisation along the way as we implemented our plans. Yet we were less interested in "disruptive change," which has lately been the rage, and rather focused on change that was informed by data, experimentation, and the experiences and perspectives of others (when there were any to draw upon). Of course, some of our approaches have disrupted the way we did things before, but data-driven decision-making can be very effective in changing attitudes. Today, this might be called design thinking or effective strategic planning. We saw it as developing holistic plans to meet the deeply felt needs and aspirations of both the UMBC community and the communities we serve.

There were times when efforts on our campus to address real problems, such as minority underrepresentation in the faculty, were not wholehearted and fell short of our goals. We have come to understand that this was often because changes were implemented to meet some externally imposed goal, and therefore there was no real internal champion to lead change. When we did succeed, it was because university leaders, administrators, faculty, staff, or students saw a need, found the tools to address it, engaged others in sometimes difficult conversations, built consensus for the project, recruited key people to the work, and then undertook that work. This required years of deep engagement and closing the loop on effective assessment.

Change can be the response to demands from many sources, sometimes external and sometimes internal. Often change responds to both external and internal pressures and opportunities at once. One school of thought suggests that it can occur in response to the "cognitive dissonance" that emerges when organizational structures and needs are out of alignment.[8]

For UMBC, external forces have been as varied as concern for black males in American society, a report from the Massachusetts Institute of Technology (MIT) on the status of women in its science faculty, the deployment of technology (the introduction of Wi-Fi was "disruptive"), interest in supporting entrepreneurship in the American economy, and the availability of funding that incentivized our work. Outside funding that provided incentives for us included Corporation for National Service grants for service learning, Kauffman Foundation grants for entrepreneurship, National Science Foundation (NSF) ADVANCE grants to support women faculty in science and engineering, and University System of Maryland grants for course redesign. We have benefited from the support of federal agencies, including the NSF, the National Institutes of Health, the National Security Agency, the National Aeronautics and Space Administration, and the US Department of Energy, as well as support from companies like Northrop Grumman, which helps fund our Center for Women in Technology, our cyber scholars program, and our K–12 initiatives in the city of Baltimore. Substantial gifts from Robert Meyerhoff, George and Betsy Sherman, and Earl and Darielle Linehan have launched and supported key academic initiatives.

Internal needs also lead to change when students, faculty, and staff articulate those needs and take the initiative. Black student protests about our racial climate led to changes in residential life and academic programs to support minority students. Women challenged us to do more to support female faculty in the sciences and engineering. Faculty decided we could simply do much better when it came to improving learning outcomes in such diverse classes as Introduction to Chemistry, Introduction to Psychology, English Composition, and Classical Mythology. With regard to the last of these, UMBC ancient studies professor Timothy Phin redesigned Mythology because he wanted to reach his students more effectively than he could using the traditional large lecture course. Using technology, he created a hybrid course that brings students more personalized content and learning. Sometimes, necessity really is the mother of invention.

Sometimes resistance becomes an obstacle, whether the motivation for change is internal or external. We will always encounter moments of conflict because individuals or groups bring different, and sometimes divergent, interests and agendas to the table. We may encounter indifference in the face of a problem and strong opposition to proposed solutions, but many will express concerns simply because they don't see why change is necessary, don't understand why they should be involved in implementing change, feel uncertain about the impact of change upon their work, or have not yet understood how to change. Information and negotiation—both essential to deeper conversations—can help resolve conflicts. Change is more likely to occur and be sustainable when individuals with a variety of agendas come together and find common ground in an initiative.

And that's not the end of it. Once you've enacted change, you face the hardest part—sustaining it. People are most excited by and interested in investing in something that is new, whether you are talking about senior leadership, faculty investing their time, or the federal government investing their funding. Once it's no longer "new," or once a grant that supported an initiative expires, the energy that is required to sustain an innovation often diminishes. Leaders in a position of authority, such as the provost or vice provost, must be vigilant, talking with staff and faculty involved in a program, asking hard questions, and reviewing the data to make sure that progress stays on track. When our ADVANCE grant expired after we made great progress in hiring women faculty in the natural sciences, our progress plateaued and then began to decline. After we realized this, we redoubled our efforts and committed institutional resources to restore and sustain progress.

Whether talking about course redesign or how to diversify the faculty, we are challenged as leaders to continuously monitor progress to ensure that it endures and that we don't regress toward the former state. Most backsliding comes because we stop pushing forward on an innovation and it is human nature to fall back into prior habits, or because we involve new people who are unaware of the reasons why the changes we had made were so important. This could be a new dean, department chair, faculty member, or students. So, when new people join our campus community, we must be sure to educate them about our culture, our approaches, and our history. We must give new members of our community the time to understand our culture, to reflect on their own experiences, and to become passionate about the success of our students.

Change is hard. Success is never final. But there are tools we can use to empower leaders, staff, faculty, and students to enact and sustain change.

4

Leadership and Empowerment

Changing culture to change practice requires leadership *and* empowerment.

Many presidents know firsthand that change originating from the top of an organization can certainly provide "short-term dividends," but it does not necessarily lead to sustainable change or create the healthy organization that activates and sustains innovative work over the long term. As my colleague Ken Maton and I argue in our "social transformation theory of change," what does lead to those outcomes is an authentic and potent engagement between strong leaders and empowered actors, a deep and supportive interaction that brings out the best and the most in everyone.[1]

Leadership

Senior campus leaders play a critical role in developing a community vision, a culture that enables innovation, and the support needed for successful change. Presidents, provosts, deans, and faculty identify and focus attention on a problem, signaling to the campus that the institution takes the issue seriously and supports faculty and staff who take the lead in enacting solutions. "Presidents should be expected to promote risk-taking and experimentation and should not be afraid to 'rock-the-boat,'" Bill Bowen and

Mike McPherson have argued. "This is especially true in the area of teaching methods, which must continue to evolve in new ways, with rigorous assessment of what works and what doesn't work at each step along the way."[2]

As mentioned earlier, I recently served with a group of college presidents, brought together by the Aspen Institute, who reported out ways to strengthen the college presidency through hiring, mentoring, and professional development. We acknowledged the many challenges university presidents face today and the consequences of these for recruiting and sustaining successful presidents. Few enter the role fully prepared, the job is now harder than ever, and the environment is more uncertain and unpredictable, our report notes. But we saw a way forward that suggests that we not only can recruit good people to leadership but also can help them be strong leaders who can promote the risk-taking and experimentation that we need.[3]

The Aspen report makes suggestions for recruiting and supporting presidents. First, we can cast a wide net when recruiting new presidents. Every campus is different, so the primary goal is to find the person who is the right fit for the campus at that point in time, with its particular culture, resources, and issues. Sometimes the appropriate leader will have the traditional academic background, someone who began in the faculty and rose through the administration. Sometimes it will be someone internal, other times a proven leader from another campus. Sometimes a nontraditional candidate could be the right person for the job since, while it is not always popular to bring in someone from outside academia, that person could be the best choice given the set of issues a campus is facing at a particular time. Given changing demographics in our society, we should also seek a broad, diverse pool of candidates so that we are sure to tap all of our available talent. We need leaders from diverse backgrounds who can prepare for the forthcoming challenges that we are not even aware of yet.[4]

Second, we must provide mentoring and professional development for both new and seasoned presidents. Boards can play a role in helping presidents, especially new ones. For that to happen, boards must be knowledgeable about both their institutions and best practice. The report recommends training board members on how to hire and support presidents. Boards can work to develop transition plans for new presidents and ongoing professional development for both new and current leaders.[5]

One of the most significant recommendations is bringing greater clarity to expectations and plans for the first year of a presidency. The report offers the following ideas for a successful first year:

- Create a first-year development plan.
- Listen closely to constituents on campus.
- Learn about institutional decision-making and the campus culture.
- Generate a "campus dashboard" with indicators about key areas—academic, financial, and administrative—from research to student success.
- Develop a network of peers and friends who can be supportive both for the work and for physical and emotional well-being.
- Stay abreast of national developments and the ways higher education fits into the national context.

Understanding the campus—its people, culture, budget, student achievement, research, and community relations—is central to informing senior leaders, beginning with the president, so that they can focus on shaping campus culture, working with colleagues, and implementing the practices that will make a difference.[6]

This is how we develop senior leaders who are prepared to lead a healthy campus that activates and sustains innovative work over the long term. Presidents must be adept at leading organizational change, articulating vision and values, and outlining for constituents both goals and actions. They must engage in shared governance, manage ever more partnerships, communicate to internal and external constituencies, and support change agents on campus as they work to change processes and practices. They must collaborate with others in making decisions under conditions of uncertainty, managing complex finances in an era of declining state appropriations, working with faculty and staff to effectively deploy information technology, and analyzing the data to identify areas of improvement and support student success.[7]

Empowering Settings

Senior leaders are necessary but not sufficient to tackle this complicated array of challenges and opportunities. This is shared work that requires our senior leaders to engage stakeholders across campus and to empower those who will initiate, lead, and sustain innovative new work.

Empowerment is a vitally important value and activity for us. At UMBC, we have intentionally created empowering settings for leaders, administrators, staff, faculty, and students:

- While some universities have moved away from shared governance, we have deeply embraced it.
- In the late 1980s, we initiated annual campus retreats. In the early years, we invited the President's Council. After I became president in 1993, we expanded attendance to include about two hundred faculty, staff, and leaders to discuss campus issues.
- We devoted a great deal of effort and time to our recent strategic planning process, which was carefully designed to be highly collaborative and inclusive. While the trend in business and higher education has been to substantially shorten the time devoted to strategic planning, we chose to take the time necessary to listen to and include our entire campus community.
- We hold periodic focus group sessions on campus, with students, faculty, and staff. I love these opportunities to listen and learn, discuss and interact.
- We have instituted incentive grant programs for faculty that

empower their efforts to redesign courses or infuse their classes with entrepreneurship or civic engagement.

- We also empower our students in several ways: we instill high expectations; we encourage community building and group work; we design courses in which they become responsible for—empowered to take control of—their own learning through active, team-based work.

Those who lead change may be senior leaders, but almost anyone on campus can and should be a critical agent of change. Students, faculty, and staff have all led change on our campus:

- Students advocated for a dedicated twenty-four-hour group study space in the library with tables they can configure, whiteboards, and snack machines. This effort led to the creation of the Retriever Learning Center on the first floor of our library. I often take guests on a campus tour to this center—it's a great place to see students deep in work.
- Faculty have led our course and curricular redesign efforts and have also been central to our efforts to increase faculty diversity.
- Staff have been the agents for infusing entrepreneurship into the academic core and the student experience.
- A group of faculty, staff, and students launched Breaking-Ground, a movement to support and enable civic and community action on our campus, in and out of the classroom, which inspired the administration to fund the infusion of community engagement into courses in the same way entrepreneurship had been integrated into the curriculum. This initiative represents a major partnership between students, faculty, and student affairs on the campus.

Effective change in an academic environment does not occur just by leaders telling faculty what to do. The work requires the involvement, commitment, and hard work of many stakeholders.

Faculty or staff who become champions, change agents, and allies are necessary for the success and sustainability of any campus innovation. When respected faculty are involved, they can be powerful as both change agents and role models. We'll see below how senior faculty have supported the Meyerhoff Scholars Program, faculty diversity, infusing entrepreneurship in courses, and course redesign. For our work in diversifying the faculty, we have used the STRIDE program (based on best practice from the University of Michigan), which recruits majority faculty to educate their peers on both the importance of diversity and the tools needed for success in searches and working with new faculty hires.

Shared Governance

As presidents, provosts, and other campus leaders, we often feel as though we move from crisis to crisis. We are constantly putting out fires. For example, four deaths in just four weeks among our students, staff, and faculty from health issues, suicide, and a tragic off-campus murder left our campus reeling. These were difficult times. But what allowed us to come together and to heal in this situation was that we had already established a strong community in times of calm that we could draw on in times of crisis. This takes proactive work. On our campus, we have already learned how to listen, and so, in crisis, we listen as we always do.

We have already established community, learned to listen, and practiced problem-solving through shared governance. As with democracy, shared governance can be messy, with differences in perception, conflict about goals, and diverse opinions about solutions. But shared governance that is founded on a set of shared values is critical and worth investing in for both the short and long term.

Long-term, consistent interaction and conversations among campus leadership, faculty, staff, and students create the foundation of shared governance. At UMBC, both the president and the provost attend meetings of the faculty senate, and the president of the faculty senate and chair of the senate's academic planning and budget committee are members of the President's Council, which also comprises the president, provost, other vice presidents, deans, and key staff leadership. Further, several of our key administrators, including, for example, our provost, are former presidents of the faculty senate. Integration of leadership like this allows for transparency and information sharing, providing a platform for collaborative decision-making.

This shared governance is based on a shared culture, one in which we talk about UMBC itself as an experiment and a place where we encourage experimentation.[8] We designed campus-wide projects, including strategic planning and self-assessment for accreditation, to be broadly collective and inclusive. Along with this, we have an annual two-day retreat just before the fall semester begins that also includes broad participation from faculty and staff and contributed to both of these recent efforts. As we researched this book, we talked with many people on our campus about what either encouraged or discouraged their willingness to initiate innovative approaches in their work. We listened to several of our faculty colleagues talk about challenges they faced with their departments, chairs, and fellow faculty members when trying to implement innovative practices, and it was eye opening for me. In some cases, we had no idea about the obstacles and challenges people had to overcome even on a campus like ours that embraces innovation. This encapsulates the benefits of inclusion and listening.

At its heart, what matters is collaboratively developing a campus culture that embraces innovation as a "habit of mind" that prompts us to always look in the mirror, question what we are doing and why, and ask how we can do better. It is critical that we, as leaders, listen with an open mind about what does and does not work well. It is also important to avoid becoming defensive when problems are aired, as we want to encourage people to say what they really think.

Beyond listening, we must also communicate with our campus community when there is an issue or development of general concern. But how often? In the current political climate, people expect campus leaders to speak out, almost in real time, when the administration in Washington announces a major policy decision on a sensitive issue that affects our campus community. When new policies are inconsistent with the values we express, my colleagues and I have worked to craft and send an email to the university community that states the facts clearly, articulates our values, acknowledges varying points of view, and describes in clear terms the action(s) we are taking, if any. We are very careful with the language and vet our communications at multiple levels. We understand that, regardless of the communication, there will be people who disagree with our message. This is the nature of a diverse academic community. Sometimes, when I receive heated responses, I invite the correspondent to my office. Students who are invited typically believe they are going to be punished in some way, but I simply listen to their perspectives and then give sincere responses.

Difficult Conversations

A healthy campus is one in which its members can have difficult conversations, ask probing questions, consider the evidence, and work collaboratively toward solutions. I enjoy telling the story about Nobel Laureate Isidor Isaac Rabi. When he came home from school each day, his mother didn't ask, as many others do, "What did you learn today?" He said that when he came home, his mother asked, "Did you ask a good question?" and that developing this curiosity made all the difference for him. That's what we need, a willingness to ask good questions, a culture of curiosity.

At the heart of such a culture is a space in which everyone can breathe deeply and have honest conversations that surface issues, information, and potential solutions. These conversations provide an opportunity for us to disentangle complicated issues, such as how we might change our racial climate, improve retention and graduation, or redesign courses to improve teaching and learning. They help us identify problems and engage them together to find creative solutions. They enable us to forge new relationships or partnerships that empower stakeholders across campus, overcome resistance, enable buy-in, and lead to the development of champions and allies crucial to sustainable success.

Striving to understand means hearing all voices, discovering the challenges and possibilities, and also bringing forth evidence in the most transparent way possible for everyone to consider and discuss. It is so easy to make uninformed decisions based on anecdotes. We have all done it. But it is not the right thing to do, and we would not be modeling the way we expect our students to learn and act in college, their professional careers, or their contribution to civic life. Today, advances in data collection, data accessibility, and statistical and predictive analytics provide powerful tools for analyzing problems, assessing programs, and providing data to support decision-making. Such tools provide critical insight into the challenges we are addressing, particularly in the area of student success and progression.

Even before we had the sophisticated tools now at our disposal, simply diving into available data was helpful for us in driving change. For example, when we looked at student success in the late 1980s, we examined the data on student achievement and found that black students had lower median grade point averages (GPAs) in STEM courses than other students, and much lower than we expected. But whites and Asian Americans also weren't succeeding in STEM. They also had low median GPAs. This informed our view of both the problem and the solutions. We realized that there were issues with the way science and mathematics were taught as well as the achievement of minority students in these areas.

Another source of evidence to consider is "best practice." Drawing on the experiences of others as they have addressed similar problems or opportunities allows you to capitalize on information about what works and avoid the pitfalls of what doesn't. When it came to developing the Meyerhoff Scholars Program, I looked for predominantly white institutions that were successful in supporting black students in an intentional way in the natural sciences and put them on a path to graduate school. There weren't any, and that was important information. However, I did find experimental work by Uri Treisman at Berkeley that successfully supported minorities in mathematics, and we drew on that to inform program design. I also drew on the supportive practices of historically black colleges and universities that have been proven to increase learning, persistence, and success for black students. In developing a new design for Introduction to Chemistry, the department chair drew on a decade of work by colleagues who were experimenting with new approaches to chemistry education. Our faculty have taken similar approaches to evidence-based improvements in teaching and learning from English to Psychology to Computer Science.

Careful self-reflection and robust dialogue lead to a shared institutional vision, problem identification, and agenda setting. For example, realizing our shared vision of inclusive excellence required the clear articulation of strategic goals, initiatives, and values; coordinating across multiple levels and units; and developing policies and procedures for supporting students at the high levels. For the Meyerhoff program, "a vision was generated to develop a more positive climate for students of color by creating a cadre of science and engineering African American students who would become leaders and role models for the country." The elements of the program followed from that.[9]

Just as we aim to be informed in our decision-making by data and not anecdotes, we aim to manage our initiatives by embedding assessment in the work from the outset. Willie Pearson, now professor of sociology at Georgia Institute of Technology, and I developed an evaluation component for the Meyerhoff Scholars Program that Kenneth Maton, professor of psychology at UMBC, has since overseen for nearly thirty years. This work was embedded in the program from its inception and has included formative assessments that have provided information to the program in real time for ongoing course corrections. Our emphasis on summative assessment has led to the Meyerhoff Scholars Program becoming a national model for inclusive excellence.

5

Grit and Greatness

I often quote Aristotle: "Excellence is never an accident. It is always the result of high intentions, sincere effort, and intelligent execution. It represents the wisest choice of many alternatives—choice, not chance, determines your destiny."

When I used this quote at the end of my "Founders' Day" speech in 2016, marking the fiftieth anniversary of our campus, I followed it by saying, "It takes grit to achieve greatness!" I did so because I wanted to emphasize that we achieve our aspirations not by chance, but by the choices we make and the hard work it takes to follow through on them. I wanted our campus to think about this because our fiftieth anniversary was not an end point, but rather a milestone on a long journey. "We are not yet done," I insisted. "Success is never final. However good you are, you can always improve. As we move forward we are looking in the mirror, asking questions: What are our challenges? What are our goals? How can we address the great issues of our day?"

I went on to note that, even though we have received accolades for innovation, we continue to face important challenges as a campus, including the funding needed per student to effectively execute our mission, the expensive nature of some of our academic programs, retaining our outstanding faculty when other campuses try to recruit them away, improving the diversity of our faculty, strengthening the learning experience of our undergraduate and graduate students across disciplines—a key component of our ongoing effort to improve student success—and growing research, with initiatives in selected areas.[1]

Furthermore, we have important strategic questions that are related to our goals for supporting students and extending our engagement with our communities:

- For our academic programs:
  - What is the appropriate level and balance of enrollments across our academic programs, and how do we align enrollment growth with available resources?
  - How can we increase student retention and degree completion while reducing time to degree? Which student success initiatives have the greatest impact and can be brought to scale to benefit the largest number of students?
  - Can we extend to all students the benefits of practice pioneered in our scholars programs?
  - How can we provide experiential learning and greater cultural and global competence for all students?
  - How can we deepen our innovation in teaching and learning, improve advising and mentoring, and more fully capitalize on student analytics and assessment?
  - How do we best invest in faculty and staff to increase our capacity in interdisciplinary and multidisciplinary research, scholarship, and creative activity?
- For our broader engagement:
  - How can we take the traditional themes of community engagement and service and more effectively merge them with the concept of engaged scholarship and learning?
  - How can we continue to build our partnerships with other research universities, within our university system and beyond?

 o How can we become the anchor institution for our region, advancing our role and reputation as a vital stakeholder in Maryland's innovation economy?

These are critical questions. Addressing our future challenges and opportunities will take vision and hard work, building on what we achieved during the journey of our first half century.[2]

A Valuable Asset

As I spoke with the university presidents at the White House Summit, I could not help but consider UMBC's first fifty years and the two decades I had served as president of the university. We have progressed so far during these years—a result of far more commitment and hard work than any one person could accomplish. I believe that the key to our success has always been a culture that is founded on a set of shared values that are supported by a system of effective shared governance, honest and open conversation, respect for differing viewpoints, collection and analysis of facts, and collaborative approaches to problem-solving. This does not mean that there is universal agreement about important issues, that we never encounter resistance to change, or that there is no backsliding if we take our eyes off the ball. However, it does mean that leading sustainable change means taking the long view, listening carefully, immersing oneself in substantive conversations that create a shared vision of the future, and then building a collaborative effort that addresses important issues.

The story of our campus begins two decades before my arrival. The state of Maryland in the early 1960s observed increasing student demand for higher education and recognized the need for a new public research university that would contribute to the Baltimore region's economic growth and civic life, just as the University of Maryland campus located in College Park served as a stimulus to the greater Washington, DC, region. Demand for higher education opportunities from high-achieving students rose sharply in the 1960s, particularly in the Baltimore metropolitan area, home to more than half of Maryland's population. Indeed, a 1960 study projected that "within a decade, Maryland college enrollment may grow more than in all past history. Conservative estimates lead to the conclusion that the number of Maryland students attending college will double by 1970 and triple by 1980."[3]

As demand grew faster than could be accommodated at the University of Maryland's College Park campus, with much of that growing demand in Baltimore, the sensible solution was a new campus in that region. In the midst of the unprecedented national expansion of higher education in the 1960s, and in order to meet the growing need for higher education capacity in the state, the Maryland General Assembly authorized in 1963 the establishment of a new campus in Baltimore County, charging it with providing a "nucleus for scientific research and development" and fueling science-based industry in the Baltimore region.[4]

Adding to the growing general demand was mounting pressure for inclusion following the *Brown* decision in 1954 and the civil rights movement that ensued. When UMBC opened its doors in 1966, it became the first campus in the state to enroll students of all backgrounds at its founding. Our initial freshman class in the fall of 1966 comprised 750 students, only a small number of whom were black. Yet the number and percentage of underrepresented minority students began to grow, particularly during the 1970s, when a Maryland commission criticized the campus for underrepresentation of blacks. By 1977, about a decade after we opened our doors, our undergraduate student population was one-fifth black, and black student enrollment and success would become a central part of our story. Now, forty years later, our incoming freshman class is half white and half minority.

At our opening in 1966 Albin Kuhn, the first chancellor of UMBC, said, "Just like a youngster, we don't have all the answers, but we do want to develop our own personality and become part of the Baltimore metropolitan area."[5] For our first twenty years, UMBC started small, primarily serving an educational role as an institution whose students were largely commuters. The campus was a wise bargain for everyone: commuters saved money by living at home, the state initially saved money by forgoing the cost of residence halls, and the university had a narrow mission to focus on as it became established.

As the campus matured, it was clear that it could become an even more valuable asset to the state of Maryland and the nation. And so, since the mid-1980s, we have become something else—an inclusive, student-focused, residential, research university. Michael Hooker, UMBC's fourth chancellor, expanded UMBC's aspirations when he said at his installation in 1986, UMBC's twentieth year, "My [vision] . . . is for UMBC to be a model university for the twenty-first century, and to be the best public university of its size in the country." Hooker argued that to capitalize on the university's potential and make this vision a reality, the campus should be "progressive," by being forward-looking; "responsive," by embracing our community and its needs; "selective," by growing and achieving excellence in key areas; and "metropolitan," by being a partner for the region, a force for addressing its social problems and economic development needs.[6]

At my own installation in 1993, I remarked that at the founding of Stanford University—or even at that university's twenty-fifth anniversary—no one could have envisioned what it would one day become. Its transformation lay well in the future during World War II, the Cold War, and the tech boom in Silicon Valley. Similarly, at our founding no one could then have fully envisioned what we could one day become either, I noted. My point was that we had to set our sights high. "We are a university on the move. We know what we want to become and how to get there. We will work to become one of the best research universities of our size in the world, and we are determined that our dream will not be deferred."[7]

We have since fulfilled Hooker's vision and, more importantly, become a national model for inclusive excellence. Our success can be traced to many factors. We have an inclusive notion of leadership and shared governance—and many of our administrators today were once leaders in our senates. We embrace risk—the willingness to try something new—and we act on this impulse because, as a scrappy, young institution, this is how we achieve far more than one would expect given our resources. Our most distinctive quality is our emphasis on experimentation and assessment based on evidence-based practices, particularly in the area of student success. We had early success in supporting students in the social sciences, with many students, including African Americans, going on to law school, legal careers, and judgeships—and built on that success in preparing students of all backgrounds in the STEM fields and by creating a robust research park. We believe in hard work represented by the collective effort of our entire campus community—faculty, staff, and students. And that commitment is directed toward our common goals of making a difference in the lives of our students through engaged teaching and social change through engaged scholarship that, together, constitute the core of what Ernest Boyer called "the New American College."

Today, with awards of $99.4 million in research and training grants, UMBC has taken its place among our nation's research universities—the Carnegie Foundation for the Advancement of Teaching has classified our institution as a "Doctoral University—High Research Activity." Almost all of our growth in funded research has occurred in the past twenty-five years, with funding in the natural sciences and engineering from the NSF, the National Institutes of Health (NIH), the National Aeronautics and Space Administration (NASA), and the Department of Defense, and funding in the arts, humanities, and social sciences from agencies like the National Endowment for the Humanities and the Mellon Foundation. We have also benefited from generous research support from companies such as Northrop Grumman and from foundations such as the Howard Hughes Medical Institute. UMBC operates three major collaborative centers with the NASA Goddard Space Flight Center, employing over 160 scientists and researchers. One of these, the Joint Center for Earth Systems Technology (JCET), aligns with NASA's earth science interests: engineering, atmospheric processes, climate and radiation, and atmospheric chemistry and dynamics. UMBC is ranked among the top twenty institutions in the nation with NASA support.

Recognition of our success can be seen in many of the national rankings produced in the media. *US News and World Report* ranked UMBC as the nation's number one up-and-coming national university for six years in a row (2009–14), and then in the top ten on a newly created list of the nation's "most innovative" national universities (2015–18). It has also consistently ranked UMBC among the nation's leading institutions for "Best Undergraduate Teaching." For the eighth consecutive year, *Kiplinger's Personal Finance* named UMBC a "Best Value College." The *Chronicle of Higher Education* has placed UMBC on its list of "great colleges to work for" nine years in a row, and we are just one of ten large universities to be featured on the distinguished "Honor Roll" for institutions that excel in nearly every measured category.

Of course, it is one thing to find affirmation of UMBC's success in such national rankings—often dismissed as "beauty pageants," with some reason—but we have also seen our success reflected in rigorous external reviews. In November 2016, we hosted our ten-year accreditation site visit by the Middle States Commission. The visit was preceded by a rigorous campus self-study that included a review of our mission and goals and a thorough institutional assessment. After reviewing our self-study report and spending three days meeting with students, faculty, and staff on our main campus and at Shady Grove, the Middle States review team reported that UMBC met all standards for accreditation and that they had no additional recommendations. A report from early 2017 providing formal notification of this result stated the following: "UMBC should be commended for the degree to which it's various plans—academic, enrollment, facilities, research, and most important, financial—are interrelated. This is a sign of effective institutional planning." This success results from the dedication and hard work of hundreds of colleagues, students, and supporters who shared in these planning and reaccreditation efforts.

Since 2000, we have known that we had become a special place, as it became clear that our hard work to achieve "inclusive excellence" had succeeded and people had started to take notice:

- In 2002, an American Society for Biochemistry and Molecular Biology study of 1998–99 academic year data ranked UMBC first nationally in the total number of undergraduate chemistry and biochemistry degrees awarded to African American students (twenty-one), well ahead of any other institution, and about one-third of those in the nation. When we saw these data, we knew we had achieved something special, and so did others.[8]
- In 2003, a blue-ribbon panel commissioned by Building Engineering and Science Talent (BEST) selected UMBC's Meyerhoff Scholars Program as one of three "BEST Exemplary Higher Education Programs for Undergraduates."[9]
- In 2006, the *New York Times* wrote that UMBC "opened for business in a former cow pasture not far from downtown just forty years ago. Still in its infancy as universities go, UMBC is less well known than Maryland's venerable flagship campus at College Park or the blue-blooded giant Johns Hopkins. But the upstart campus in the pasture is rocking the house when it comes to the increasingly critical mission of turning American college students into scientists."[10]
- In 2011, an analysis by the National Academies of Sciences, Engineering, and Medicine, using data from the NSF, found that among predominantly white institutions (PWIs), UMBC was the number one producer of African American undergraduates who continue on to earn doctorates in the natural sciences and engineering. When we followed up with the NSF to update the data in 2018, we found that UMBC remained the top baccalaureate-origin university among PWIs and was ranked second overall, behind only Howard University. What we also learned, while analyzing data from the Association of American Medical Colleges (AAMC), was that

UMBC is the number one university *of any type* in producing African American undergraduates who go on to earn an MD-PhD.[11]

- On November 13, 2011, CBS's *60 Minutes* aired a segment about UMBC and our Meyerhoff Scholars Program. After that, the phone calls, emails, and campus visits doubled, then tripled.
- In April 2012, the *Washington Post* editorial board called us "one of the nation's premier universities," noting the way we "combine the best of a major research center while keeping [our] focus on undergraduates."[12]

With accolades like these, it is clear that we have come a long way in the thirty years since the mid-1980s, when we were still a struggling young commuter school with a problematic racial climate. We are now preparing for new challenges and opportunities and to create the innovative approaches to teaching, learning, research, creative activity, administration, and community engagement that they demand.

The House of Grit

At the time of our fiftieth anniversary, we adopted "Grit and Greatness" as part of our celebratory branding. Personally, I suggested that it might be perceived as a bit immodest and premature to use "greatness," but it had consonance with "grit," a notion that our campus embodied, so I went along, and it provided an opportunity to talk about how it takes "grit" to move toward moments of "greatness."

Early in my time as president, my personal mantra for our campus was "It's cool to be smart." We wanted our students to believe in themselves as highly capable scholars and to adopt the high expectations aligned with that idea. Over time, though, we moved away from this notion to focus on "grit" as a key concept in describing our campus culture. We wanted to emphasize that all of our students could succeed if they had the determination and were willing to put in the work. The name of our mascot, the Chesapeake Bay Retriever, is "True Grit." We call ourselves the "House of Grit," and while I often speak about the work of Dweck and Duckworth when discussing the power of grit and a growth mindset, we had already embraced the term "grit" for decades before it become popular. In fact, we were happy to see their work as affirming and adding to what we were already doing.[13]

My installation address made the point of saying we were a "university on the move." So, along with grit, we wanted to cultivate the notion that we are adaptable and agile. As a young university, we were not bureaucratic or ossified; we would not be defined by what we did in the past, but by what we would do to construct our future. We are able to change and innovate, free from the inertia of tradition.

We also placed a great emphasis on thinking differently about choices. As Aristotle said, excellence is the result of the choices we make. When confronted with choices, we are often presented with dichotomies, for example, "Is your institution a liberal arts college or a research university?" Many dichotomies are false. So, we have rejected what Jim Collins has called the "tyranny of the 'Or'" and instead embraced "the genius of the 'And.'"[14] This allows us to think differently.

Indeed, as our campus developed, we appeared to face a choice between two futures: remain a campus founded on the liberal arts, or grow into a research university, a model that was sometimes referred to as "College Park North." The way forward, it turned out, was to reject the dichotomy, embrace both ideals, and aspire to be an institution that provides a strong liberal arts education to students, teaches them skills for their careers, and promotes research involving both undergraduates and graduate students, who could be pulled into it for the benefit of both the students and faculty. It meant finding our niche and focusing on the complement of our educational and research programs.

We have emphasized our approach to our state legislators, explaining how a student learns while working on a research project, and that this is a form of teaching and learning that is every bit as effective as spending time in a classroom. Many campuses say they want to be both, but we have the proof that we have done it. You can see it in the work our students do, what our students publish in student-refereed and academic journals, and the impressive percentage (40%) of our undergraduates in the natural sciences who go on to graduate school.

We also emphasize that while success can be measured by graduation rates, it must also be measured by the quality of the education a student receives en route to graduation. It means the provision of authentic research opportunities for students, and it means faculty working closely with students in advancing scholarship. It means transforming courses and the student experience. An award from the Ewing Marion Kauffman Foundation allowed us to provide grants to faculty who have infused seventy courses with entrepreneurship. We have established a BreakingGround initiative that similarly provides grants to faculty so they can infuse their courses with community and civic engagement. We have established new programs in gender and women's studies; media and communications studies; global studies; and languages, literacy, and culture. Awards from the Carnegie Corporation and the Heinz Foundation have endowed our Hrabowski Innovation Fund, which provides grants to faculty and staff to study student success and to redesign their courses and learning experiences. A grant from the Bill and Melinda Gates Foundation has allowed us to redesign and enhance the transfer process for students in STEM fields who come to us from partner community colleges.

We have become a university that is in sync with its environment. We are located in the Baltimore-Washington corridor. We have developed strengths in public policy and community engagement that address the challenging local social and economic problems of the Baltimore metropolitan area and also national policy issues in partnership with the nearby Social Security Administration and Centers for Medicare and Medicaid Services. We have developed a particular niche in financial economics in partnership with such financial institutions as T. Rowe Price and Legg Mason, both headquartered in Baltimore. We have developed strengths in STEM, with a particular focus on computing and cybersecurity, that align with the needs of key partners in our area, including the NSA and Northrop Grumman. We have developed strengths in environmental research, from addressing urban environmental issues to earth science, the latter through our partnership with nearby NASA Goddard Space Flight Center. We hosted the annual Imagining America conference on social justice and the arts, focusing on the challenges and opportunities for collaborative work with colleagues in the city of Baltimore.

Embracing each of these—an emphasis on grit, the genius of the "And," an institution that is both liberal arts college and research university, outside funding to innovate in our academic program, and partnerships for education and research—required our culture to evolve in new ways. They required us to recalibrate our conception of what is possible and how we might achieve our aspirational goals. They required us to think of ourselves as a university on the move, to believe that we could innovate, that we could thrive as an institution, that our students could thrive as scholars and citizens and go on to exciting opportunities in graduate school and their careers, and that we could make a difference in our society.

Strategic Choices

Tick-tick, tick-tick . . . the clock ticks as the *60 Minutes* segment opens. CBS News chief national correspondent Byron Pitts stares into the camera and brings the viewer into a conversation about our work: "UMBC . . . was once known as a commuter school. Today, this midsized state university has earned a reputation as one of the most innovative schools in the country, especially when it comes to getting students into math and science and keeping them there." Later in the segment, Kafui Dzirasa, an alumnus who went on to earn an MD-PhD and join the faculty at Duke Medical School, says,

"The most beneficial thing I got out of UMBC was believing in my-self as a scientist and learning how to work with others; how to think deeply, how to seek others who were great in other areas without being intimidated, and building teams to solve problems together." These words from Pitts and Dzirasa distill the essence of the story of our first fifty years as we were transformed from a commuter school into a midsized research university with a rep-utation for innovation, a transformation that required us to ele-vate our expectations, change our culture, make strategic choices, and innovate in our practices. We developed creative approaches to teaching and learning; we empowered faculty and staff to be in-novative and students to aim high and succeed; we encouraged col-laborative approaches to innovation, community-building among students, and team approaches to learning; and we supported risk-taking, hard work, and persistence among everyone—and we call it "grit."

When Chancellor Hooker urged us to be a model university for the twenty-first century and the best research university of our size, we built on the pioneering spirit of the faculty who had estab-lished UMBC in its first two decades. Through the collective choices we made, we sought to become that aspirational institution that developed communities of learners, redesigned courses, infused courses with entrepreneurship, embodied the notion of inclusive excellence, and increased diversity in the faculty. The choices we made led to those deep changes in culture and practice that evolved and affected the overall institutional culture and subtly, but sub-stantially, affected our ideas of who we were and what we could do.

Changing our physical environment was one of the more pro-saic changes that has made a difference in our culture. Founded in the 1960s, our campus was characterized by the architecture of that era. The utilitarian appearance of our buildings and concrete walkways was not always aligned with our desire to be an aspira-tional institution. Over the years, we have systematically improved the campus environment, replacing concrete with more aesthetic alternatives and creating more green space with trees, bushes, and flowers along our pathways. As we have built new buildings, the architecture has become more interesting and pleasing. Our landscaping has brought our campus a lush feeling and much color.

When I was the interim president in 1992, Governor William Donald Schaefer visited, and I took him up on the roof of the Administration Building to show him the campus. While we looked out over the buildings and I described what we hoped to do, the governor turned to me and said, "Freeman, what can I do to support your candidacy to become president?" He said, "I'm going to call the Regents and ask them to make you president." I asked him not to. I said, "Please, do not contact the Board of Regents." That would have seemed like I was trying to pressure the regents to hire me through the governor, and I didn't want my campus to think I had gotten the job because of him. So, when I politely declined his offer to intercede on my behalf, he then asked what he could do, noting that he didn't have a lot of money to throw around. I said, "Give me trees!" After he left, he called the Maryland Department of Natural Resources and asked them to plant trees all over campus. Those trees are now 25 years old, and they have brought much beauty to our campus, literally and visually making this a different place. When I pass those trees, I always think about Governor Schaefer.

As were many campuses founded in the 1960s, we were initially regarded as a commuter school, another characteristic that suggested we were just a run-of-the-mill place, a campus that students came to when they could not afford or gain admission to a well-established residential university, and often a place that students came to for a few years with the intent of transferring. We worked over many years to shift UMBC from a commuter school to a residential university. It takes a long time. The transformation came about by, first, continuing to hire scholars who care about teaching and, second, refining our admissions process to ensure that accepted students had a reasonable chance of success, improving student services, and very gradually adding more residence halls.

Perceptions take even longer to change than the number of beds in your residence halls. Many in the state still think of UMBC as a commuter school, which impacts who applies, who decides to enroll, and whether the students want to live on campus. But UMBC's transformation into a residential campus has happened, and this has profoundly reshaped the culture of our campus by allowing us to build community in ways we were not previously able to. It has allowed us to provide cocurricular programming that enhances the educational experience. It has brought us students with higher expectations, and that, in turn, has elevated our academic culture.

In the meantime, we have continued to support our students who live nearby and commute, understanding that not every student has the means or opportunity to live on campus. Twenty years ago, we began to listen more carefully to them about their needs. They articulated two concerns. First, many commuters said that there just wasn't any place for them to congregate, sit with friends, and talk. Second, they felt that the campus lacked a sense of community. We made a conscious decision to create many more places for students—both commuters and residents—to sit and talk with each other and with faculty, both inside and outside our buildings. We listened to their voices, and the changes we instituted went far toward building community.

As we evolved from a commuter school into a residential campus, we also began to evolve as a research university. At one point, there was even serious discussion about merging UMBC with the professional school campus at the University of Maryland, Baltimore, which precipitated an identity crisis for us. Would we be a liberal arts college or a research university? And would we emphasize the natural sciences and engineering over the arts, humanities, and social sciences? As I've noted above, our discussion about embracing the genius of the "And" was critical to finding a common path forward. To make sure that the campus understood our support for all disciplines, we highlighted the research productivity of all of our faculty and departments. We made sure that we measured research excellence not only by the amount of research funding but also by awards, fellowships, books, and articles.

But words only get you so far. Facilities and infrastructure also help to shape the campus culture. While we have been fortunate to be able to build new facilities for the natural sciences and engineering, we also obtained funding from the state to build our beautiful, state-of-the-art Performing Arts and Humanities Building (PAHB) and then revitalize our Fine Arts Building too, so that we can support those disciplines as well. As the most expensive building on campus, the PAHB has sent a signal that we support all disciplines and believe strongly in providing a broad liberal arts education.

Another act of deliberate culture change was Michael Hooker's plan to establish a research park at UMBC.[15] Hooker hoped that such a park would achieve three things: (1) send a signal to the state and federal governments that we were a serious research university, deserving of the resources and research grants of such an institution; (2) create opportunities for faculty research and student internships and jobs; and (3) provide an instrument through which the university could contribute directly to the economic development of our region. It has been a success. Today, the park—now called bwtech@UMBC—houses over 140 companies, an incubator, and space for two federal agencies, but it almost never came to be.

The park was a complex initiative that took years to bring to fruition. Hooker and I traveled to Silicon Valley in California, Research Triangle Park in North Carolina, and the Route 28 corridor in Boston to observe how universities could be major players in technology transfer, start-ups, and economic growth. It was impressive to see how many hundreds of companies have emerged from the work of MIT faculty, students, and alumni. We were excited about the way a research park could be transformative for UMBC and the Baltimore-Washington corridor. After Hooker left, my colleagues and I continued to push for the park with the help of Mark Behm, vice president for administration and finance. We developed plans and sought appropriate approvals.

However, many did not see our vision the same way, and our plans were met with significant opposition on campus and off. On campus, some faculty were generally supportive, because they were interested in technology commercialization as it related to their research. Other faculty were concerned that the project would siphon university resources for our students and alter the academic mission of the university. Some members of our community argued that the facility would have negative impacts on the local environment.

Meanwhile, off campus, community opposition developed in neighboring communities, and things were about to get nasty. Community opponents raised concerns about the possibility of increased traffic and also about whether biological research would pose an environmental risk to the surrounding community. During a community meeting, community members rose and voiced their concerns. Someone even asked whether I was pushing the research park just to get rich. "Is the president going to be on the boards of the companies in the research park and how much more money is he going to get being on the boards?" As I listened to the arguments against the park, I composed myself by writing on my pad rather than quickly becoming defensive. Some in the community got the idea that I must be writing down thoughts that would embarrass me if they were made public, so one evening while the cleaning crew was working on my floor someone walked into my office after I left, stole my notes, and gave them to a local paper to publish them. I was not embarrassed. Whenever my mother was upset, she would just say "Sweet Jesus." I had been writing that over and over on my pad, and that's the worst thing I had written.

Eventually, we were able to move forward, though in stages. When Lockheed and Martin-Marietta merged, they vacated a building near our campus. Staff at UMBC suggested we purchase the building and land to launch the research park without the new construction that was the source of most opposition. Even then, people laughed at the thought of our proceeding in this way. I was asked in a town hall meeting how we could purchase the building when we were experiencing financial challenges at the time. The response from me and our leadership team was that we had to take the long view. The financial challenges were short-term issues that we would overcome, and the facility could be purchased with long-term debt. This was not about today or tomorrow but what was good for the best interests of the institution in the long run. Senior leaders, led by Mark Behm, worked with the University System of Maryland, the Board of Regents, and the state to obtain financing so that UMBC could purchase the building. This first phase did allow us to demonstrate the benefits of the park and show the detractors that it could work and would not have the negative externalities they feared. To ameliorate concerns about the environmental impact, we agreed to reduce square footage for the new buildings to be built in phase two and to the establishment of the UMBC Conservation and Environmental Research Area (CERA).

This was culture change. We listened to those who opposed the research park. We found ways to negotiate, to accommodate concerns, and to demonstrate value. Faculty worked collaboratively with the administration for the good of UMBC. We also changed our attitudes. We embraced the notion that research and economic development were part of our mission in a significant way. We embraced the importance of experiential learning for students and research for faculty. We accepted that we were evolving and that our mission was changing.

As we became a more residential campus and grew into a research university, we also changed our approaches to admissions and academics, which also required us to change our goals, values, beliefs, and behaviors. In our early years, we admitted most students who applied. However, we expected them to perform at a high level once they arrived. There was a disconnect. A joke about our campus—that we had an Ivy League faculty and a community college student population—summed up the problem. And the result could be seen in our six-year graduation rate, which was just 35 percent in 1988.

In the late 1980s, our leadership, beginning with the then chancellor Michael Hooker, sought to reshape both our undergraduate population and the experiences we provided to our students. As our applicant pool grew, we made our admissions process more selective while also identifying students from low-income and under-represented groups who could succeed at UMBC. To attract more highly qualified students, we established an Honors College and a program designed to support high-achieving African Americans in the natural sciences and engineering, the Meyerhoff Scholars Program. The implementation and eventual success of the Meyer-hoff program would change our campus profoundly, leading to higher expectations for African American students but also for students generally, a focus on community building among students, and multicultural inclusion. The program also highlighted the importance of external fundraising, pulling faculty into innovation, and the critical importance of assessment, built into the Meyer-hoff program from its inception. Later, our faculty would redesign courses through active, team-based learning and experiential learning. We would also buck the trend seen in many public universities toward greater use of adjunct professors by increasing the number of lecturers and full-time teaching professors, hence decreasing our reliance on part-time adjuncts. All of these changes required identifying problems and opportunities, deep conversations about goals and actions, and follow-through.

A final major change in our culture has been the evolution of UMBC into a multicultural campus. Our doors were open to applicants of all backgrounds beginning with our first class, which matriculated in the fall of 1966. In our early years, the undergraduate population was overwhelmingly white, averaging about 85 percent, but also included a significant African American population, about 15 percent, a number that fluctuated over time. Our success in the 1990s with the Meyerhoff Scholars Program brought more African Americans to our campus, especially more high achievers. At the same time, we also experienced an increase in Asian American students as many highly educated Asian Americans began to make their homes in the Baltimore-Washington corridor. More recently, the Latino population of Maryland has increased, and we have seen a surge in students from those families as well.

Consequently, our student population is now about half white and half minority—Asian American, African American, Hispanic, and Native American. We also have students from over one hundred countries. UMBC is no longer a "predominantly white institution." It would be also wrong to characterize it as simply a "minority-serving institution." Yet with the way our nation characterizes institutions, we are often forced to pick one or the other. To reflect our multicultural campus, we have taken to describing ourselves as a "historically diverse institution," signaling that we have served a sizable black population since our founding and that we now reflect the incredible multicultural diversity of Maryland and our nation.

Multiculturalism is not just defined by numbers. To be a truly multicultural campus requires a culture of inclusion and engagement for all groups by all groups. Our campus was not always a place with a welcoming racial climate. One could argue that, like other universities, we had a very challenging racial climate during our early decades, with recurring racial incidents. Within a few weeks of starting my first job at UMBC in April 1987, the Black Student Union even took over the chancellor's office on the tenth floor of the Administration Building to protest recent upsetting incidents in our residence halls and the way they were handled by staff.

We were able to change this culture through difficult conversations, changes in approaches to support for African American students that altered perceptions about who could succeed at UMBC, and changes in other aspects of student life, from orientation to student affairs to student judicial proceedings. One of the critical aspects of the work, though, was finding ways, in a variety of academic and nonacademic settings, of bringing students of different backgrounds together. Some of this happens naturally in athletics, as sports teams are composed of diverse students. We brought a similar dynamic to academics through team-based learning, in which students were randomly assigned to groups. This, too, brings students of diverse backgrounds together and allows greater familiarity, understanding, acceptance, and inclusion. That changes perceptions and behaviors—it changes the culture.

Our nation is now at a critical historical moment, a crossroads if you will. Enabling an inclusive, multicultural environment at our institutions has never been more critical to the success of our institutions, our students, and America. We turn to this next.

Part II

6

At the Crossroads

The United States has arrived at a crossroads.

In the nation's growing knowledge economy, driven by technology and talent, higher education matters more than ever. This economy thrives on educated talent, workers with at least some postsecondary education, typically a bachelor's degree, and often an advanced degree.

The Center for Education and Workforce (CEW) at Georgetown University reported in June 2016, just months before the most recent presidential election, that America had experienced a "divided recovery" since the end of the Great Recession in 2009. Of the 7.2 million jobs lost during the recession, 5.6 million were held by workers with a high school diploma or less. Since then, only 800,000 jobs had been created for those with a high school diploma or less. Meanwhile, workers with a bachelor's degree or higher gained 8.4 million jobs.

The CEW report, *America's Divided Recovery*, concluded, "The post–Great Recession economy has divided the country along a fault line demarcated by college education. For those with at least some college education, the job market is robust. The economy has added 11.6 million jobs since the recession bottomed out—11.5 million, or 99 percent of them, have gone to workers with at least some college education. By contrast, workers with a high school diploma or less hear about an economic recovery and wonder what people are talking about." The report observes that these trends began much earlier, but the Great Recession and the recovery since "have intensified the long-term trends of differential opportunities between workers with and without a college education, reinforced by skill-biased technological and structural change."[1]

At the same time that our economy is changing, so is our nation's population. Policies of the current administration notwithstanding, we are on an unstoppable demographic trajectory that will produce a majority-minority population nationally within a quarter century. Indeed, already in 2019, the majority of our children in the United States are from minority groups: Asian American, African American, Hispanic, Native American, Alaska Native, or Pacific Islander. In our state of Maryland the non-Hispanic white population was 51 percent in 2016, a proportion reflected in our campus demographics as well.[2]

What makes these combined trends alarming is that we are not fully engaged in the hard work of integrating them into the powerful force for prosperity that they could be. As STEM fields grow in importance in our economy, the nation's demographic groups that are growing the fastest are the most underrepresented in these fields. This is where higher education—and what we do in our institutions of higher education to support students of all backgrounds—can make such a difference. Achieving major national goals takes time, hard work, and the participation of all actors, including federal and state government, the private sector, foundations, and our institutions of higher education. Achieving major national goals requires from higher education ideas, innovations, pilot projects, proof of concept, dissemination of best practice, and adaptation across many institutions. They require that we take the long view and accept that our goals require hard work over the long run.

The Crossroads

In 2008, I accepted an invitation from the National Academy of Sciences to chair a study committee that would engage in a national conversation about what we, at UMBC, had come to call "inclusive excellence." The committee would write a report on enhancing the participation and success of underrepresented minority students in STEM fields, the focus of my academic research and my work at UMBC over many years. What made the offer especially appealing was that this study would be a direct follow-up to the most significant report on the science and engineering enterprise in some time, *Rising above the Gathering Storm: Energizing and Employing America for a Brighter Economic Future*. I believed that positioning our work as an extension of the *Gathering Storm* report would significantly enhance its potential impact.

The National Academies had produced *Rising above the Gathering Storm* in response to a congressional request for "the top ten actions . . . federal policymakers could take to enhance the science and technology enterprise so the United States can successfully compete, prosper, and be secure in the global community of the 21st century."[3] The *Gathering Storm* report argued that while America's capabilities in science and engineering were as strong as ever in 2005, our dominance in these fields had diminished as other countries invested in and grew their research and educational capacities. The report urged that for the United States to maintain its global leadership position in STEM and enhance its economic competitiveness, the nation had to commit to significant investments in research, enact policies that encouraged innovation, and implement programs that would grow a strong and talented science and technology workforce.[4]

In November 2006, Senators Barbara Mikulski (D-MD), Edward Kennedy (D-MA), Hillary Rodham Clinton (D-NY), and Patty Murray (D-WA) wrote a letter to the National Academies requesting a follow-up report to the *Gathering Storm* report that would more fully address the issue of workforce development and diversity in STEM education and the ways the federal government and others could work to expand underrepresented minority participation and success. Later, when Congress passed the America COMPETES Act—the legislation implementing most of the recommendations of the

Gathering Storm report—it included a directive to the National Academies to undertake the study that I was about to lead.

After fundraising and the appointment of a strong study committee, the work got underway, and in 2011 we released *Expanding Underrepresented Minority Participation: America's Science and Technology Talent at the Crossroads*. Often referred to as the *Crossroads* report, our study presented compelling evidence that the success of underrepresented minority students in STEM (referred to as science and engineering, or S&E, in the report) was critical to our national success and competitiveness in science and technology:

> The importance of S&E to the United States has been documented in a series of reports over more than half a century. Nevertheless, critical issues for the nation's S&E infrastructure remain unsettled. Among them, America faces a demographic challenge with regard to its S&E workforce: Minorities are seriously underrepresented in science and engineering, yet they are also the most rapidly growing segment of the population. *Gathering Storm* provided compelling recommendations for sustaining and increasing our knowledge workforce as part of a larger plan to sustain the nation's scientific and technological leadership. These workforce recommendations focused on improving K–12 STEM education as well as providing incentives for students to pursue S&E education at the undergraduate and graduate levels. We fully support these recommendations, but they are insufficient to meet the emerging demographic realities. The United States stands again at the **crossroads**: A national effort to sustain and strengthen S&E must also include a strategy for ensuring that we draw on the minds and talents of all Americans, including minorities who are underrepresented in S&E and currently embody a vastly underused resource and a lost opportunity for meeting our nation's technology needs.[5]

Our report reflected on the fact that our nation has never been close to drawing fully on our nation's science and technology pool of talent. And, unfortunately, at the time of this writing that goal is now receding further from our grasp, as our society grows more divided rather than united in its robust and powerful diversity and commitment to inclusion. As our report clearly demonstrates, if we turn our backs on minorities and immigrants, who have the greatest potential to energize our national science and technology enterprise, we will do so to the detriment of our society, our economy, and our global competitiveness. However, if we take the deliberate steps needed to expand the participation and success of underrepresented minorities in STEM fields—those who represent the fastest-growing part of the US population—we will have a diverse pool that draws from all of our talent and provides the graduates needed by private, public, and nonprofit employers to meet the economic, security, health, and other national goals the American people prize.[6]

Dimensions of the Problem

The *Crossroads* report identified significant underrepresentation of African Americans, Hispanics, and Native Americans in science and engineering, which continues eight years later. The percentage of the nation's science and engineering workforce (academic and nonacademic) that was underrepresented minority increased from 9.1 to 12.8 percent between 2006 and 2015. However, between 2006 and 2014, the percentage of the nation's population that was composed of underrepresented minorities increased from 28.5 to 32.6 percent.[7] The increasing participation of minorities in the science and education workforce is not keeping pace with changing demographics in our society.

The *Crossroads* report found that "underrepresentation of this magnitude in the S&E workforce stems from the underproduction of minorities in S&E at every step of postsecondary education, with a progressive loss of representation as we proceed up the academic ladder."[8] In 2016, to mark the fifth anniversary of the *Crossroads* report, we revisited the issues we examined in that study and then published an article in *Issues in Science and Technology* that contained our findings.[9] What was true in 2000 and remained true in 2012 (the most recent year available for data when the article was published) was this: despite increases in underrepresented minority participation in postsecondary education and science and increased numbers of degrees earned at all levels, we still see significant underrepresentation in STEM fields. In 2012, underrepresented minorities composed 34.6 percent of undergraduates, but only 18.9 percent of those earning STEM bachelor's degrees, 13.7 percent of those awarded S&E master's degrees, and just 7.3 percent of doctoral awards in these fields.[10]

Our study committee was not surprised to discover, given the findings described above, that most underrepresented minority undergraduates left STEM majors prior to completing a college degree. According to analysis by UCLA's Higher Education Research Institute (HERI), just 18.4 percent of blacks, 22.1 percent of Latinos, and 18.8 percent of Native Americans who matriculated at four-year institutions seeking a bachelor's degree in a STEM field earned one within five years.[11] We concluded, based on this evidence and the success of some institutions in producing much better results, that there existed "a cadre of qualified underrepresented minorities who already attend college, declared an interest in majoring in the natural sciences or engineering, and either did not complete a degree or switched out of STEM before graduating." We recommended comprehensive support for minority college undergraduates in these fields—even as we also support K–12 academic preparation—and that financial support for these students "be provided through higher education institutions along with programs that simultaneously integrate academic, social, and professional development."[12]

As a committee, we were surprised at another finding from the HERI study. While underrepresented minority students had low levels of persistence in STEM majors, the rate of success of white and Asian American students was higher but still significantly below the levels of success we need for undergraduates of all backgrounds in STEM: 33 percent of whites and 42 percent of Asian Americans who aspire to earn a bachelor's degree in a STEM field had done so within five years. Indeed, what we see in these STEM persistence rates is a national crisis. While we have a compelling obligation to support underrepresented minorities in STEM, we must also find ways to improve teaching and learning in the natural sciences and engineering for all undergraduates. We'll turn to this later.

Models to Learn From

At the time we released the *Crossroads* report in 2011, we observed that while we had barely moved the needle on expanding underrepresented minority success in STEM fields, we as a nation had an excellent opportunity to succeed since we already had clear, best-practice examples of what worked and, therefore, what we needed to do. Indeed, reports from the National Academies, the White House Office of Science and Technology Policy, and other organizations have now clearly described the problem of underrepresentation in STEM and offered evidence-based findings and thoughtful recommendations for creating the pipeline for the talent we need.[13] The nation has at hand successful models of inclusive excellence in STEM education that are ready to be adapted at other colleges and universities. This can be understood if we look at the evidence: data disaggregated by field and institution. This level of analysis identifies universities that are already succeeding in educating underrepresented minorities in these fields. It is imperative that we should build on and adapt this work nationally.

Where should federal agencies, corporate foundations, and private philanthropies invest their funds to boost the success of underrepresented minorities in STEM? An analysis of the institutions that educate undergraduate African Americans who go on to earn PhDs in the natural sciences and engineering reveals a diverse range of institutions that can support underrepresented minority success in STEM. As shown in table 1, twelve of the top twenty baccalaureate-origin institutions are historically black colleges and universities and eight are predominantly white institutions. With just one exception, all of these institutions are either HBCUs or very large "Research–Very High" institutions as defined by the

TABLE 1

Top thirty US baccalaureate-origin institutions of 2007–16 black science and engineering doctorate recipients, by institutional control, 2010 Carnegie classification, and HBCU status

Rank	Baccalaureate institution	Institutional control	2010 Carnegie classification	HBCU status	2007–16 Black S&E doctorate recipients
	All black S&E doctorate recipients	n/a	n/a	n/a	7,206
	From US institutions	n/a	n/a	n/a	6,104
	From foreign institutions	n/a	n/a	n/a	905
	From unreported institutions	n/a	n/a	n/a	197
1	Howard U.	Private	Research–high	Yes	130
2	U. Maryland, Baltimore County	Public	Research–high	No	119
3	Florida A&M U.	Public	Doctoral/research	Yes	112
4	North Carolina Agricultural and Technical State U.	Public	Doctoral/research	Yes	108
5	Xavier U. Louisiana	Private	Baccalaureate	Yes	103
6	Spelman C.	Private	Baccalaureate	Yes	102
7	Morgan State U.	Public	Doctoral/research	Yes	85
8	Southern U. and A&M C., Baton Rouge	Public	Masters granting	Yes	78
9	Hampton U.	Private	Masters granting	Yes	75
9	U. Florida	Public	Research–very high	No	75
11	Morehouse C.	Private	Baccalaureate	Yes	69
12	U. Maryland, College Park	Public	Research–very high	No	63
13	Jackson State U.	Public	Research–high	Yes	62
13	Tuskegee U.	Private	Baccalaureate	Yes	62
15	Massachusetts Institute of Technology	Private	Research–very high	No	61
16	U. Michigan, Ann Arbor	Public	Research–very high	No	60
17	Tennessee State U.	Public	Doctoral/research	Yes	54
18	U. Illinois, Urbana-Champaign	Public	Research–very high	No	52
19	Georgia Institute of Technology	Public	Research–very high	No	49
20	U. North Carolina, Chapel Hill	Public	Research–very high	No	46
21	North Carolina State U.	Public	Research–very high	No	44
22	Alabama A&M U.	Public	Masters granting	Yes	43
23	Florida State U.	Public	Research–very high	No	42
24	Clemson U.	Public	Research–high	No	41
24	Rutgers, State U. New Jersey, New Brunswick	Public	Research–very high	No	41
24	U. Virginia, Charlottesville	Public	Research–very high	No	41
27	CUNY, City C.	Public	Masters granting	No	38
28	Cornell U.	Private	Research–very high	No	37
28	Harvard U.	Private	Research–very high	No	37
28	Prairie View A&M U.	Public	Masters granting	Yes	37

Source: National Science Foundation, National Center for Science and Engineering Statistics, 2016 Survey of Earned Doctorates; special tabulation (October 2018).

Notes: Includes only US citizens and permanent residents. Institutions with the same number of doctorate recipients are listed alphabetically. For the purposes of this table, science and engineering includes health and excludes psychology and social sciences. HBCU = historically black college and university; n/a = not applicable; S&E = science and engineering.

2010 Carnegie Classification. The solitary exception among all of these baccalaureate-origin institutions is UMBC, a medium-size, predominantly white yet historically diverse research university ("Research–High" in the Carnegie Classification). UMBC places number two in the list for African American PhDs, well ahead of the next PWI (University of Florida, at no. 9). UMBC has focused on "inclusive excellence," delivering results in a manner that is quite unexpected given this context. Meanwhile, as seen in table 2, all of the top twenty baccalaureate-origin institutions for Hispanic PhDs in the natural sciences and engineering are without exception Hispanic-serving institutions or very large "Research–Very High" institutions.

The HBCUs are Howard, Florida A&M, North Carolina A&T, Xavier, Spelman, Morgan State, Southern, Hampton, Morehouse, Jackson State, Tuskegee, and Tennessee State. The PWIs are UMBC; Florida; University of Maryland, College Park; MIT; Michigan; Illinois; Georgia Tech; and the University of North Carolina at Chapel Hill. The efforts of these PWIs are important, though even the highest-producing predominantly white, Research–Very High universities are only graduating a relatively small number of African Americans each year who go on to earn PhDs in the natural sciences or engineering—about four to eight per year. And this is often without a deliberate program. With a concerted effort, as we discuss below, we believe that these universities could more than double or triple those numbers.

Clearly, HBCUs are critical. According to the National Center for Education Statistics, there are one hundred HBCUs in nineteen states, the District of Columbia, and the US Virgin Islands. They represent just 3 percent of postsecondary institutions, but they enroll 8 percent of all black undergraduates. They award 15 percent of bachelor's degrees earned by blacks, 19 percent of STEM bachelor's degrees earned by blacks, and 35 percent of bachelor's degrees earned by blacks who go on to receive PhDs in STEM. HBCUs continue to be a critical resource in educating and preparing blacks for our nation's science and engineering workforce.[14]

TABLE 2

Top thirty US baccalaureate-origin institutions of 2007–16 Hispanic or Latino science and
engineering doctorate recipients, by institutional control, 2010 Carnegie classification, and HSI status

Rank	Baccalaureate institution	Institutional control	2010 Carnegie classification	HSI status	2007–16 Hispanic S&E doctorate recipients
	All Hispanic or Latino S&E doctorate recipients	n/a	n/a	n/a	9,083
	From US institutions	n/a	n/a	n/a	7,852
	From foreign institutions	n/a	n/a	n/a	1,044
	From unreported institutions	n/a	n/a	n/a	187
1	U. Puerto Rico, Mayaguez	Public	Doctoral/research	Yes	559
2	U. Puerto Rico, Rio Piedras	Public	Research–high	Yes	326
3	U. Texas, El Paso	Public	Research–high	Yes	189
4	U. Florida	Public	Research–very high	No	184
5	U. California, Los Angeles	Public	Research–very high	No	144
6	U. California, Berkeley	Public	Research–very high	No	134
7	U. Texas, Austin	Public	Research–very high	No	132
8	Massachusetts Institute of Technology	Private	Research–very high	No	129
9	Florida International U.	Public	Research–high	Yes	128
10	U. California, Davis	Public	Research–very high	No	117
11	Texas A&M U., College Station and Health Science Center	Public	Research–very high	No	101
11	U. California, Irvine	Public	Research–very high	Yes	101
13	U. Arizona	Public	Research–very high	Yes	93
14	U. California, San Diego	Public	Research–very high	No	92
15	Cornell U.	Private	Research–very high	No	89
16	U. New Mexico, Albuquerque	Public	Research–very high	Yes	85
17	U. Puerto Rico, Humacao	Public	Baccalaureate	Yes	84
18	New Mexico State U., Las Cruces	Public	Research–high	Yes	81
19	U. Miami	Private	Research–very high	No	80
20	U. California, Santa Cruz	Public	Research–very high	Yes	70
21	U. California, Riverside	Public	Research–very high	Yes	66
22	Florida State U.	Public	Research–very high	No	64
23	U. Puerto Rico, Cayey	Public	Baccalaureate	Yes	62
24	Stanford U.	Private	Research–very high	No	57
24	U. California, Santa Barbara	Public	Research–very high	Yes	57
26	U. Texas, San Antonio	Public	Research–high	Yes	55
27	Arizona State U.	Public	Research–very high	No	52
27	Rice U.	Private	Research–very high	No	52
29	California State U., Los Angeles	Public	Masters granting	Yes	51
30	U. Michigan, Ann Arbor	Public	Research–very high	No	50

Source: National Science Foundation, National Center for Science and Engineering Statistics, 2016 Survey of Earned
Doctorates; special tabulation (October 2018).
Notes: Includes only US citizens and permanent residents. Includes only institutions in the United States. Institutions
with the same number of doctorate recipients are listed alphabetically. For the purposes of this table, science and
engineering includes health and excludes psychology and social sciences. HSI = Hispanic-serving institution; n/a = not
applicable; S&E = science and engineering.

However, since the overwhelming majority of black undergraduates (92%) are enrolled in institutions that are not HBCUs, we must not ignore the responsibility of those institutions to make a significant difference in educating blacks in the STEM fields. At the graduate level, PWIs award 88 percent of doctorates to blacks: 26 percent of blacks earn a bachelor's degree at an HBCU and then earn a doctorate at a PWI, and 62 percent of blacks earn both the bachelor's degree and PhD at a PWI. There is some variation by field in the percentage of PhDs awarded to blacks by PWIs: these institutions award 96 percent of mathematics and computer science PhDs, 91 percent of engineering PhDs, 87 percent of physical sciences PhDs, 86 percent of biological and biomedical sciences PhDs, and 73 percent of PhDs in agriculture.[15]

Given that most African American students are enrolled in PWIs, replicating the success of those PWIs that have done well in educating African Americans in STEM—and building on the lessons learned from successful HBCUs—would be a logical place to focus investment. UMBC is one of those institutions, because we developed innovative approaches to supporting African American students, financially, socially, and academically, and provided that support through a focused initiative, the Meyerhoff Scholars Program.

Evolving Context

The participation of African American students in American higher education has grown dramatically since the 1960s. In 1966, the year UMBC opened, just 3.8 percent of blacks age 25 years and older had completed four years of college. Because of de jure segregation, most college-educated African Americans at that time had attended one of our nation's HBCUs, typically the only institutions available to them. These institutions played a critical role for the black community during this period—and still do as that role evolves. Like many who attended an HBCU, I have great pride in my alma mater, Hampton University. Two decades later, the landscape had changed. By 1986, 10.9 percent of African Americans over age 25 had earned a four-year degree. They had done so at a much wider array of higher education institutions. The number of African American students enrolling at HBCUs was not declining, but as the number of black students going to college went up, the increase was entirely in attendance at PWIs. By the early 1970s the percentage of black undergraduates who were enrolled at HBCUs fell below 50 percent, and by 1980 just 17 percent of black undergraduates were enrolled at HBCUs; most were enrolled at PWIs like UMBC.[16]

Change did not come easily, and it was possible only because many actors played a determined role over a long period. These increased levels of participation and success had been facilitated by the Supreme Court's 1954 decision in *Brown v. Board of Education*, the Civil Rights Act of 1964, the creation and implementation of federal financial aid programs in 1965, and the expansion of those programs to include the Pell Grant in 1972. The modern civil rights movement worked hard—and often against violent opposition— to tear down segregation in the South and make good the promise of the *Brown* decision that black students could enroll at state universities there in the late 1950s and early 1960s. Change was also facilitated by the hard work of black families who sacrificed to send their children to college and by those students themselves who worked hard to achieve something that often no one in their family had ever achieved before. And once black students were admitted to universities across the country—in the South and the North— they often encountered more challenges to their success. Sometimes they had to deal with the inadequate preparation their high schools had given them; other times they encountered situations in which they felt unwelcome or had to confront outright racism.

Against this backdrop, our UMBC campus was built in the mid-1960s on the edge of the Baltimore metropolitan area, nearly in the geographic center of Maryland, which was then in the throes of racial change. As a Southern state, Maryland had been racially segregated for decades. Public schools and colleges, movie theaters and amusement parks, residential neighborhoods, and public facilities were segregated and neighborhoods redlined. Yet this regime was contested, and as our campus came to life, segregation was eroding. In the 1930s, the National Association for the Advancement of Colored People sued to force the University of Maryland Law School to admit blacks because no similar law school was made available for black students under a "separate but equal" policy. Donald Gaines Murray, represented by Charles Hamilton Houston and Thurgood Marshall, won this case, setting an important precedent on the road to *Brown v. Board of Education* in 1954. In 1952, two years before the *Brown* decision, the Baltimore City School Board admitted twelve black students to Baltimore Polytechnic Institute, a magnet secondary school, because no similar program was available for black students. Following the *Brown* decision, public schools and universities in Maryland were desegregated, and segregation in general in Maryland slowly began to collapse. The Gwynn Oak Amusement Park just two miles from UMBC in Baltimore County, for example, was integrated in 1963 after several protests. A daughter of an employee at the nearby Social Security Administration was the first African American to enjoy a ride at Gwynn Oak when she rode the carousel.[17]

The advance of civil rights and the removal of racial barriers brought both heartbreak and opportunity. In 1968, following the assassination of the Reverend Dr. Martin Luther King Jr., Baltimore erupted in riots and fires that left many African American neighborhoods in the city devastated, as frustration decades in the making boiled over. Afterward, with the passage of fair housing laws that same year, black families joined white families in moving to suburban areas like Woodlawn in Baltimore County and the new planned community of Columbia, founded at the same time as UMBC and just a stone's throw away in Howard County. Columbia would grow over time into a city of 100,000 and would also become one of the most racially integrated and tolerant communities not only in Maryland but also in the United States. It was, in the 1960s and 1970s, one of the few places in Maryland and even the United States where interracial couples were welcome. As that town grew, its high schools would become some of the largest feeder schools for UMBC.

The Baltimore-Washington corridor, where UMBC is located, grew increasingly integrated as the federal presence grew significantly in the 1960s and after. The region surrounding our campus became home to many large federal agencies and installations, including the Social Security Administration, the Centers for Medicare and Medicaid Services, the NASA Goddard Space Flight Center, and the National Security Agency at Fort Meade. While there were also challenges to integrating the federal workforce—which had been deliberately segregated under Woodrow Wilson's administration—these federal agencies were often among the leaders in hiring black professionals, increasing substantially the black middle class in the Baltimore area. At the same time, many black federal employees moved their families from the District of Columbia to neighboring Prince George's County in Maryland at the southern end of the Baltimore-Washington corridor. The Washington and Baltimore metropolitan areas stand today as first and third in the nation, respectively, for median black household income.

Because of the *Brown* decision, the work of the modern civil rights movement, and these changes in our community, when UMBC enrolled its first students in the fall of 1966, we were poised to provide a different experience for students of all backgrounds. We were the first campus in Maryland open to students of all races from its beginning, and newly empowered black families in the Baltimore-Washington region, just like other families, sent their children to places like UMBC for the opportunities that a college education could provide. From 1966 to 1971, black undergraduate enrollment at UMBC increased from 2 to 8 percent. That was a start, but the Maryland Human Relations Commission argued in 1972 that this 8 percent (just 287 of 3,772 undergraduates) was still inexcusably lower than the percentage of the metropolitan area's population that was black. They also noted that just 8 out of 187 faculty were black. So, we took steps to increase black enrollment further. By 1973, it had more than doubled to 613, or 12 percent of the student population. By 1977, with black enrollment at 1,057, it momentarily reached an all-time high of 21 percent of our undergraduates, before declining and leveling off in the ensuing decade at around 13 percent, primarily because of poor academic persistence.

This roller-coaster ride of African American enrollment at UMBC during these early years is the backstory to a major transformation on our campus. Trying to do the right thing, we had adopted many of the same admissions practices as our peer institutions. We admitted many students, black and white, without ensuring that they were adequately prepared for the academic work before them, and without ensuring that the campus was prepared to welcome, integrate, and support them. I had seen the same phenomenon earlier while a graduate student at the University of Illinois. In an effort to integrate and increase the number and percent of black students at the University of Illinois at Urbana-Champaign, administrators who had good intentions opened the door to many blacks, often from places like Chicago. Unfortunately, like the rest of American higher education, they had not given much thought to the minimum level of preparation one needs in order to succeed at the university, so the "open door" soon became known as the "revolving door." I then saw this same phenomenon at UMBC as well. We had high enrollment but low persistence and completion. And low grades and students flunking out, in turn, lead to frustration.

Changing the Climate and Outcomes

I started work as vice provost at UMBC on April Fools' Day—April 1, 1987—so I should have known there would be a surprise in store for me.[18] And so here I was on April 15, trying to make my way to my office, walking carefully among the students sitting on the floor of the hallway chanting, "We're gonna beat back, this racist attack! We're gonna beat back, this racist attack!" I had once participated in a civil rights protest in my hometown of Birmingham, Alabama, at age 12 and spent five terrifying nights in jail for it. Now, I wondered to myself, had I become "the man"? I found the one black person besides me who worked on the tenth floor and asked what was going on. She said, "Oh, don't worry, this happens every spring at UMBC."

She was more or less right about the frequency of black student protest at UMBC. There had been periodic protests and sit-ins over racial incidents at UMBC during its first two decades, not every year but often enough to suggest that there were deep unaddressed issues. The last protest had occurred one year before in April 1986, motivated by two incidents in UMBC's residence halls in which white and black students had come into conflict and by the manner in which they were handled by UMBC administrators. In one of the incidents, two young men, one white and one black, had been involved in a late-night altercation over noise and partying. However, only the black male had been investigated and sanctioned. The Student Judicial Board found the black male guilty of "behavior that jeopardized the safety or well-being of another person" and of violating residential life regulations, and they sentenced him to probation and fifteen hours of community service. However, the director of residential life, who was white, took the unusual step of appealing that relatively light sentence to the vice president of student affairs, also white, who handed down more severe sanctions that included suspension of the student's residential contract for a year. While the administrators involved followed established procedures "to the letter" and the penalties handed down by the vice president for student affairs matched the sanctions handed down in similar, previous cases, many African American students were upset. Investigating only the black male appeared biased. Appealing the sentence and imposing a much harsher one added insult to injury. Not surprisingly, students felt a strong need to vent their frustration, formed a "Coalition against Injustice," and drew up a list of demands. On April 18, 1986, the coalition occupied the chancellor's office and the tenth floor of the Administration Building and presented their list of demands to Chancellor Dorsey.

What happened next is the kind of tragicomic dance that can only happen at a campus in which the climate is toxic and there is little trust. Chancellor Dorsey, just months away from retirement, left the unresolved matter for his successor, Michael Hooker, who took office as chancellor in the summer of 1986. Dorsey had promised that the administration would take action following a review of the events, and the students had ended their sit-in, saying they would await a response. Hooker took the coalition's demands seriously. He met with the university's Task Force on Desegregation in July 1986, asking them to review the incidents of the previous academic year and provide him with recommendations for action. He then also met with the student protest leaders in October 1986, saying he would take action once the task force had submitted its report. When the task force submitted an interim report on March 4, 1987, the coalition leaders said Hooker had enough information to act and insisted on a response to their demands by noon on April 15. Hooker told the students that the final report of the task force was to be delivered on April 16 and that he would be more than happy to meet with them on either Friday, April 17, or Monday, April 20, to discuss both the coalition's demands and the findings and recommendations of the task force. Neither the students nor the chancellor gave ground. When Hooker did not respond by noon on April 15, the coalition marched to the Administration Building and took over the tenth floor. They chanted, "Chancellor Hooker, you better fear! We won't take this another year!"

During the period from 1965 to 1972, when black students first arrived in numbers on traditionally white campuses after the passage of the Civil Rights Act, black protests erupted on campuses in response to racism, real and perceived, and also frustration with the pace of progress toward African American academic success. Black students and their allies, as they did at UMBC in 1986 and 1987, demanded greater inclusion and more substantive support. Some of these protests, like the takeover of Willard Straight Hall at Cornell, turned dangerous and left bitter feelings for many involved among protesters, administration, and faculty. These black protests have echoed over the years, including quite recently. After a series of racially charged incidents, black student protests came to the University of Missouri in the fall of 2015. Students organized two "Racism Lives Here" events on September 24 and October 1 and eventually submitted a list of demands to the leadership of the campus and the University of Missouri System. The consequences of the racial incidents, the protests, and the manner in which the system and campus administrations responded to these controversies included the resignations of both the campus chancellor and the system president, a 35 percent decline in freshmen enrollment at the Columbia campus, national controversy over safe spaces and free speech, and the spread of protests to eighty other campuses nationwide.

As protests spread, students issued demands of the campus administrators. A December 2015 *Chronicle of Higher Education* article reviewed a ranking of demands from groups at fifty-one campuses by FiveThirtyEight. The most common demands included increasing faculty diversity (with an emphasis on hiring black faculty), increasing student diversity and working to retain more minority students, requiring diversity or sensitivity training, funding cultural centers, changes in the curriculum and in courses required for students, and expanded mental health resources. In some instances, students demanded the removal of specific administration officials.[19]

The demands of the coalition at UMBC in 1986–87 read like a distant echo of the demands we hear on today's campuses. They included the dismissal of personnel and students believed to have acted in a racist manner, reforming student judicial processes, special funding for the Black Student Union, creation of an office of minority affairs, and the recruitment of black faculty members. As additional voices joined the conversation, the issues under discussion broadened to also include staff sensitivity training on the one hand and student support, retention, and academic success on the other, both of which opened additional areas of discussion and work.

Several of the demands were met and helped diffuse, over time, the immediate conflict. Key personnel departed UMBC or were transferred to other offices. New personnel in student affairs brought expertise and experience with intercultural communication. A review of student judicial processes led to policy and procedural changes that made processes clearer and fairer. Student affairs established sensitivity training programs for staff and students. The chancellor provided funds to the Black Student Union for orientation, cultural events, and other special projects.

Deep problems are not solved overnight but require an environment characterized by substantive and authentic discussions and significant effort over a sustained period of time. At his installation in 1986, Chancellor Hooker had outlined a long-term vision for UMBC that would strengthen both its effectiveness and reputation: improve academic performance for all students, increase the size and quality of faculty research, engage our community as a partner, and become an economic driver for the region. In April 1987, one might have concluded that our problems were largely racial in nature, yet we soon found that when we peeled back the layers on issues of race, they were deeply intertwined with issues of academic performance. This gave us an opportunity to refocus our conversations on academic improvement for all students, including African American students.

We changed the lens through which we looked at our campus and changed the conversation to focus on student success. As a society, we were tearing down segregation in higher education and opening opportunity for students of all backgrounds. We had a growing number of black families that took advantage of that opportunity. At a time when higher education was becoming more important to securing and maintaining a position in the American middle class, their children had "made it" to campus. Yet access alone was not enough. The campus environment had not yet developed to adequately support student learning and success. The six-year graduation rate at UMBC in the late 1980s was 35 percent for all groups and 10 points lower for African American students; indeed, students of all races were not making it. Even today I meet people who were students in the early decades who tell me they

"attended" UMBC—they don't say they "graduated from" UMBC—
and I can see in their eyes what they mean and feel. They feel as
though they failed, but I know that, back then, our institution just
as often failed them.

So while the protests were a momentary "cause célèbre," what
mattered more in the long run was the hard work to come of
changing campus culture and improving student success, and that
required a different kind of engagement. A report on the protests
by a campus task force argued that the "case could well serve as
a textbook example in the social dynamics of campus interracial
peace and politics." For more than a decade we had had periodic
racial incidents and protests. This was a "conversation" of sorts,
but not a productive one for our campus. Students wanted us to
take them seriously, they wanted to be heard, and they wanted
our help. Students who receive low grades, and ultimately students
who don't make it, experience terrible frustration. Success in higher
education, and the American dream that came with it, was so close,
and yet so far away.

Our faculty and staff were very committed to students and
worked hard to build our campus, but from our leadership on down
we had not yet found a way to have the difficult conversations with
students, faculty, and staff that could be transformational. The
response to protests by campus leaders had often been to avoid
discussion, and the "campus conversation," such as it was, just as
often deteriorated into protest chants. An alternative approach
would have been to say, "Come in and let me listen to you."

What I have learned over the years is that having the opportunity to listen to different voices and perspectives and being seen
as genuinely interested in understanding the challenges that students or faculty are facing can lead to greater trust among groups
and more productive interchange of ideas. Counterintuitively, a
leader's hand is actually strengthened when the environment encourages open and robust dialogue and problem-solving and we
convince people that leadership is not about "the leader," but about
collaboration across the campus. I am often asked whether I have

made major mistakes at one point or another as president. My answer is always a resounding "yes." But I have learned that mistakes can still lead to progress when I am truthful, ask for help, show the humility to allow that I don't know something, and, perhaps just as importantly, show the confidence that we can address issues and solve problems together, that we can continue to improve. Being honest and receptive goes a long way.

Chancellor Hooker was honest and receptive. He had previously served as a dean at the Johns Hopkins University and then president of Bennington College and readily admitted having no prior experience in dealing with racial climate issues. This did not stop him from reaching out, securing help, and finding a way forward for our campus that could be transformational. He consulted with the state's black legislative caucus, which encouraged him to diversify his senior staff. He hired two African Americans into senior positions that carried broad responsibility—and, very importantly, not just responsibility for promoting diversity and supporting minority students. One of these hires was me. I came on board as vice provost, a new position to focus on the undergraduate academic experience. The other was Thomas Malone, hired as associate vice chancellor for graduate studies and research. This immediately changed the character of the campus administration.

As vice provost, I was charged with overseeing and improving the undergraduate academic experience for all students, with enhancing student success for African American undergraduates as a critical element in an overall strategy. Having already served as vice president for academic affairs at nearby Coppin State College, my primary responsibility in this new position would be to focus on the academic performance of undergraduates. Faculty and staff at UMBC were supportive of our students, black and white. Some black students had been performing well in the social sciences and the humanities, disciplines that had produced graduates who went on to law school and a variety of careers. But the performance of black students in the natural sciences and engineering was especially problematic, because in their foundational coursework these students generally earned Bs and (more often) Cs at best. I held focus groups with students and asked them why they thought they were not getting better grades. The black students reflexively said that they thought it was due to "racism." I probed further. Some said that when blacks and whites were in the same class, black students typically received lower grades than white students. Since the teacher was white, they assumed that this perceived difference must be due to racial bias. What else could it be? Yet many white students were also not doing well. When I probed further with them, they said it was because the academic environment they encountered at UMBC was "cold" and "unsupportive."

We changed this culture through conversations with our students and faculty and then changed the way we approached the support for African American students. These changes led to successes that fundamentally altered perceptions about who could succeed at UMBC. We succeeded by identifying the key challenges. We found that a disproportionately high percentage of African Americans were not succeeding, especially in the natural sciences and engineering. Rather than addressing this problem by focusing on remediation, we flipped the paradigm and concentrated on finding resources to attract and support high-achieving African American students in the natural sciences with a view to preparing them for success in graduate school. We determined the minimum level of preparation that students needed to be ready to do the work and succeed at UMBC in the natural sciences and established those standards as the threshold for admissions.

While we encountered some opposition to this approach, we were able to bring along enough people to allow us to proceed and see whether we could succeed. Some admissions staff were concerned about the impact changing admissions standards would have on enrollment. Based on their prior experience, some faculty were concerned that African American students would not succeed in higher-level science classes or take advantage of the undergraduate research opportunities that were a distinctive component of UMBC's approach to preparing the next generation of scientists and engineers. Some members of the campus community were concerned that this approach would lead to the reallocation of scarce resources to a small group of students.

What helped convince enough people to be supportive was the notion that what we proposed was an "experiment." We are all researchers. We have identified a problem. We have a hypothesis describing a solution that will work. Let's try it, collect data, and evaluate it using the same methodology as we would in experimental scientific research. If it works, we will have proof of concept and a potential national model. If it doesn't, then we can step back, understand the lessons learned, and consider alternative approaches. As it turned out, this was a persuasive argument and one that garnered enough allies for us to launch the Meyerhoff Scholars Program (discussed in more detail in the next chapter). We included robust evaluation from program inception. The data we collected proved beyond a doubt that the program was successful in reaching its goals. Its notions of innovation, experimentation, evaluation, inclusion, hard work, and high expectations would spawn other innovations and change the culture of our campus.

During the campus protests, students demanded, and leaders promised, the creation of an office of minority affairs, but we eventually developed a different approach and structure that has worked well for our campus. We have a broad range of offices that focus on the work of diversity and inclusion, including the Office of Multicultural Affairs in the Division of Student Affairs, a vice provost for enrollment management who looks at issues of diversity within the broader landscape of admissions and enrollment, and a vice provost for faculty affairs who is charged with enhancing faculty diversity with the assistance of a program coordinator. Equally important, diversity and inclusion are considered a strong core value for our university, and senior leaders across the campus consider questions of diversity a critical component of their work.

When I was hired as vice provost and charged with improving the academic success of all undergraduate students, including African Americans, this became the implicit model for all members of the campus community. There would be no comprehensive "office of minority affairs" at UMBC. Instead, a positive campus climate and the academic success of minorities was to be a mission critical responsibility of every staff member, administrator, and senior leader. This responsibility and mission would not be separate, siloed, and, thus, potentially marginalized. It would become central to our mission and who we would become as a campus. When we hire senior leaders, we look to ensure that they have affirmatively demonstrated a commitment to diversity and inclusivity so that they come to us already on board with our culture. This approach, of course, differs significantly from that of many other campuses nationwide that have created an office of minority affairs or an office of diversity, typically led by a committed staff member with a title such as "chief diversity officer" (CDO).

I have been invited to speak to CDOs, and perhaps the question I hear most frequently is, "How do I convince my president and other senior leaders to make a substantive commitment to diversifying the campus?" I note that I have had the opportunity to work with presidents, provosts, and CDOs from both public universities and private liberal arts colleges and have found that the most effective teams of leaders are those that understand that the responsibility for bringing about substantive change on the campus is not the role of the CDO alone. While that person can be helpful in facilitating change, the ultimate responsibility rests with the president, chief academic officer, and other senior leaders on the campus, including, perhaps even equally importantly, the senior faculty. The most successful CDOs have the strong support of both senior leaders and faculty. The ineluctable questions are as follows: "What difference has any university initiative made in not just the number of people hired but also the academic success of students or professional success of staff and faculty on that campus?" "Is the environment welcoming and supportive of people who have been traditionally underrepresented on the campus?"

We have learned that when new staff are hired and come on board we must educate them about UMBC's history and culture. If they are sensitive to issues of diversity, they often see a lack of an office of diversity as a signal that "this place doesn't care about diversity," even though the opposite is actually true. They see the absence of such an office as a lack of support. These new staff must be educated about what has been accomplished at UMBC not just despite that but because there is no office of diversity. If we don't provide this important context, then this can lead to new problems.

The innovations we have described were particularly timely as our campus was about to become even more diverse and multicultural. We had been the first (and only) public institution founded in Maryland after *Brown v. Board of Education*, so our doors were open to applicants of all backgrounds beginning with our first class, which matriculated in the fall of 1966. In our early years, the undergraduate population was overwhelmingly white, averaging about 85–90 percent, but it also included a significant African American population, about 10–15 percent, a number that fluctuated over time. Beginning in the late 1980s, we experienced an increase in Asian American students as many highly educated Asian Americans began to make their homes in the Baltimore-Washington corridor. The number of Asian Americans exceeded that of African Americans among undergraduates in 1999 and has composed about 20 percent of our total student population since 2000. More recently, the Latino population of Maryland has increased, and we have seen a surge in students from those families as well. Consequently, our student population is now about half white and half minority (Asian American, African American, and Hispanic), and we have students from over one hundred countries.

However, success is never final. The work of sustaining inclusive excellence is never done on a campus that exists in a society that has not yet fully embraced that notion. On April 12, 2015, Baltimore City police officers arrested Freddie Gray, a 25-year-old African American, who died a week later from injuries he sustained while in police custody. Protesters congregated in downtown Baltimore to demand prosecution of the officers who had arrested Gray and that authorities address the ongoing issue of police brutality. The

Baltimore Uprising was a multifaceted response to both a specific incident and a general frustration, and UMBC's relationship with it was similarly complicated. UMBC students were among the protesters. In solidarity with those seeking racial justice, students hung a banner from the side of the Administration Building here at UMBC that proclaimed "WE ARE BALTIMORE." As a campus administration, we sought to be supportive of students, staff, and faculty who wished to peaceably exercise their constitutional rights for freedom of assembly and to demand redress for heartfelt grievances. Our faculty, across departments, struggled with how they could support students who wanted to talk about what they were doing and feeling. They understood the need to support our students by facilitating such discussions but didn't feel they had the expertise to effectively do so. However, some of our faculty felt confident in their ability to hold deep discussions around issues related to race and criminal justice, and in addition to organizing such discussions with our students, they worked with our Faculty Development Center to provide support and training for their faculty.

We held a teach-in at UMBC on May 1, 2015, on issues related to the long history of racism in Baltimore, the issues involved in the Freddie Gray incident, and the long-term nature of the work that still remained before us. There were presentations about the history of racial residential segregation in Baltimore, cumulative disadvantage related to the intersection of race and poverty, the educational and mental health needs of lower-income black Baltimoreans, and the importance of long-term community listening, engagement, partnership, and service. UMBC's deputy police chief provided perspective on community policing. I personally attended and spoke about the long-term nature of the work of addressing both inclusion and opportunity. "Thirty-five years ago, the father of Freddie Gray was a student at Coppin when I was an administrator there," I said. "And so this is all . . . very personal for me. Because 35 years ago, I thought that we were educating in a way that the world would be so different by the time you were born. And while in some ways it is, in many ways we still face the same challenges."

The conversations did not end there but continued in a setting that allowed for interchange in a national venue. In the fall of 2015, UMBC hosted the annual national conference "Imagining America: Artists and Scholars in Public Life." This national consortium of colleges, universities, and organizations dedicated to advancing the public and civic purposes of arts, humanities, and design had selected Baltimore as the location of the conference well before the death of Freddie Gray, but his death, the ensuing protests, and the surfacing of deep concerns around policing and poverty added great urgency to both the meeting and our role in it. "As we collectively find new footing in our examination of real-world issues," the organizers noted, "Imagining America provides a source for information and ideas in support of engaged undergraduate and graduate pedagogies, public scholarship, and institutional-change initiatives." The selection of Baltimore "is a testament to the long record of powerful civic work underway at UMBC, and to campus leaders' commitment to fostering civic agency, engaged scholarship, and a culture of innovation and inclusive excellence." The UMBC organizing team of staff, faculty, alumni, and graduate and undergraduate students included Baltimore grassroots organizations, nonprofit organizations, and our university partners— Maryland Institute College of Art, Morgan State University, and Towson University—"to ensure sustainable impact in Baltimore beyond 2015."[20]

The conversations also led to collective thinking among faculty about our scholarship and curriculum as they pertain to race and social justice. Several UMBC faculty initiated an ongoing project to "Preserve the Baltimore Uprising 2015." This digital history project has collected photos, videos, and stories surrounding the arrest, death, and funeral of Freddie Gray, as well as the protests and civil unrest that followed.[21] Our College of Arts, Humanities, and Social Sciences developed a list of courses and experiences available to undergraduate and graduate students that focus on or include the themes of race, equity, inclusion, and justice. These courses can be found in Africana studies; American studies; anthropology; computer science; economics; education; English; geography and environmental science; gender and women's studies; history; language, literacy, and culture; media and communication studies; music; philosophy; political science; psychology; and sociology.

As we had worked hard to create an inclusive and supportive environment at UMBC over nearly three decades and had more recently supported students, faculty, and staff throughout the uprising and the Imagining America conference, we were taken by surprise when controversy and protest came to UMBC in the fall of 2015 about the same time as the protests at the University of Missouri. A UMBC student had posted a photo of himself with a dark acne cream mask on his face and the caption, "I'm finally black." The incident was investigated. The student in question, who was an Asian immigrant, said he did not know the history of "blackface" in the United States and apologized. But, in the context of racial protests on campuses nationally, it led to one at UMBC. On November 4, the Black Student Union led a march across campus from the Commons to the Administration Building. Just as they had back in the 1980s, they chanted. This time the chant was "Black Students Matter, say it loud. I am black and I am proud." Once they arrived at the Administration Building, the students held a rally, and speakers noted that while UMBC was well known and celebrated for diversity and inclusiveness, it was still critically important to confront racism on campus and in American society.[22]

Provost Philip Rous and I issued a statement on November 4 in response to this specific incident and the protest and then also issued two further statements later in the month about diversity in general and faculty diversity initiatives in particular. Our November 4 statement read as follows:

> UMBC is a community of students, faculty, and staff committed to sustaining a supportive learning environment built on a foundation of mutual respect. We take great pride in our inclusive community and know that collaboration across differences to solve problems is a core strength of the campus. We are greatly troubled to see recent

material on social media that fails to honor these, our most fundamental, campus values.

Our Community does not support or condone hurtful, racist, or
offensive language, imagery, or actions in any forms. As members of
this community, all of us have a role to play in helping others recognize that such actions, intentional or otherwise, are deeply harmful
and can have a destructive impact on our community and our mission
of inclusive excellence.

We commend and support the strong response from the campus
community, including student organizations, expressing concern over
racist language and calling on us all to work together to uphold and
reaffirm our community values. Your work is at the heart of helping us
restore relationships tested by this incident, and it is shaping our path
as a university striving to be a model of a truly welcoming, diverse
community.[23]

Beyond the "response to campus" statement from the provost and
me, what helped the campus heal quickly was the response from
our Division of Student Affairs, which includes experts in conflict
resolution. Applying techniques of "restorative justice," student affairs brought together students involved in this incident, allowing
them to share with and learn from one another about their perspectives. This worked to not only resolve the matter but also improve the climate for the future.

There were many lessons learned to guide us forward and that
we are still discussing even now. One outcome that arose from this
incident was a better understanding of how social media ampli-
fied what might otherwise have been an invisible episode, both on
and off campus. Indeed, it was through social media that those
off campus who complained the loudest, parents and others, even
learned of the incident. This occurrence underscored the fact that
progress in our society and on our campus requires vigilance and
unwavering commitment to the ongoing work. It also brought renewed focus to the need to educate new members of our community about the values we have collectively built over time and now

share—a critically important process for a university where large numbers of new students, faculty, and staff join the campus every year. Finally, we reminded ourselves that we had more work to do, particularly with regard to increasing the racial and ethnic diversity of our faculty.

1

Pillars of Success

It was a moment that gave us goose bumps.

In the summer of 2002, the American Society for Biochemistry and Molecular Biology (ASBMB) reported that something unexpected and special was happening at UMBC. In a study of 1998/99 data, ASBMB ranked the leading producers of chemistry and biochemistry bachelor's degrees. UMBC was among them. It also ranked universities on the number of those degrees awarded to minority students. We were second. It also ranked universities on the award of these degrees to African Americans. UMBC was first. In its journal, ASBMB stated that, out of sixty-six undergraduate chemistry and biochemistry degrees awarded to African American students nationwide that year, UMBC had awarded twenty-one of them, well ahead of any other institution of any type. This was an important moment for UMBC, representing a milestone in its history and acknowledging the important work that had been done by the campus community.[1]

For campus leaders, faculty, and staff, this success confirmed that we had developed a national model for supporting high-achieving African Americans in STEM, the Meyerhoff Scholars Program, and vindicated much of our hard work over many years. Indeed, it had been fifteen years since we had begun the discussions that led to the establishment of the program in the fall of 1989. There is a key message in this: work that matters—particularly work that involves changing the culture of an institution around issues such as race, gender, academic performance, teaching, and learning—is not accomplished overnight. It necessarily involves passion, but also a fundamental commitment to deliberate execution, vigilance in its use of evaluation for continuous improvement, and patience in its anticipation of a successful outcome. This form of persistence in the face of significant change is what, at UMBC, we call "grit."

Understanding Student Success

In the late 1980s, most students were not succeeding at UMBC. Just one-third of students who matriculated as first-time, full-time freshmen in the fall of 1982 had graduated from UMBC six years later in the spring of 1988. A portion of this low completion rate was due to students attending UMBC for a time and then transferring to another institution to complete a different major that we could not offer at UMBC. Many of our students who left, though, simply weren't prepared for the level of work expected at UMBC, and we were not providing the level of support required for most of these students to be successful.

As we discussed our low graduation rates, we found three dimensions to the problem of preparation and persistence. First, as a public university we were deeply committed to access for students of all backgrounds, and in the early years, this ideal often translated into a willingness to admit as many students to UMBC as possible in order to give them the opportunity to benefit from the highest levels of academic rigor that we had established for our degree programs. This well-meaning approach produced a harsh reality: our admission standards were relatively low given the high expectations we had for our students. In other words, there was a significant disconnect between what students hoped to achieve and their actual academic performance. Second, we were granting admission to students even if they were from poorly performing schools in underserved areas, such as Baltimore City, and even if they were not fully prepared for college. As a consequence, we had a racial achievement gap wherein our African American students had a completion rate that was over ten percentage points lower than that of our white students. Third, students majoring in the natural sciences, mathematics, and engineering were less success-ful than those majoring in the arts, humanities, and social sciences. Many students in the STEM fields were challenged by our lack of infrastructure to support even well-prepared students once they arrived on campus. Students majoring in these fields who wanted to go on to medical school were more often than not disappointed.

We learned about these aspects of student persistence and com-pletion, particularly differences by race and field, through a wide array of discussions. Some of these conversations were informal or held in small groups, such as when the chancellor (now the pres-ident) discussed issues and initiatives with the provost and vice provost. Many were in more formal settings. As we dove deeper into the many dimensions of student achievement, we discussed data, issues, and potential programming in the bi-weekly meetings of our Chancellor's Management Committee (now called the Pres-ident's Council), consisting of the university's chancellor, provost, vice provost, vice chancellors, and deans. In the 1987/88 academic year, I organized with my colleagues in the Office of the Provost a series of focus groups with students, science and engineering de-partment chairs, and faculty and administrators who had an inter-est in understanding how students were doing and what it would take for them to improve their performance.

We began by talking with students in the natural sciences about their perceptions of our academic environment and programs. We quickly gained insight into the work we needed to do. African Amer-ican students expressed a need for social support as minorities in a predominantly white institution; students of all backgrounds expressed the need for academic support and new approaches to teaching and learning, particularly in our foundational science and mathematics courses, which were often described as "cold," "cut-throat," or "weed-out."

We also analyzed grade point averages for students in the natural sciences, and what we saw reinforced the multidimensional nature of the problem facing us and the need for a multifaceted response that addressed both racial climate and our approaches to teaching and learning. The average GPAs for black students at UMBC were 1.9 for men and 2.0 for women. White students had higher GPAs, and Asian Americans had the highest, but their GPAs were not so much higher that we were able to avoid concluding that while the best-prepared white and Asian American students in the natural sciences performed well and some were able to go on to medical or graduate school, large numbers of students of all races were not achieving what they had come to UMBC to accomplish.

We held focus groups with department chairs, program directors, and faculty in the natural sciences. They were deeply committed to our students and especially concerned about improving the achievement of our black students. They wanted to understand what could be done to improve the racial climate on our campus and what more they could do to help students succeed. However, we were starting from a challenging place. It was difficult to lay out a vision that would lead to success for the majority of our African American students when our experience was that most of these students struggled academically in our foundational courses. While a few African American students had done well enough to go on to medical school, the number of US-born African Americans who had earned As in their science courses and had shown the type of promise necessary to go on to graduate school was relatively small. The question in the minds of many was, "Is it realistic to think that we could produce large numbers of blacks who could perform well in STEM areas or who would be willing to go to graduate school in these fields?" This question echoed the response we received when we discussed African American achievement in STEM at a prestigious foundation, whose staff suggested that "perhaps it would take another generation before we could expect to see large numbers going on to graduate school."

Despite these challenges, we began to believe that if we found and recruited African American students who were academically well prepared and if we changed the learning environment to be more supportive, we could create a model program that would produce successful minority students, even in the STEM fields. So, we decided to look for and learn from the work of other PWIs that had already initiated programs to support minority students in these fields. We planned to contact institutions that had graduated at least ten such students each year in order to learn about their best practices. However, when we received from the NSF its data on the leading undergraduate institutions that produced blacks who went on to earn PhDs in STEM fields, we were shocked to find that there was not even one institution that hit the mark. The only institutions that were producing a substantial number were a handful of HBCUs, including my alma mater, Hampton, where I had experienced a nurturing environment and faculty who engaged with me and other students.

This discovery only lent greater urgency to our work. I was fortunate to learn about Uri Treisman's work with minority students in mathematics at the University of California, Berkeley. His Emerging Scholars Program had aggressively recruited a diverse group of students in mathematics and was producing results. It was not a remedial program but one that focused on helping students earn As and Bs in gateway mathematics courses, master the content, and develop the skills to succeed in more advanced courses. Program staff were honest with the students about the hard work needed to become mathematicians, but they also provided a community and peer support that ensured that students would thrive in large first-year mathematics courses rather than succumb to the debilitating sense of isolation and discouragement many students feel.[2] However, even Berkeley was not producing more than one or two African Americans per year who went on to earn PhDs.

It was becoming clear to me and my colleagues that we had not considered carefully enough the relationship between the actual level of preparation of the students we admitted and the amount of academic support we were offering. We concluded that we needed to rebalance both ends of this equation, and this observation led us to the notion of a "strengths-based" program for our students. Rather than a deficits-based approach, one that would have focused on remediating deficiencies in student preparation, we would recruit talented, well-prepared students and then build on their knowledge and skills through a combination of high expectations and a transformative academic and social environment.[3]

Empowering Students

In my 2013 TED Talk, entitled "The Four Pillars of College Success," I talk about the ways in which we can better support and empower our students of all backgrounds. The TED Talk focuses on our work at UMBC supporting the success of underrepresented minority students and what we learned from that work to support students more generally. Central to this work has been the notion that students can be empowered to take ownership of their education, that students can be taught to be passionate and effective learners, to ask good questions, and to support each other as members of a community of scholars rather than competitors. Our support and their empowerment can be fostered through these four pillars: high expectations, building community, faculty and student engagement, and continuous improvement through the mechanism of program assessment.

For the first pillar, we help students to not just survive but thrive through high expectations. We admit students who are already high achieving in their high schools. While some are better prepared than others, this means that they have performed well in rigorous precollege coursework and have high scores on standardized tests. However, that is not enough. They must also have a positive attitude and passion. We underpin this by helping students understand that they do have what it takes to succeed and setting for them the personal milestones of graduating, going on to graduate school, earning a PhD, and ultimately pursuing the goal of career in research. We reinforce the path we lay out for them by emphasizing the fact that they can reach this goal through hard work. It takes passion, personal commitment, and hard work, what we call fire in the belly.

Second, we build a community of learners. In many universities, introductory science classes are often perceived by students as "weed-out" courses. Since it appears that "only a few are chosen," the environment is competitive, which discourages students from supporting each other in their learning. We take the opposite approach. We help students support each other socially and academically. They belong to a community with similar goals and objectives, they are members of a cohort, and they are required to work together in groups to support the success of their colleagues. In this way not only do students learn to trust and help each other but they also enhance their learning by explaining concepts that they understand to others and having concepts that they are struggling to grasp clarified by others. This sense of community is self-reinforcing, since it is one thing for you to earn an A in a challenging course but quite another to help someone else succeed as well. Your learning is deeper, your sense of responsibility is developed, and your sense of personal accomplishment and community engagement is stronger.

Third, we like to say that "it takes researchers to produce researchers." A centerpiece of our program is the participation of faculty who not only teach in the classroom but also pull students into their research, whether it is in the field, the library, or the laboratory. This form of experiential learning is powerful. It reinforces and applies skills and knowledge acquired in the classroom and strengthens the participating student's identity as a scientist or an engineer.

Fourth, we evaluate our work and engage in a cycle of continuous improvement. From its inception, we incorporated assessment into the program with the invaluable help of Willie Pearson, a sociologist then with Wake Forest University and now with Georgia Tech. Our collaborative assessment effort led to our first coauthored paper, "Recruiting and Retaining Talented African American Males in College Science and Engineering."[4] Ken Maton, professor of psychology at UMBC, has continued the assessment and evaluation of the program over the years. This drove cycles of continuous improvement and provided the rigorous data needed to establish the proof of concept given the significant outcomes gains of program participants relative to control groups.

Using insights that we obtained from assessment, my colleagues and I have written extensively in articles and books about how we created the Meyerhoff Scholars Program, its key elements, and its program outcomes.[5] I have told the full story of the founding and development of the Meyerhoff Scholars Program most recently in *Holding Fast to Dreams.*[6] Our purpose here is to summarize the types of conversations needed to develop program champions and allies and to launch the program. These conversations began with those described above in which we asked difficult questions to learn about student success on our campus. They continued with further conversations that provided opportunities for broader input and buy-in.

The most critical conversations were those I had with Robert Meyerhoff, a real estate developer and Baltimore philanthropist. Robert Embry, president of the Abell Foundation and former Baltimore City school board president, connected me to Bob, and when we first met, his desire to make a difference in the lives of black males was clear. Bob was exasperated that whenever black males were discussed in the news, the story was typically about either crime or sports. He wanted to invest in a program that would change that. He said, "I want the country to understand that if you support black males they can do as well as anybody else, if not better." When I told him about our plan to develop a program to support black students in STEM fields on campus, he was intrigued and asked for a proposal. We met several times to discuss what such a program might look like. He gave us $500,000 to start the program—the Meyerhoff Scholars Program—in the fall of 1989 with a cohort of black male college freshmen.

Next, we held conversations with potential students and their families to create excitement about a program that did not yet exist. Most of these high-achieving black students, recommended to us by school principals, guidance counselors, and science and mathematics teachers, were focused on admission to highly selective institutions, so we had to be persuasive. We invited these prospective students to campus for a "Meyerhoff Weekend." This was an opportunity for them to discuss college opportunities and meet the other high-achieving black students from Maryland who would be there—and twenty-five came. We discussed the significance of being a young, gifted African American man pursuing a career in science, the challenges that they often face in college, and how our program would prepare them to become PhD-level researchers. We talked about our program, how it would work, and the financial support we could offer. The weekend was a success. One of the most powerful aspects of this event was simply the act of bringing these students together since many of them attended integrated high schools in which they were the "only one" in advanced mathematics or science courses. Being part of a group of gifted African American male students for the weekend was moving, and we could feel the energy build within the group. Nineteen of the twenty-five young men who came to campus that weekend enrolled at UMBC and became the first Meyerhoff cohort.[7]

Throughout our discussions, we had been talking to selected faculty. We needed their active participation in the program. While some of my well-meaning colleagues expressed the concern that some students would not have the necessary preparation, others argued that it was "unfair" to provide a program that benefited just one group of students. Nevertheless, many faculty members were eager to embrace our experiment and find out, along with us, if it would work. Our Chemistry Department chair, Catherine Fenselau, who had moved to UMBC from a professorship at Johns Hopkins University, shared an important insight: almost every student admitted to medical school eventually completes the MD since that outcome was embedded in the culture of those schools. She noted that, by contrast, in science it was generally accepted that most students would not make it. For our new program to be successful, this culture had to change.

Michael Summers, a Howard Hughes Medical Institute (HHMI) investigator and professor of chemistry and biochemistry, embraced the Meyerhoff program and its students at its inception, bringing both high-quality academic work and legitimacy to the program, particularly in the eyes of other faculty. In fact, he has become one of the leading mentors in the nation of undergraduate and graduate underrepresented minority students (especially African Americans) who go on to earn a PhD. Inspired by the undergraduate program, he and Catherine created a graduate Meyerhoff program that Mike has led for the past twenty years. The program recently celebrated the award of its first one hundred PhDs in conjunction with the University of Maryland School of Medicine (doctoral awards are now up to 113). He has mentored many minority undergraduate and graduate students in his laboratory, which explores the structures of retroviruses, including HIV-1. Many other faculty have been enormously important to the program, and once we had their commitment, they made it their goal to work for the success of the students, provided research opportunities for the students, and then helped them grow as scientists and engineers. Without this buy-in from faculty, the program would not have been the success that it has been.

Lastly, we had conversations with admissions office staff, academic administrators, and interested faculty about how we used standardized test scores in admissions. Some argued that well-prepared minority students still might not perform well on standardized tests, so we should not give those tests much weight in our admission decisions. Others, including me, argued that while standardized test scores alone are not sufficient to predict college-level success, they are an important indicator—along with grades, level of rigor in coursework, and noncognitive factors such as "fire in the belly," interest in and commitment to pursuing a career in science, and willingness to listen to advice. Coming out of these conversations, Ken Maton and I looked at data collected over a twenty-year period, examining the correlation between SAT scores, high school GPAs, and performance in undergraduate STEM courses at UMBC. We determined that students usually needed a minimum score of 600 for the mathematics section of the SAT and preparation through rigorous science and mathematics courses in high school to be successful in the natural sciences or engineering, and we established this as a minimum threshold for admission to the Meyerhoff Scholars Program.

The Road Taken

We found ourselves at a crossroads in the late 1980s and took a path that we had to build as we went along. The implementation of the Meyerhoff Scholars Program over three decades has empowered students, changed our university in numerous ways, and served as a model for other institutions.

The Meyerhoff Scholars Program has made a tremendous difference to the students who have been enrolled. Compared to program applicants who were offered admission but declined, participants are more than five times as likely to have graduated from or currently attend a STEM PhD or MD-PhD program.[8] As of October 2017, program alumni had earned 273 PhDs, including 49 MD-PhDs, 1 DDS-PhD, and 1 DVM-PhD. Our graduates had also earned 107 MDs, as well as 261 master's degrees, primarily in engineering and computer science. Another 300 alumni were enrolled in graduate and professional degree programs.[9]

We have compared our student outcomes to those of other universities by examining the NSF data on the baccalaureate origins of African American PhDs in the natural sciences and engineering—the same data we looked at back in 1987 to see if we could identify successful institutions—as well as data from the Association of American Medical Colleges.[10] We have found the following:

- UMBC was the number two baccalaureate-origin institution for black students who went on to complete a PhD in the natural sciences or engineering from 2007 to 2016. We were number one among PWIs.

- UMBC ranked as the number two baccalaureate-origin institution, behind Howard University, for blacks completing a PhD in the life sciences from 2007 to 2016. We were number one among PWIs.
- The Massachusetts Institute of Technology had the highest percentage of its African American undergraduates go on to earn PhDs in the natural sciences and engineering. UMBC was second, followed by Cornell, Princeton, and Johns Hopkins.
- UMBC ranked as the number one baccalaureate-origin institution for African Americans who earned the MD-PhD from academic years 2000/2001 to 2016/17. UMBC had forty-two. Harvard University was second with fifteen.

We have demonstrated clearly the success of our model. This success has led to further scholars programs at UMBC and to efforts now underway to replicate or adapt the Meyerhoff program at other institutions.

Not only have our Meyerhoff Scholars benefited from the program, but their presence and success have also changed the culture of our campus in profound ways. Mike Summers has noted how powerful the program has been in shaping faculty perceptions. "When you have nine smart, engaged black males sitting in the front row of your science class for the first time," he says, "it changes your notion of what's possible." The success of the program gave us a sense that we could be diverse while also offering a challenging experience to all of our students, and that we could embrace the values of both inclusiveness and excellence. A positive unanticipated benefit of African American males leading the way is that the majority of our African American students are male, a fact that is counter to trends at almost every other higher education institution.

Still, the road to inclusive excellence has its bumps. Scholars were members of a special program; received financial support, books, and computers; and lived together on one floor of a residence hall that included other students who did not receive any of these privileges. We did not anticipate how many of these other students would perceive the program. Seeing its perquisites daily, some argued that the program was "not fair" and a form of "reverse discrimination." Residence Life staff who mediated the backlash that had erupted reviewed the literature on racial integration to understand what might work better as we moved forward. They found that if you put into proximity people of different backgrounds who had similar levels of financial support, there would be less conflict. So, we made Susquehanna Hall into a residence for students in the Meyerhoff Scholars Program and also students from the Honors College, who at that time were mainly white and Asian. This created a more level playing field from a student perspective.

There was a more serious, existential challenge to the Meyerhoff program that we also had to navigate. To address the underrepresentation of blacks on their campus, the University of Maryland, College Park had established the Banneker Program to provide scholarships to African American students. Parents of white students brought a lawsuit against the university, arguing that the program could not be based on race and provide awards only to African American students. The university defended the program as part of its desegregation plan, but it ultimately lost the case. In 1995, the Supreme Court let stand a Court of Appeals ruling that College Park could not have an all-minority program and, effectively, dismantled it.

This ruling put the Meyerhoff program into immediate jeopardy, so we took steps to protect it. We dropped the requirement that participants had to be African American and replaced it with the requirement that scholars, no matter what their racial or ethnic background, had to demonstrate a strong commitment to supporting diversity and inclusion in the natural sciences and engineering. Many in Maryland's black community were upset that the strength of the program, known for excellence in African American achievement, would be diluted if it did not continue to focus on African Americans. The program still had the broad purpose of addressing underrepresentation in science for African Americans, women, and people from low-income backgrounds, but the change in requirements did alter the diversity of the program. For the 2017/18 academic year, for example, the 260 students enrolled in the program were 63 percent African American, 15 percent Caucasian, 11 percent Asian, 10 percent Hispanic, and 1 percent Native American.

In the long run, having students in the program who are not underrepresented actually strengthened the program. We have found that a diversity program can teach students of all races how to live and work effectively together, and this is culture change too. They come to understand the challenges that each group faces, how they are different, and what they have in common. This change, along with other efforts on our campus to increase the interaction of people from different backgrounds, has meant that we had created a university that was authentically multicultural—not just in terms of numbers, but in terms of the way people get to know others.

Fundamentally, the Meyerhoff program and the success of its participants set a new tone for our campus and profoundly changed its culture in ways we did not expect but eventually capitalized on. The program demonstrated that academic innovation could work and further innovation would be supported. It established the notion that a comprehensive set of program elements could support students in a holistic way: high expectations, institutional support, faculty buy-in, financial support, community building, advising and mentoring, summer bridge, tutoring, group work, participation in research, professional development, community service, and assessment. It proved that, among those elements, community building and group work were powerful interventions that promoted academic success and should be the center of any new academic innovations.

Building Communities

Innovations—especially successful, high-profile ones—can and should stimulate further conversations. As the Meyerhoff program began to show promise, faculty in other disciplines began advocating for "scholars" programs that would enhance the student experience in other fields. Over time we have established six more scholars programs that have drawn on the elements of the Meyerhoff program, including building community through cohorts, shared values and goals, group work, living-learning environments, and community service. Beyond our institution, two universities are also adapting the Meyerhoff program for students on their campuses.[11]

Humanities, Linehan, and Sondheim Scholars

In the early 1990s, our colleagues in the arts, humanities, and social sciences asked what we could do to support students in disciplines outside of the natural sciences and engineering. As a growing university we had established a core liberal arts program for all of our students. Yet as UMBC evolved as a research institution, we were quickly becoming known as a "strong STEM school," partly because of Meyerhoff but also because we strengthened our undergraduate programs in the natural sciences, mathematics, engineering, and information sciences and these programs saw significant increases in enrollment. We sought to balance this growth by recommitting to our traditional strengths across the broad range of fields that are critical to a balanced liberal arts program and by establishing new scholars programs in these fields. We established the Humanities Scholars Program, housed in the Dresher Center for the Humanities, in 1992, the Linehan Artist Scholars Program in 1995, and the Sondheim Public Affairs Scholars Program in 1999.

The Humanities Scholars Program supports undergraduates who have demonstrated deep interest and talent in the humanities. As the program website describes, we enable their growth as creative thinkers who can explore and understand cultural products and practices from a range of perspectives. The program provides scholars with educational opportunities and support for learning, research, and civic engagement. Our goal is to enable the scholars to pursue work in the humanities, impact and diversify the intellectual life of our campus, and contribute significantly to our culture and society. We expect Humanities Scholars to ask probing questions, learn about the values and traditions of different cultures, discover what makes a great work of art or how history is made, and prepare for engagement with a range of social and career settings for the betterment of society. Majors include Africana studies, Asian studies, American studies, history, ancient studies, English, gender and women's studies, media and communication studies, cultural anthropology, modern languages, philosophy, and interdisciplinary studies.[12]

With generous support from Earl and Darielle Linehan, the Linehan Artist Scholars Program, as its website notes, supports students who have academic and artistic ability and seek to develop as artists in multiple fields. Linehan Scholars major in dance, music, theatre, visual arts, or interdisciplinary studies; they work with faculty who are composers, choreographers, directors, designers, photographers, computer artists, painters, filmmakers, video animators, art historians, and performers and who actively engage students in creative and analytical work. Linehan Artist Scholars take a first-year seminar for their cohort and live in the Visual and Performing Arts Living-Learning Community during freshman and sophomore years. They work in a community-based nurturing environment that includes weekly seminars, workshops with arts faculty and artists-in-residence, digital storytelling workshops, grant writing, and making artworks to investigate significant ideas in contemporary art. They join trips to performances and museums to develop their knowledge and creativity. They are offered research opportunities through the Linehan Summer Research and Study Award, the Undergraduate Research Award, and the UMBC Study Abroad Program.[13]

Walter Sondheim had long been an inspiration for our university and the greater Baltimore community. Walter was a department store executive who was also committed to Baltimore and public service. A long-time member of the Baltimore City Board of Education, he was among a handful of business leaders who envisioned the renaissance of Baltimore's downtown, including its harbor front. He was a personal friend and mentor to me. So, it was natural that when we created a scholars program focused on public service in 1999, it would be dedicated to him. At that time, Provost Arthur Johnson created the Public Affairs Scholars Program to support talented undergraduates interested in public service who aspire to careers in government, law, nonprofits, education, health care, and environmental sustainability. Beginning in 2002, a multimillion-dollar campaign was begun to endow the program as the Walter Sondheim Public Affairs Scholars Program. We were successful in reaching our goal through major gifts from local foundations. While Sondheim Scholars typically major in political science, economics, history, psychology, social work, environmental studies, global studies, or health administration and policy, the program is open to students of any major, and we have included students from such fields as computer science in the program.

The Sondheim Scholars Program brings together like-minded students interested in public service. As is also true of the Meyerhoff Scholars, Sondheim Scholars enter the university and program as part of a cohort of about fifteen students and take two courses together: the Public Affairs Seminar and English Composition. First-year students are mentored by upperclassmen, who are also required to complete a service-learning activity. The program provides scholars with intensive advising and mentoring and assistance in finding internships, research opportunities, and leadership positions on and off campus. Scholars have many opportunities to engage experts in the fields of public policy and the social sciences through exclusive events and UMBC's Social Sciences Forum, which sponsors public lecturers on current, vital issues. Over one hundred students have participated in this program, and its alumni have "gone on to top law and graduate schools across the U.S. and abroad, and serve the community as policy analysts, lawyers, social workers, justice activists, environmental experts, corporate leaders and teachers."[14]

CWIT and Cyber Scholars

UMBC created its Center for Women in Information Technology (CWIT) in 1998 to increase the representation of women in the computing and information sciences—a significant issue at the height of the 1990s internet boom. In order to pursue this goal, the center launched the CWIT Scholars Program with a focus on increasing the number of women and minorities in UMBC's computing and engineering programs. Data show that the percentage of IT bachelor's degree recipients in the United States who are women has actually decreased from 36 to 18 percent since the program was begun in 2000. However, at UMBC, our programs in information technology have bucked the trend and are educating many more women in these fields. With funding from the state of Maryland, our current CWIT Scholars are 89 percent women and, more specifically, 9 percent women of color.

In 2010, the center also established the Cyber Scholars Program as our rapid response to the need for increasing the representation of women and underrepresented minority men and women in the emerging field of cybersecurity. The Cyber Scholars Program supports undergraduates who are 44 percent women and 33 percent underrepresented minorities. These programs provide academic, mentoring, and financial support for students who support gender diversity and inclusion in computing and engineering. The Cyber Scholars Program, which attracted early funding from Northrop Grumman, is a university-corporate partnership that is ensuring that graduates obtain good jobs and employers get the skilled workers they need in a rapidly growing field. The scholars —undergraduates in cybersecurity—are supported financially and incorporated into a scholarship community that includes a CWIT

Living-Learning Community in one of our residence halls, courses tailored to the needs of CWIT scholars, mentoring, and the chance to take part in cybersecurity research and internships early in their academic careers. Graduates of the program have gone on to substantive jobs at Northrop Grumman and the NSA.[15]

The Baltimore-Washington corridor has a particular economic niche in cybersecurity, and a recent study suggested that there is robust demand for staff with skills in this IT submarket. Among the top research universities for undergraduates majoring in computer and information sciences, UMBC was well positioned geographically and programmatically to very quickly establish a program in response to workforce demand as cybersecurity has developed into a strong growth area in our state. We have undergraduate, graduate, and professional training programs in IT and cybersecurity.

As we spend down the initial funding for the Cyber Scholars Program, the primary challenge for this program is sustainability, an issue we are now having conversations about. There are many demands on the university's resources, and most of our scholars programs have achieved sustainability through endowments funded from outside sources. The current discussion among university and program leadership focuses on grant writing, fundraising, and allocation of university funds. The university will need to invest its own resources to ensure institutionalization, but we have a multi-year budgeting process that assumes, in the long term, that these programs will build endowments through charitable gifts from private donors and foundations.

Sherman STEM Teacher Scholars

The need for an increased number of prepared high-quality teachers in the sciences and mathematics is also well documented. The National Academies' seminal report on competitiveness, *Rising above the Gathering Storm*, listed the production of such teachers as its number one priority.[16] The President's Council of Advisors in Science and Technology subsequently reasserted this need, recommending that the United States produce 10,000 more qualified science and mathematics teachers annually.[17]

In 2006, shortly after the *Gathering Storm* report identified K–12 STEM teacher preparation as a critical national issue, I had a conversation with George and Betsy Sherman. George, an engineer, was executive vice president at the Black and Decker Corporation, then president and CEO of Danaher Corporation, and most recently founder and president of Cypress Group. Betsy Sherman, a graduate from Tufts University with a degree in early childhood education, was the first Head Start teacher in Kentucky and taught in rural Virginia, experiences that led to her passion for helping disadvantaged youth. She was the only white teacher in an all-minority school, and this experience gave her special insights about and appreciation for teachers, regardless of race, who care deeply about their students.

As this conversation began, it focused on the pipeline for STEM graduates. By the time it was finished, the Shermans were convinced they could help address an important social and economic need by focusing attention and resources on producing STEM teachers for K–12 schools, particularly those serving disadvantaged students. The Shermans believed that strong teachers would "capture" the interest of students who want to go on to college in STEM. Inspired by UMBC's success with the Meyerhoff program, they committed generous funding to launch and support the Sherman STEM Teacher Scholars Program in 2006. As we worked through the details, both of the Shermans brought their own life experiences to the conversations. They asked hard questions about program objectives and ways to assess the outcomes of the work.

We established the Sherman Scholars as a joint program of the College of Natural and Mathematical Sciences, the Department of Mechanical Engineering, the Department of Education, and the Interdisciplinary Studies program. Drawing on the core elements of the Meyerhoff program, its mission is to provide students majoring in engineering and the natural or mathematical sciences with training and preparation for teaching and then place these students in public schools in the Baltimore area.[18] Complementing the work of the Sherman Scholars Program, departments in the College of Natural and Mathematical Sciences have taken science education more seriously and created content-rich academic programs in collaboration with our Department of Education that are designed to prepare students who wish to become educators. These programs, which include bachelor's degrees in chemistry, physics, and biology education, allow students to develop a solid foundation in the discipline and to complete the coursework needed for certification to teach at the secondary level.[19]

The Sherman Scholars Program enrolled its first cohort at UMBC in the fall of 2007, had its first graduates in 2011, and is showing promising program outcomes. As of November 2018, we have ninety-three program alumni, including eight-one who are currently teaching. They are currently working in Baltimore City (twelve), Baltimore County (fifteen), Anne Arundel County (fourteen), Howard County (eleven), Montgomery County (eleven), and Prince George's County (five), as well as other jurisdictions in Maryland (five), independent schools (three), and out of state (five). Corey Carter, a graduate of the Sherman program, was named Baltimore County Teacher of the Year for school year 2016/17. Recently, Amy Connor was one of thirty-two teachers nationally selected by the National Science Teachers Association for their new teacher's fellowship. This year Christine Van Norstrand was one of six teachers selected by the Maryland Council of Teachers of Math for their Outstanding Math Educator award.

Yet there have been challenges. The first was budgetary. While the Shermans generously provided a substantial endowment, it took several years before there was enough funding in the scholarship budget to offer major financial support to our students. The second challenge has been adapting the Meyerhoff model to a program with a much more diverse population of students. The Meyerhoff program admits students as freshmen, but Sherman Scholars can enter UMBC as freshmen, transfer students, or even as graduate students who have decided to pursue STEM teaching seriously as a career. While most Sherman Scholars are typical college-age students, there is a large age range, and students bring to the program diverse experiences. While this diversity adds richness to the program, it also makes it difficult to implement some successful components of the Meyerhoff program, such as a common summer bridge experience.

The third challenge is the relationship of the program with the Baltimore City Public Schools (BCPS). When the school district recently experienced difficulties in recruiting teachers, it signed contracts with nonprofits, like Teach for America (TFA), to fill teacher slots not filled through regular hiring practices. Moreover, the BCPS prefers TFA students, as they typically come from highly selective colleges and the school system hopes they will move into administration. By the time the BCPS has recruited TFA students and regular hires, many Sherman graduates have already taken offers from other jurisdictions. Consequently, Sherman Scholars are teaching in schools with challenging environments across the region. Our newest initiative involves the establishment of the Sherman Center, which expands the university's efforts to build a strong foundation for learning for young children in Baltimore City and establish best practices for urban schools through applied research, teacher professional development, and partnerships.

In 2013, we created a partnership with Lakeland Elementary/ Middle School and surrounding schools that involves the Sherman Scholars Program.[20] Concerned about K–12 educational outcomes for disadvantaged youth, a potential donor approached UMBC with an offer to fund a university-administered charter school, noting that other universities have developed such schools to serve as models for academic success. UMBC staff considered the offer but instead explored how a holistic program might enhance student success in an existing public school. We engaged in discussions with partners about the academic needs of students, community goals, and the ways in which we could deploy our resources and expertise in an engaged way that would solve problems while facilitating agency by partners. Following a series of discussions, we formed a partnership with the BCPS centered on Lakeland Elementary/Middle School, a pre-K through eighth-grade school in Baltimore City, and several surrounding schools. The partnership is generously supported by funding from George and Betsy Sherman and a 21st Century Community Learning Center grant funded by the Maryland State Department of Education.[21]

Beginning in its first year, the work of the partnership included the following components to address community needs in a holistic way:

- implementation of the 21st Century Community Learning Center grant to form an after-school and summer program for first to fourth graders (five years of funding);
- recruiting preservice teachers from UMBC's Sherman STEM Teacher Scholars Program into applied-learning placements at Lakeland to support after-school and summer activities and targeted STEM classrooms;
- teaming UMBC math education faculty with Lakeland teachers to work on the transition to Common Core–aligned curriculum and Partnership for Assessment of Readiness for College and Careers (PARCC) testing;
- professional development for science and mathematics teachers by providing them with opportunities to attend trainings and conferences of national associations;
- placing a team of Shriver Center Choice Program Fellows to work intensively with forty students who were identified as at-risk by the school owing to high absenteeism and/or classroom disruption;
- supporting Lakeland's effort to serve parents and the broader community by pairing two Shriver Peaceworker Fellows with Lakeland's community schools coordinator.

More recently, funding from Northrop Grumman has facilitated the development of a community-based STEAM (science, technology, engineering, arts, and mathematics) center.

The academic support we provide at these schools has already provided dividends. Our support includes student teaching in science and mathematics by Sherman STEM Teacher Scholars. It also includes UMBC students who serve as math coaches, working with small groups of students to help them more deeply understand concepts they are learning in the classroom. These additional resources have played a role in helping Lakeland students boost their standardized scores in mathematics. From 2016 to 2017, the percentage of fourth-grade students scoring 4 or 5 (passing) on the PARCC exam more than doubled from 19 percent to just over 43 percent.

Expanding to New Fields

At the time *Expanding Underrepresented Minority Participation* was published in 2011, UMBC was one of the top ten baccalaureate institutions for African American undergraduates who go on to complete PhDs in the biological sciences. Historically, we have had a focus on the life sciences within the Meyerhoff Scholars Program since many of our key faculty partners have been in the biological sciences and biochemistry. Our funding from several NIH institutes has reinforced this focus.

Inspired by the way the Meyerhoff program has supported minority students in the natural sciences and other scholars programs now support students in a range of fields, we are also exploring how we can expand the Meyerhoff program to new fields with similar deliberate and focused efforts. Recently, we have had success expanding support to students in the physical sciences. In 2011, UMBC was not a top ten institution for educating African Americans in the physical sciences who go on to doctoral studies. Since then, we have made a conscious decision to focus on the discipline and have made progress. Through an even closer partnership with the agencies that support the physical sciences, in particular the NSA, we have been able to support more students in mathematics and the physical sciences. Our increased success with African

American students in these fields has recently moved our institution into the top ten.

We are now also developing initiatives that will allow us to broaden the Meyerhoff program itself to support diversity in new fields. We have just received a major $1.3 million grant from the Alfred P. Sloan Foundation to expand the Meyerhoff program to include the field of quantitative economics. This effort will include students of all backgrounds, but we are particularly hopeful that we can use the program to nurture young African Americans, who are deeply underrepresented in this field.[22]

In addition, we are also now looking at how we can help more students of color, and in particular black males, go on to medical school to pursue an MD. UMBC ranks first in the nation in producing African American undergraduates who go on to earn the MD-PhD. Our success is remarkable. We have educated forty-two African American undergraduates who have gone on to earn the MD-PhD since 2000, more than any other institution, and more than twice as many as the next institution, Harvard University. If we can do that, then surely we can support African Americans who want to earn an MD. At present, UMBC ranks twenty-fifth when it comes to producing African Americans who go on to medical school and earn an MD or MD-PhD. As our efforts to produce more minority PhDs have focused on increasing exposure to research and research careers, we may have discouraged students from going to medical school. With a concerted effort focused on this particular mission and appropriate funding, we could double or triple the current number of ten UMBC African American graduates who earn the MD or MD-PhD each year. We would need to produce five more per year to be in the top ten. Given the dearth of black males in medicine, this is an urgent goal.

We are now exploring how we can include African American students interested in medical school in the Meyerhoff program, particularly black males, who are substantially underrepresented in medical professions. We will need to be careful about student selection and deliberate in obtaining faculty engagement. We will need to support those who are doing reasonably well in their science courses, prepare them for the MCAT, establish academic pathways they can follow, build for them the kind of community that sustains students, and provide scholarship assistance that allows them to focus on their work.

Meyerhoff Adaptation Partnership

When many presidents, provosts, and deans learn about the success of UMBC's Meyerhoff Scholars Program, they wonder what they would have to do to create a similar program at their own institution. Some are eager to delve into the program and learn more about it. Others are less so. Over the years I have heard presidents dismiss the program as "expensive" or suggest that it is only successful because UMBC is a "unique place with an African American president" who is the program's champion in a way that cannot be duplicated.

While it is true that I founded the Meyerhoff Scholars Program with Robert Meyerhoff and have worked with committed colleagues to establish the program on our campus, these critics miss several key points. First, I was vice provost tasked with overseeing academic affairs (not president) when we started the program, so it was my job to tackle issues like this. Second, while I was deeply involved in the program in its early years, it has since its inception been led and managed by a director and staff, and the program would not be successful without the direct involvement and commitment of senior faculty. Our Meyerhoff program directors over the years—Susan Boyer, Earnestine Baker, LaMont Tolbert, and Keith Harmon—have been critical to the program's success. It "takes a village" to educate and nurture a Meyerhoff Scholar, and the success of the program cannot be attributed to just one person.

Further, these questions about replicability are being put to the test in a more experimental way. Based on the notion that we should learn from institutions that have been successful in educating minority scientists and engineers, a recommendation of *Ex-*

panding Underrepresented Minority Participation, HHMI took a closer look at UMBC's Meyerhoff Scholars Program. At the same time, in 2011, we began discussions with leaders at the University of North Carolina at Chapel Hill (UNC) and Pennsylvania State University (PSU) about organizing a partnership to "replicate" the Meyerhoff program at those institutions.

The stars had aligned. HHMI awarded a Phase 1 grant for UMBC and UNC to establish the Chancellor's Scholars Program at UNC and for UMBC to work with PSU as it established the Millennium Scholars Program there. Both institutions recruited their first student cohorts in the summer of 2013. Since then, UMBC, UNC, and PSU have developed a four-year partnership—the Meyerhoff Adaptation Partnership (MAP)—to continue the work. HHMI, through a Phase 2 grant, has now funded all three institutions. HHMI's total investment in this effort is $8 million over five years. There is deep institutional commitment to these programs at both UNC and PSU. There was turnover in their leadership after the establishment of their new programs, but the subsequent university heads— UNC chancellor, Carol Folt, and PSU president, Eric Barron—were just as supportive as their predecessors were. Indeed, the programs not only have survived turnover in institutional leadership—always a test—but also have been strengthened. The current leadership at UNC and PSU has allocated several million dollars in institutional funding for student support and raised millions more from external sources.

MAP's March 2017 progress report describes the goal of the program as follows:

> The overarching goal of the resulting "Meyerhoff Adaptation Partnership" (MAP) is to determine if Meyerhoff-like outcomes can be achieved at larger research institutions with different histories, geographies, and institutional cultures. Specific aims include (i) developing Meyerhoff-like STEM inclusion activities at UNC-CH and PSU that lead to significant, quantifiable increases in URM academic performance, retention in STEM, and matriculation to STEM doctoral

programs; (ii) enhancing inclusive institutional cultures at UNC-CH and PSU; and (iii) determining if this type of inter-institutional partnership could serve as a general mechanism for disseminating effective STEM practices. Prompted by HHMI, a fourth aim was to (iv) develop a more granular understanding of the goals and benefits of individual elements of the Meyerhoff program. Finally, because institutional culture, history, local environment, and resources differ among the three academic institutions, we prioritized (v) documenting and assessing the implementation and outcomes of the different programmatic elements at each institution, and to determine which [Meyerhoff Scholars Program] elements could not be easily replicated and required institution-specific adaptation.[23]

As with UMBC, the success of the MAP and the individual programs at UNC and PSU will depend on the buy-in and deep involvement of faculty and staff beyond broad institutional leadership. As with the original Meyerhoff program at UMBC, this adaptation effort includes a rigorous and ongoing evaluation program that serves to both inform program development and validate proof of concept. So far, results look positive with respect to student academic success and student retention in STEM majors.[24] The progress report notes that "climate change is also occurring on both campuses. Faculty are expressing interest in joining program activities and recruiting students to their laboratories." The report quotes one faculty member as saying, "These kids are the reason I get up in the morning."

8

An Honors University

One look at the data told me we had work to do. In 1988, I was hired as vice provost, a new position with a mandate to improve student learning and the success of our undergraduates. And this was where we were starting from: that year, UMBC had a six-year graduation rate of 33 percent for our full-time new freshmen who had entered in the fall of 1982. Clearly, we had much room for improvement.

We have come a long way since then. We grew our academic program. We established programs to support high-achieving students and adapted what we learned from those programs to better support students from all backgrounds. We designed, implemented, and assessed initiatives to meet student needs and improve outcomes. We redesigned courses and infused them with experiential learning. Building on a culture of assessment, we developed our capacity to collect and analyze data to identify interventions that support students. This work has made a strong difference. By 2005, the full-time, freshmen completion rate had risen to 55 percent; by 2016, almost 65 percent of freshmen graduated from UMBC within six years, and another 10 percent had earned a postsecondary degree at another institution.[1]

Boosting Student Success

Building our academic program to meet the interests and needs of our students has played a central role in boosting student success. We used to have several programs for students who began their studies at UMBC but finished elsewhere, a situation that required our students to transfer and, in so doing, also reduced our completion rate. In our early years, for example, nursing students began their undergraduate program at UMBC and completed at our nearby sister institution, the University of Maryland, Baltimore (UMB). Today, nursing students begin and complete at UMB, so their course of study no longer affects our completion rate. We had a similar arrangement in engineering, but the evolution of our programs in this field followed a different path. During our first two decades, undergraduate engineering students took three years of coursework at UMBC and then typically transferred to College Park for the fourth year of advanced coursework and completion of their degrees. In the 1980s, the state approved full undergraduate programs at UMBC in chemical, biological, and industrial engineering and graduate programs in all engineering fields. This allowed us to form a College of Engineering in 1992, which has continued to evolve and now offers bachelor's programs in mechanical engineering, chemical engineering, business technology administration, computer science, computer engineering, and information systems. That same year we also completed construction of our first engineering and computer science building. Our faculty and students in these fields eagerly moved out of temporary trailers into a state-of-the art facility. A decade later, as we grew rapidly in computing, we completed construction of a second information technology (IT) and engineering building that allowed us to colocate all academic units in computing and information science in the same building.

The transformation of our academic programs in computer and information sciences was a defining moment for us. For the first time, the state provided us with operating funds for equipment in addition to construction funds for our original engineering building. We used these resources to replace decade-old computing equipment with new computing resources for our faculty and students that increased productivity exponentially. We built ten state-of-the-art computing laboratories and installed high-end workstations, becoming one of the first universities in the nation to have such powerful computing infrastructure. This investment put our academic programs in the computer and information sciences on a new trajectory just as the internet boom started in 1994. The labs and equipment enabled our faculty to offer instruction using cutting-edge tools; for example, we began teaching our first cohorts of students in the emerging field of computer animation. In a virtuous cycle of improvement, our improved infrastructure allowed us to recruit better-prepared students; these students then achieved at a higher level; their success allowed us to recruit even better-prepared students; and so on. Today, our College of Engineering and Information Technology (COEIT) awards about one-third of bachelor's degrees in computer and information sciences in Maryland and is a top producer nationally.

These facilities and other investments also supported cutting-edge research, not only in the computing and information sciences but also across all of engineering, the natural sciences, and visual arts. Our first strategic investment in technology, in 1987, was $250,000 for a computer that would be used in the Imaging Research Center (IRC), an interdisciplinary center for computer animation and imaging. In 1992, the IRC moved to the Engineering Building and acquired a professional-level animation system capable of producing graphics for professional film development. In 1987, we had purchased our first UNIX workstation, which was used by biochemist Mike Summers. In 1994, we purchased a high-performance computer from Silicon Graphics, one of the 500 most powerful in the world at the time, along with 240 workstations installed in the new Engineering Building. This immediately boosted research performance. Summers in biochemistry, Larrabee Strow in physics, and Curtis Menyuk in electrical engineering all used this new computing power, immediately boosting their research productivity. These and other faculty would also pull students into their research, further enhancing the academic program.[2]

Just as we built our program in engineering and IT, we also built our program in the arts, humanities, and social sciences to meet student interests and needs. To preclude program duplication, the state of Maryland has barred UMBC from offering undergraduate programs in several popular majors, including business, journalism, education, and electrical engineering. So in our early years, many students who matriculated at UMBC and completed introductory courses later transferred to another institution to complete a major that was not offered at UMBC. While these restrictions on our program base remain, in the intervening years we have created majors that appeal to students who might otherwise transfer. For example, we have established majors in financial economics, which appeals to students who might major in business; media and communications studies, of interest to some who might major in journalism or communications; and computer engineering, for students who might major in electrical engineering. We have also established the Sherman STEM Teacher Scholars Program, which is of interest to students who might otherwise major in education and teaching. Students who find what they are looking for in these programs now stay and complete degrees at UMBC.

While we evolved our academic program, we also established programs to better support high-achieving students. In 1988, building on an earlier honors program, we organized the Honors College to offer talented students a challenging and interdisciplinary academic program within the broader university. Today, about 500 students (just under 5% of the undergraduate student body) are members of the Honors College, and they participate in small classes that allow close engagement with faculty members and work in an environment that builds their writing, research, and critical thinking skills.[3] Meanwhile, the Meyerhoff program began to produce results for minorities in the natural sciences, and our newly fortified programs in engineering and IT expanded and evolved, transforming UMBC into a destination for high-achieving students interested in STEM.[4] As these efforts bore fruit, we simultaneously raised admissions standards and student preparation, increased undergraduate enrollment and retention, and boosted both student learning and completion. Eventually, we were confident enough in our trajectory that we rebranded UMBC as "An Honors University in Maryland." As this signature became widely accepted, it further enhanced the pool of applicants to the university and the preparation of the students for the work.

Most UMBC students, however, are not participants in special programs, and we have taken the initiative to increase the support that helps boost their success as well. In the late 1980s, white students had a six-year graduation rate of 35 percent and black students had a six-year graduation rate of just 25 percent. Many of our students, frankly, were not prepared for the work at UMBC or were simply distracted, citing job pressures or financial problems as reasons for withdrawing from UMBC. So, we also implemented initiatives and programs to improve learning, persistence, and completion among our students more broadly. Features of the Meyerhoff Scholars Program that our assessment program identified as particularly effective served as models for initiatives we began to take to scale for the larger undergraduate population beginning in the early 1990s. We strengthened tutoring for our undergraduates by expanding our Learning Resources Center (LRC). We built academic community among students by encouraging them to work together in study groups outside of the classroom. Students readily embraced group work, and at the request of, and in collaboration with, our students, we established and completed construction of the Retriever Learning Center (RLC) on the first floor of our library in 2010. The RLC is a dedicated group study space open twenty-four hours a day, filled with moveable tables, chairs, and whiteboards that can be rearranged by students so that they can work effectively together. Food and drink are allowed in the RLC, and we have even included snack machines in the space. When I take visitors on tours around campus, I often take them to the RLC.

It is always filled with students working in groups, and I can typically find whiteboards covered with solutions to math or chemistry problems.

Participation in undergraduate research has also proved an effective component of the Meyerhoff program, so we have extended this idea to the larger student population through programs that support both research and creative activities. We established the Undergraduate Research Awards (URA) program in 1996, the Undergraduate Research and Creative Achievement Day (URCAD) in 1997, and the *UMBC Review* in 2000.[5] URCAD is a full-day exhibition that provides UMBC undergraduates an opportunity to showcase their research, scholarship, and creative work in a professional context. The *UMBC Review* is a venue for the publication of undergraduate research articles.[6] It complements UMBC's annual journal *Bartleby*, which provides peer review and publication of student work in fiction, creative nonfiction, poetry, and visual art.[7] All of these further complement the work we do to encourage and support experiential learning through internships, entrepreneurship, and community engagement.

Also following the example of the Meyerhoff program, the Honors College and many of our scholars programs include a residential component to enhance cohort building and provide both a sense of community and opportunities to engage in group work. The entering cohort for each program lives together in a "Living-Learning Community" (LLC) during their first two years on campus. Emerging from the community-building component of the Meyerhoff program, this concept has resulted in the creation of eight such communities on campus, beginning in 2000. One of our recently created communities is the Discovery Scholars LLC, which focuses on merit scholars and other academically talented students who have not yet declared a major.[8] Through our analysis of student persistence, we have found that students who are affiliated with a group on campus—a scholars program, an LLC, an athletic team, or another community group—are more likely to persist and succeed. Students whose major is "undeclared" at matriculation are a particularly vulnerable group since they have no home department or major. We established the Discovery Scholars LLC to provide these undeclared students with both an affiliation and a community where they "belong." We have also recently established the STEM LLC, which provides opportunities for students majoring in these disciplines opportunities to connect socially and academically with other STEM students at UMBC. The STEM LLC offers both tutoring and social gatherings to enhance academic success and social support.[9]

When we adopted "An Honors University in Maryland" as our signature, Diane Lee, professor of education, wrote a letter to me in which she argued that we had to redouble our efforts at undergraduate student success to make sure the "honors university" became a reality for all students and not an empty promise. I met with Diane and listened carefully to her. I appreciated her perspective and began to involve her more deeply in our work. In 2005, we established the Office of Undergraduate Education (OUE), led by a vice provost and dean for undergraduate education to oversee and coordinate programs and initiatives in academic affairs. I asked Diane to serve in this position and help lead further innovation. She agreed.

One of the concerns for OUE, under Diane's leadership, continued to be retention and completion. By 2005, our six-year graduation rate had climbed from 33 percent to about 55 percent, yet we aimed to increase the rate to at least 67 percent, the level that the *US News & World Report* then published as our "expected" six-year completion rate. We estimated that about half of our increase in six-year completion rates from 1990 to 2005 was accomplished by retaining students who would have transferred to other institutions that had popular programs that we were not allowed to offer at UMBC. Going forward, we aimed to implement additional initiatives to increase student learning and retention.[10] We enhanced our advising capability and focused on making students feel "connected" through affiliations with programs, communities, teams, or clubs. We supported the first-year student transition to college, for both freshmen and transfer students. We developed cocurricular experiences and experiential learning. Through our Faculty Development Center and several incentive grants programs we supported faculty adoption of new teaching strategies, including active and team-based learning. All of this made a difference: between 2005 and 2010, the number of students transferring out of UMBC to other four-year institutions decreased by over 40 percent, and our six-year graduation rate grew by ten percentage points to 65 percent.

We also recognized that students needed support during their first year, a critical transition period during which new students adapt to college life and college-level academic expectations. We launched a set of activities for first-year students that we have now packaged together as UMBC's "First-Year Experience." We had been providing seminars on academic success skills for first-year students for some time. When we branded UMBC as "An Honors University in Maryland" in 2002, we expanded and formalized these as "Introduction to an Honors University" (IHU) seminars. These are provided not as stand-alone courses but as supplements to regular first-year foundational courses. We saw rapid growth in student participation in IHU seminars in the first several years, and since then, the number of IHU sections has been stable at about forty per year, each with an enrollment of approximately twenty students. In 2005, we also instituted our First Year Seminars, in which a faculty member and class participants study a topic in an interactive, small-group environment, focusing on learning by sharing knowledge and experience through writing, discussions, and presentations. A significant fraction of our incoming class now participates in these seminars. Assessment of the impact of these seminars on student success has demonstrated that they have longer-term benefits beyond the narrow learning experience of the course itself. For example, we found that entering freshmen who had not yet declared a major but completed a first-year seminar had significantly higher retention and six-year completion rates compared to those who had not. In 2004, we established the New

Student Book Experience. Each new student—first-year or transfer student—reads a recommended book that is discussed in small groups during Welcome Week. This activity provides an opportunity for a common experience, community building, and early intellectual interaction with peers and faculty in a small-group setting. Assigned books in recent years have included *Half the Sky*, *The Immortal Life of Henrietta Lacks*, *An Unquiet Mind*, *Not in My Neighborhood*, and *Enrique's Journey*. More recently, we developed our Collegiate Success Institute (CSI), which offers a summer bridge program to new freshmen who want to get a jump start on the introductory mathematics and writing courses required for first-year students.[11]

We also initiated programming for our transfer students, who constitute nearly half of our new student population each year and also benefit from support during their transition. We piloted transfer student seminars in 2008 and 2009 and then instituted them formally in 2011. With funding from the Bill and Melinda Gates Foundation, we also established a program to support students in STEM fields who transfer to UMBC from one of four partner community colleges. This program has involved close collaboration with our community college partners, who received some of the grant funding to work with us to develop closer curricular alignment (including course redesign), academic planning, career counseling, and mentoring from UMBC students who were community college alumni. This successful program has been sustained after the grant period ended using university funds. While this program included pre- and post-transfer activities and supports, the basic concept was to move away from the notion of managing the transition from community college to UMBC and instead develop a consistent student experience from the day that a student entered community college to the day they graduated from UMBC.[12]

A major grant in 2014 from the NIH's Building Infrastructure Leading to Diversity (BUILD) initiative has allowed us to further extend what we have learned from the Meyerhoff Scholars Program to the broader undergraduate population in the life sciences at UMBC. The STEM BUILD at UMBC program funded by this grant targets promising STEM students who enter as freshmen or as transfer students and is only available to students who otherwise would not qualify for other significant university or scholarship support.[13] The BUILD Training Program provides financial support, extensive advising, special programming, career exploration, a series of group research opportunities, and academic support. Through this program and its components, we are infusing the mentoring and training elements found in the Meyerhoff program into the broader undergraduate experience. The BUILD Training Program and the BUILD LLC also foster community, scientific identity, and resilience. Bill LaCourse, our dean of the College of Natural and Mathematical Sciences and program co-PI along with our provost, writes,

> At the heart of STEM BUILD at UMBC is the development of BUILD Group Research (BGR), a sequence of experiences designed to overcome the challenges that undergraduates without programmatic support often encounter (e.g., limited internship opportunities, mentorships, and research positions for which top STEM students are favored). BUILD Training Program (BTP) Trainees serve as pioneers in this initiative, which is potentially a national model for universities as they address the call to retain and graduate more students in STEM disciplines—especially those from underrepresented groups.[14]

Information Technology, Assessment, and Data Analytics

If our aim here is to discuss student success, it might seem a digression to detour into a history of computing services at UMBC. However, the development of our IT program within our organization has positioned it to be an innovative partner in our drive to both support students and develop evidence-based approaches to ensuring their success. Our Division of Information Technology (DoIT) has partnered powerfully with institutional research, enrollment management, and our academic program to develop a data analytics capacity that advances teaching and learning, as well as student persistence and completion.

Evolving Computing Services

The development of our campus computing services has played a special role in our overall advancement as an institution. In our early years, computing services developed in a haphazard way. Beginning in 1985, UMBC had two separate computing programs, one for academics and another for administration. In the early 1990s, as email became popular, our academic and administrative computing units had adopted different email systems and local area networks for faculty and staff, respectively. These different email systems made communication between faculty/students and administrators challenging; it was difficult to even send email messages between the two systems. In 1995, Provost Joanne Argersinger engaged Philip Long to conduct an external review of computing at UMBC. Long, who was in computing at Yale University and would go on to serve as chief information officer (CIO) there for a decade, recommended merging our two computing organizations. Later that year, Argersinger acted on the suggestion and combined the two units to create University Computing Services, led by the academic computing director, Bill Scott, who reported to vice provost Tom Roth. Two years later, Jack Suess, a UMBC alumnus, assumed the position of director of University Computing Services.[15]

In the 2000s, our computing services evolved further. In 2000, we merged Instructional Technology and University Computing Services by creating the Office of Information Technology, with Suess as the director and our CIO. We also purchased PeopleSoft applications for finance, human resources, student information, and performance management. In 2001, we began our PeopleSoft implementation with finance and human resources under the direction of a project manager reporting to the vice president of administration. When that manager left the following year, Suess became the project manager, further consolidating computing and information services in one organization.

About this time, I began to appreciate how IT could be a transformative force for our university. With this in mind, I wanted to learn as much as possible about technology and how it could be deployed to support academics, research, and administration. I benefited from direct discussion with our CIO and quickly began to see how energizing it would be for him to be directly involved in conversations about institutional decisions so that IT could be integrated at the outset in our planning and administration. I did not want IT to be disruptive, but rather a constructive force aligned with campus priorities. I wanted our IT professionals to be partners in the work.

At most institutions, the CIO or director of IT reports to the provost, the vice president for finance and administration, or someone subordinate to one of them. I decided that our CIO would be a vice president and report directly to me. This decision facilitated my learning and integrated our IT evolution into the fabric of our campus life. It also sent a clear message to the campus about the importance I was giving IT.[16] Because our campus culture already embraced innovation as a value, the elevation of IT as a part of our strategic planning occurred smoothly. Indeed, once we raised the profile of computing services on campus, we saw an immediate payoff in our PeopleSoft implementation. When we first brought PeopleSoft to campus, the transition had been difficult because IT was not yet integrated with campus administration and we had problems with communication and execution. The elevation of IT opened communication and improved transition processes, making the PeopleSoft deployment much easier as stakeholders took the product more seriously and worked collaboratively to implement the transition.

Staying on the cutting edge of technology and computing has played a central role in enhancing the work of our staff, faculty, and students. Our investment in equipment in 1992 boosted our computing and information science programs. Since then, we have maintained our leadership position in these fields and further extended the benefits of cutting-edge technology to the rest of the campus. By 1995, most staff and faculty had a workstation and network connection. We then put ethernet into all of our dormitories, providing students with connections and direct access to the internet. As a result, we were selected by *Wired* magazine in 1999 as one of the top fifty "wired" campuses. Subsequently, we implemented campus-wide Wi-Fi capability. As a result of that work, Intel and Cisco named us one of the top twenty-five "wireless" campuses in the country in 2003. In 1999, the University System of Maryland (USM) finalized a Microsoft site license agreement, and all students, faculty, and staff at UMBC were provided access to Microsoft software. Meanwhile, in 1994, we had charged a faculty task force, staffed by our IT unit, to develop a multiyear plan for advancing research through IT. This led to the installation of a state-of-the-art campus computer network. As a result of this work, in 1997 UMBC was among the first fifty institutions to receive an NSF grant of $900,000 to join a new research initiative, the very high speed Backbone Network Service.

It was during this period that we also began innovating in the application of technology to directly support students. In 1997, five or more years ahead of most institutions, we developed the myUMBC portal for students and a web-based system for class registration. We had launched Electronic Access to Student Information in 1996 by developing web-based access to student records and enrollment. Building on this the next year, we adopted a learning management system (LMS), WebCT, the first USM institution to do so. This system allowed faculty to post course materials on the web, use an online gradebook, and administer online quizzes. In 2000, we moved our LMS to Blackboard. This immediately benefited faculty teaching and student learning and eventually served as a resource we could draw on to develop a data analytics program to enhance academic performance.

We have continued to ensure that our students and faculty benefit from ongoing technological advances both inside and outside of the classroom. In 2008, working with Residential Life, we began to provide wireless internet service in our residence halls, and in 2010 UMBC and Dell partnered on a $500,000 project to support virtual computing for students. That year, incoming freshmen were given Google email accounts (Gmail), and the next year all email accounts were migrated to Google. UMBC was the first school in the USM to outsource our email services. In 2012, UMBC joined twenty other Internet2 universities to engage in a web-based file service with Box.Com, now a cornerstone of our collaboration environment. Our research infrastructure also saw important up-grades. In 2008, UMBC received an NSF grant for a major high-performance computing upgrade that included the purchase of an eighty-node system. In 2015, we further upgraded high-performance computing through a large equipment donation from NASA that added two hundred additional nodes. In 2016, UMBC received the NSF CC*IIE networking award to upgrade to 100 Gbit; we became one of the first seventy-five universities to do so. All of these ad-vances support faculty research and also benefit students who are engaged with faculty in their research efforts.

Today, our DoIT is a respected organization that keeps our cam-pus on the cutting edge of technology and data. DoIT is central-ized, and our IT deployment on campus is likewise centralized, an organizational structure that is not widely shared, as many cam-puses have decentralized computing organizations. As a central-ized entity, DoIT seeks collaborative partnerships with other cam-pus units and encourages our IT staff, many of whom are UMBC graduates, to be active participants in the campus community. Further, UMBC's DoIT is viewed as a national leader in a range of computing areas as measured by the EDUCAUSE Benchmark Service and by our engagement with national organizations such as EDUCAUSE, Internet2, and IMSglobal. Jack Suess, our CIO, has served on the board of directors of all three organizations and led higher education initiatives in advancing cybersecurity, federated identity, analytics, and cloud computing.

Critically, DoIT has also become an important partner in our effort to advance student success by bringing to or developing at UMBC the best ideas and products nationally for supporting higher education. DoIT has worked with vendors to implement or develop better products. For example, UMBC staff worked with a small company, iStrategy, to develop analytical tools for student data in our LMS, Blackboard. This product was so successful that the company Blackboard purchased iStrategy, and it now serves as the core of the Blackboard Analytics product. Similarly, UMBC was one of the first universities to implement a secure web-based file service named Box. Today, Box is used by hundreds of universities and has enabled people to easily and securely work from anywhere.

Assessment and Data Analytics

When we established the Meyerhoff Scholars Program, we included an evaluation component from the outset. I had suggested that we should see the Meyerhoff program as a "scientific experiment" and collect data to understand whether, and to what extent, the initiative was meeting its goals. We used this evaluation component, funded by the Alfred P. Sloan Foundation, to collect and analyze data that would inform program operations on an ongoing basis and also examine outcomes to substantiate the program as a national model.

The use of an evidence-based approach to program inception, design, and evaluation has since become a hallmark of the culture of UMBC. In a way that affected overall campus culture, the deployment and success of program evaluation in the Meyerhoff program raised general consciousness regarding the usefulness of incorporating formative and summative assessment into new initiatives. We have incorporated evaluation and continuous improvement into many other programmatic efforts, including the Gates-funded Community College STEM Transfer initiative, the NIH-funded STEM BUILD at UMBC, and the HHMI-funded Meyerhoff Adaptation at Penn State and the University of North Carolina at Chapel Hill. Evidence-based approaches to program initiation, assessment, and continuous improvement have also been used in other areas, including the implementation of our ADVANCE grant, which was used to support recruitment, retention, and advancement of women in our science and engineering faculty and our efforts to diversify our faculty.

Through our iCubed@UMBC program, funded by a grant from the NSF, we have undertaken a large-scale educational experiment using randomized control to examine how a set of teaching and learning interventions affect student performance in STEM fields. We randomly assigned more than 1,300 undergraduate student participants into one of five intervention groups during their first year at UMBC. Four groups were treated with interventions that were scalable versions of essential components of the Meyerhoff Scholars Program: community-based study groups, direct mentoring by faculty in their majors, one-on-one guidance from professional staff specific to career goals, and participation in an active learning math course. The fifth "intervention" was no treatment as a control (participants in this group received a $50 UMBC Bookstore gift certificate). We are now analyzing our data to establish which activities are both successful and cost-effective for scaling up to benefit large numbers of future first-year STEM students at UMBC.[17]

By the early 2000s, we understood that in order to improve student success, we needed to find a way to increase collaboration, share data about the experiences of our students, and more deeply embed evidence-based decision-making into our practices. In the early part of my presidency, I had not emphasized the importance of data sharing and transparency, even though it had the potential to powerfully reshape our work. In fact, in the early 2000s, our operational culture did not insist on openly sharing data. As is typical of many organizations, people derived power through the control of information. Over time, though, we have developed a more collaborative approach to the way we manage data, facilitated in part by the centralized nature of our IT services and its work in building partnerships with other units. More specifically, and in a manner that may be unique in American higher education, Jack Suess (DoIT), Connie Pierson (Office of Institutional Research, Analysis, and Decision Support [IRADS]), and Yvette Mozie-Ross (Office of Admissions and Enrollment Management) have worked together to create a state-of-the-art data warehouse and web-based interface that provides many in the campus community with access to student-level data.[18]

In 2003, as part of our effort to improve UMBC's retention and graduation rates, we appointed a Retention Task Force, led by Diane Lee, vice provost for undergraduate education, and including Jack Suess and other administrators. Suess wrote a memo to his task force colleagues entitled "UMBC Retention Implementation Plan: Moving Strategy into Action" that laid out the systems and processes needed to develop the tools needed for exploring student-level data and understanding what initiatives, programs, and interventions work for our campus. Essentially, his plan was to build a "data warehouse," which had already been identified as a potential tool a few years earlier in our 2000 IT Strategic Plan. The development and deployment of such a database and the tools to query it would build on our culture of assessment, our growing capability in IT, and our willingness to collaborate.[19]

The first piece in the development of robust student data was the deployment of My Academic Program, which allowed faculty and staff to use a simple web form to get a spreadsheet with demographic and academic data on various student populations based on courses, majors, or some specific attributes. It also gave faculty and staff involved with advising and retention a complete view of the student—academic and nonacademic—and the ability to flag a student using "alerts" when an intervention was needed. For example, if an instructor were to suggest that a student should visit the LRC for tutoring, the coordinator for the LLC where the student lives might get an email noting that. The coordinator, who is already engaged with the student, can follow up and encourage the student to visit with the instructor during office hours and also set up a time to go to the LRC. My Academic Program was launched for students, faculty, and staff in 2005.

Meanwhile, in academic year 2004/5, our Office of Institutional Research (OIR) piloted a more expansive database by collecting and analyzing data on the incoming cohort of first-year degree-seeking students. This pilot demonstrated the benefit of ad hoc data analysis that could allow us to discern broad patterns and look at various factors affecting success. We began with a single graduate student whom we hired to write data reports. He wrote one set of reports that tried to connect student-level data from our learning management system with final grades to discover which student characteristics correlated with student success. He wrote another report that provided information on student activity on course websites and another providing data on the use of clickers in foundational courses. As we began to understand what student characteristics, activities, and interventions were correlated with student success, we were able to identify faculty who were the early adopters experimenting with technology in course delivery. We asked them to give talks at brown-bag lunch seminars as a way to inform and motivate other faculty to likewise experiment.

As a next step, we sought to deepen our analytical capability by implementing a new set of data tools that were developed through a partnership between DoIT and IRADS. In 2006, we contracted with a local business called iStrategy to help us develop reports, derived from our data warehouse and legacy student information system (SIS), that would be most useful to deans, chairs, and faculty. We were one of iStrategy's first customers. This allowed us to track admissions and retention data and drill further down into the data to look at specific student characteristics (race, ethnicity, gender, citizenship, geographic origin, major) to understand better how different groups of students were performing and why. In 2009, we went live with PeopleSoft SA, which replaced our legacy SIS and provided student administrative data on course registration, advising, financial aid, student finances, and academic progress. Then, in 2010, we began working with Blackboard, which had purchased iStrategy, to build out their product—Analytics for Learn—in combination with the data we were aggregating from PeopleSoft and other sources.

With the success of the pilot, our colleagues in OIR, DoIT, and Enrollment Management worked together to create a pioneering, robust business intelligence system supporting student success. This data warehouse, which we named REX, is a centralized data source that aggregates data from across the campus.[20] Faculty, staff, and institutional researchers can use this comprehensive resource to generate official reports required by USM, the state of Maryland, and federal government agencies. More importantly, IR staff now have the time and data to also work with the provost on deeper analytic analysis of our student success initiatives. (This change within IR has led them to be renamed as IRADS.) Most universities conduct this analytical work solely with data extracted from the SIS, which in the case of UMBC is PeopleSoft. These data are important, because they are used nationally, but they are not sufficient to fully understand student success. To get a full picture of our students and what impacts their success, we have also pulled data into REX from outside the SIS to better understand how various factors affect student success. These data include information on both the academic performance of our students and the overall student experience. REX incorporates data from our SIS, our learning management system, and electronic course materials to allow us to analyze student characteristics and course activity. It also draws in data from residential life that describe where students live and whether they are members of an LLC or other campus community. It includes information on student participation in clubs, activities, and events as a measure of engagement. This holistic data source allows us to understand which students are succeeding and which ones are at risk and why. It allows us to identify interventions that may help an individual student or a larger group.

We continue to develop our data analytics capability. In computing services there is something called the "organizational maturity curse," a notion that suggests that organizations become more bureaucratic and complacent as they develop. Any institution can fall victim to this. At UMBC, however, we like to say that "success is never final." I always encourage us all—faculty, staff, and students—to ask how we can perform better, and the broad availability of data and analyses provided the means for us to answer that question.

In 2016, we began to explore the use of predictive analytics. This project was led by associate provost Robert Carpenter. We decided to work with Civitas Learning, a leader in predictive analytics for student success. UMBC has been one of the few customers to implement Civitas by extracting data from our data warehouse rather than directly from our SIS. By using our data warehouse, we have been able to readily validate the results we have produced through Civitas and fully implement the solution in less than a year. This effort has given us new insight into many of our student success initiatives, revealing, for example, that many of our students in scholars programs have taken advantage of them, but few of our at-risk students have as we intended. Consequently, we have changed how we reach out to students in order to increase the participation of at-risk students who need the most help. As another example, in 2017 UMBC purchased Blackboard Predict. Whereas Civitas follows students who may be at risk of not persisting to the next semester, Blackboard Predict focuses on students who may be at risk in a course. In the past, we would wait until the first exam to observe which students were performing poorly and then reach out to provide additional support. We have found that when faculty make use of Blackboard for homework and quizzes, Blackboard Predict can quickly identify at-risk students and get them help before they fail the first exam. Lastly, UMBC is working closely with EAB to implement Academic Performance Solutions. As we did with Civitas, we implemented this in conjunction with REX and completed this project in less than six months. We are now using these data to work with our deans and academic chairs to help inform them of trends in their units.

By 2018, these efforts in analytics had proven so valuable that the provost and CIO formed a partnership to support these efforts. Associate Provost Carpenter joined DoIT as a deputy CIO for business intelligence and is now overseeing the analytics team as it develops dashboards to support the initiatives resulting from our strategic plan implementation. We are encouraging our data and analytics teams to work together with our college deans to develop "dashboards" that allow department chairs, faculty, advisors, and administrators to understand, in real time, how our students are performing. This effort has included the development of degree-planning tools, academic and nonacademic risk assessment, student persistence scoring, and improved early warning systems. Even more challenging, we are now deploying the tools that use "predictive analytics" to more deeply inform academic policy around curriculum, to identify groups of at-risk students to whom we can provide targeted support, and, most importantly, to identify systemic problems that require UMBC, as an institution, to change the way we do things. To this end we have been experimenting with third-party products, such as those offered by Civitas and EAB, that will assist us in this work.

We have learned, through almost two decades of work with data and analytics, that data analytics is not quite the sort of panacea that it is sometimes represented to be. Advanced data warehousing and analytical tools are critical, but we need institutional will and close collaboration among all stakeholders to adopt these tools, deploy them widely, and use them effectively. This is proactive work that is very resource intensive and requires skilled and dedicated staff. But it is work that has a high potential to pay off for our students and our university. We are also acutely aware of the potential ethical issues that surround the use of predictive data at the level of the individual student. We are actively engaged in these discussions on campus and in the national conversation.

Today, our administrative team insists on using data for evidence-based discussion of campus policies and programs. Our collaborative work speeds up data availability, iterations in querying the data, decision-making, and interventions for programs, courses, and individual students. As Yvette Mozie-Ross, our vice provost for enrollment management, has noted, we now have a healthier environment than before, one in which people can be curious and use data not to punish but to understand how to improve our work.

9

A Challenge of Quality

Quality in Teaching and Learning

The American Academy of Arts and Sciences recently focused our thoughts on the critical work we have before us in higher education when its Commission on the Future of Undergraduate Education contended, "What was once a challenge of *quantity* in American undergraduate education, of enrolling as many students as possible, is increasingly a challenge of educational *quality*, that all students receive the education they need to succeed, that they are able to complete the studies they begin, and that they can do all of this affordably, without mortgaging the very future they seek to improve."[1] The commission focused on the central fact that "only about 60 percent of students who begin a bachelor's degree actually complete one" and challenged us to do much better.[2] The other 40 percent often end up with no degree yet accumulate significant debt that they are then hard-pressed to repay without the benefit of a college degree. These outcomes are unacceptable, and even more so when we recognize that there is a significant discrepancy in college completion rates between those students who come from upper-income families and those from lower-income families. This adds an overlay of equity to the layers of concern about social mobility, individual success, civic participation, and economic prosperity.

When I was invited to join the Commission on the Future of Undergraduate Education, I agreed to serve because strengthening student educational experiences and increasing student degree completion are the leading issues we face in academia at a time when our nation's knowledge economy needs more college graduates and when a college degree is the ticket to the new middle class, composed of knowledge workers. The problem of student success is especially acute in the fields of natural sciences and engineering. I had the privilege to chair a study committee at the National Academies of Sciences, Engineering, and Medicine that focused on how we can better support underrepresented minority students in these fields. As we wrote in our report, *Expanding Underrepresented Minority Participation: America's Science and Technology Talent at the Crossroads*, we were not surprised to find minority attrition from STEM fields because that was the problem we had convened to examine. However, what was surprising was the finding that most white and Asian American students were also struggling to complete STEM degrees.[3]

Nationally, only about 20 percent of black and Hispanic students who seek to major in science and engineering graduate in five years with a STEM degree. However, similarly low completion rates are seen for white and Asian American students: 32 and 42 percent, respectively.[4] And what may appear counterintuitive is a profound reality that hurts our nation: the higher a student's SAT scores, the larger the number of Advanced Placement credits, and the more prestigious the college or university a student attends, the greater the probability that a student who starts pursuing a degree in science and engineering will switch out of STEM within the first year.[5]

It is clear that we are dealing with not only a problem that exists for minority students but also an overall American problem with undergraduate STEM completion. Most well-prepared students of all backgrounds with an interest in STEM fields and careers leave majors in those fields in the first two years of college—and this at a time when our economy needs more STEM graduates than ever before.

The *Crossroads* report, published in 2011, recommended that we —our institutions, programs, and faculty—focus on building community among our students to foster improved learning outcomes and persistence and redesigning introductory, or gateway, courses in STEM to better support the success of students. A year later, the President's Council of Advisors in Science and Technology (PCAST) released *Engage to Excel: Producing One Million Additional College Graduates with Degrees in Science, Technology, Engineering, and Mathematics*, which argued "for improving STEM education during the first two years of college . . . a crucial stage in the STEM education pathway." The PCAST report, as did ours, insisted that institutions and their faculty redesign introductory courses in the sciences and mathematics that are required for majors in those fields, as well as in engineering and medicine.[6]

Foundational, or "gateway," courses have been identified as an initial obstacle to success in STEM fields for many students. Often acting as "weed-out" courses, they have several features that discourage many students: First, they tend to be taught in a large lecture format, an environment that encourages passive absorption of knowledge rather than active engagement in learning. Second, they are often graded on a curve, creating a disincentive for students to engage in group work and collaborative learning, which have been demonstrated to boost student learning outcomes by building community among students and improving the social integration and a sense of belonging that promote persistence and completion.

There are many barriers to a quality educational experience and student completion. The methodology used by the instructor who teaches a course should not be one of them. With advances in cognitive psychology and discipline-based educational research, we now have a deeper understanding of how students learn, as well as best practices for teaching and learning by field.[7] These new approaches to teaching and learning, which are often referred to as "course redesign," include active learning, problem-focused learning, group- or team-based learning (TBL), tutoring, peer support, and flipped classrooms, among many other innovations.

Too few institutions have encouraged and, more importantly, supported their faculty members to redesign their introductory courses by employing new approaches to teaching and learning that complement, or replace, the traditional lecture method. Many institutions do not encourage students to work together or to seek help, which often leaves them fending for themselves when they might benefit from group work, tutoring, or supplemental instruction. In addition, some of the highest-achieving students are encouraged to start with advanced classes in mathematics and science, and many of these students do not compete well with more experienced students. Accustomed to performing at the highest levels, they are discouraged by their relatively poor performance and switch out of science and engineering.

As senior leaders on our campuses we must champion meaningful change in the way courses are taught so that our students are supported and succeed. Instead of allowing faculty to define "rigor" by how many students they "weed out," we must encourage them to redefine success as ensuring learning and completion of courses and degrees. The "weed-out" culture not only depresses student success overall but also tends to disproportionately dampen success and persistence for anyone who already feels insecure in an academic environment, including women, underrepresented minorities, and first-generation students.

At UMBC, we support faculty across the disciplines who are redesigning courses and transforming curricula and pedagogies to support student learning, persistence, and success. The Hrabowski Innovation Fund, administered by our Faculty Development Center (FDC), is providing seed funding to both faculty and staff for innovative course redesign and assessment efforts. The University System of Maryland is also at the forefront of providing grant funding through a similar program. A major grant from the National Institutes of Health Building Infrastructure Leading to Diversity initiative allows us to extend what we have learned from the Meyerhoff Scholars Program to the broader undergraduate population in the life sciences at UMBC. A grant from the Bill and Melinda Gates Foundation allows us to support STEM undergraduates as they transfer from our partner community colleges to UMBC and other four-year institutions, and a grant from the Howard Hughes Medical Institute allows us to redesign introductory biology courses to integrate interdisciplinary concepts from mathematics and chemistry.

Discovery as Learning

They were failing. We were failing.

Bill LaCourse looked out at his students in CHEM 101 (Introduction to Chemistry) and realized he had come to a turning point for himself, the course, and the students. LaCourse, professor of chemistry and biochemistry, had come to class that day prepared, as always, to lecture. He stood behind the lectern and, like so many other chemistry professors before him, talked about the topic of the day, whether it was the atomic-molecular theory of matter, chemical nomenclature, periodic properties, or the molecular orbital theory. But he was not reaching his students, especially the ones who needed his help the most.[8]

The traditional, expositional, pedagogical theory said that LaCourse's students would listen, take notes, and develop a foundational understanding of the principles of chemistry that they would then demonstrate through examination. But who were they kidding? The evidence right in front of him—quite literally in the form of empty seats or students in the back of the class looking at their laptops instead of him—suggested that this model of teaching did not achieve the outcomes he wanted.

In fact, experts in chemistry education can now easily enumerate the potential problems with the traditional model of teaching chemistry:

- The course covers too much material, sacrificing depth for breadth, and is generally ineffective at developing an understanding of basic concepts.
- It is taught as if students were chemistry majors, ignoring the fact that the majority of them are not.
- It uses a course or curricular design that is inconsistent with the ways students actually learn.
- The course often fails to engage student interest.[9]

If he needed more evidence that perhaps all of these were issues in his class, all LaCourse had to do was look at class grades. In the fall semester of 2004, only 32 percent of CHEM 101 students earned an A or B, while 32 percent earned a C and 36 percent earned a D or F or withdrew from the class (known as "the DFW rate"). In the context of a STEM degree, which typically involves the successful completion of a sequence of increasingly advanced courses, only those students receiving an A or B had a realistic chance of progressing toward their goal.

Students had always viewed CHEM 101 as a "weed-out course" to endure, if possible, and rolled their eyes at the thought of it. And LaCourse himself, like many instructors, preferred teaching upper-level chemistry courses because the students in those courses were more actively engaged with the material and interested in his research. But now student learning in foundational chemistry appeared to be declining as evidenced by class attendance, the results of examinations, the increasing number of students failing or dropping the course, and the decrease in the number of chemistry majors. "We were losing ground," LaCourse recalled.[10]

The decline in student performance in CHEM 101 proved, in part, to be the unintended consequence of deploying Wi-Fi across our campus, including in the Meyerhoff Chemistry Building. Connecting to Wi-Fi enabled students to tune out during lecture and tune into what was available on their laptops and phones as they sat toward the back in the lecture hall. Recapturing their attention with a dated approach that already failed at stimulating them to learn in the first place was a nonstarter. Indeed, while intentional culture change can be hard as hell, unintended culture change can occur when you least expect it. Despite its potential and obvious benefits, deployment of campus Wi-Fi was deeply disruptive to student learning. This was not just a problem for chemistry. Faculty in all disciplines found their classes affected in this way, and many raised this as a problem. The situation called for something different. The question now was how we would handle it.

Our faculty senate had several discussions about technology and the classroom. The strongest voices at first, which assumed that faculty across the campus would certainly agree with them, urged that we should backtrack. Some said, "Students should not have access to personal technology while in class. Let's just turn it off." Others, however, argued that instead of turning off the Wi-Fi, perhaps we could harness technology for learning, saying, "How could we redesign courses to capitalize on technology?"

In the summer of 2005, in the midst of this disruption, LaCourse decided that this was the time to change how CHEM 101 was taught. For many years, the course had consisted of three fifty-minute lectures for 300–350 students and multiple fifty-minute recitation sections, each for fifty to eighty students, per week. Perhaps he could take a different approach, capitalizing on technology as one element of his redesign.

Inspired by the success of the Meyerhoff Scholars Program, LaCourse understood that what works for a specific group of students could be translated and applied to a broader group of students in a specific class. As a professor of chemistry, he had encountered Meyerhoff Scholars in his classes and had seen how the program had made UMBC first in the nation in African Americans who earned bachelor's degrees in chemistry and biochemistry. He had been impressed by the holistic approach that the Meyerhoff program offered and the way it built community by encouraging students to study in groups as a strategy for enhancing both learning and persistence. In groups, students could learn from one another—the whole being greater than the sum of its parts. And, in groups, students could find a sense of belonging, a feeling proven to increase student identification with and completion of a program. This gave him a sense of the possibilities.

Further, LaCourse drew insight from ongoing national efforts to reform chemistry education that had been emerging and evolving over the previous decade to inform a redesign in Introductory Chemistry with "discovery learning." "The traditional model of teaching used in [large lecture] classes," wrote LaCourse and Ralph Pollack, the department chair at the time, "relies primarily on faculty lecturing to students, with minimal active participation by students."[11] LaCourse and Pollack had an alternative in mind. As our colleagues have summarized, "Drawing on the very successful cooperative learning pedagogies Process-Oriented Guided Inquiry Learning (POGIL) and Student-Centered Active Leaning Environment with Upside-down Pedagogies (SCALE-UP), Discovery Learning involves students working in self-managed teams on inquiry problems in a unique learning environment."[12]

LaCourse sensed that he could develop a practical approach that could really work, an active, problem-focused, student-centered approach that would put students in charge of their own learning. He would create a dedicated, active learning space in which this would happen, the Chemistry Discovery Center (CDC). In this space students would work collaboratively in groups to "discover" the basic concepts of chemistry. In their vision, LaCourse and Pollack wrote, "learners actively take knowledge, connect it to previously assimilated knowledge and make it theirs by constructing their own interpretation. Thus, students are encouraged to organize and analyze information and teaching strategies are tailored to student understanding. This model is premised on (i) students being actively engaged in learning, (ii) students learning by constructing knowledge, (iii) students learning from each other."[13]

There were two challenges beyond the redesign of the course learning methodology: money and space. Lacking both, Discovery

Learning began as a pilot project to test the idea. While based on elements of POGIL and SCALE-UP, LaCourse was really charting his own course, and it required a shakedown cruise. Pollack, as department chair, provided support for the pilot through departmental funds and space in a department-controlled classroom. When the pilot proved successful, it was time to go full scale.

Provision and availability of suitable classroom space was the largest obstacle to scaling up the pilot. The large classrooms on campus, typically lecture theaters, had immovable furniture; those classrooms with moveable furniture, typically seminar rooms, were too small. Fortuitously, at the time in which LaCourse was shopping his idea, several spaces in the University Center, previously occupied by the bursar and the bookstore, were vacated when our newly completed Commons building opened. A room became available— it was not perfect and had not been designed as a classroom, but it was about the size LaCourse was looking for. He took it.

Funding was the next challenge. LaCourse did not need a lot, but twenty group workstations required start-up capital for furniture and computers. LaCourse met with Diane Lee, dean of undergraduate education, to make his pitch and discuss his vision for a classroom laid out with workstations comprising a table, a computer, and a whiteboard. At these workstations, groups of four students would work together on carefully crafted problems that led them to "discover" chemistry concepts through an interactive, technologically enabled process. Dean Lee found $85,000 that could be repurposed for the CDC. These funds allowed LaCourse to build the dedicated CDC classroom, which debuted in the fall of 2005. Subsequently, the CDC has been maintained through funding from the College of Natural and Mathematical Sciences (CNMS) and the Chemistry Department.

With the creation of the CDC, Introductory Chemistry was reborn. Students now prepare for class using various web-based tutorials. They then attend a weekly, two-hour, mandatory "discovery" learning session, where they work on modules and materials that guide them in the development of ideas and foundational principles of chemistry—in direct contrast to rote memorization. In the CDC, students work in groups to solve problems. Students rotate through the roles of manager (leadership development), technician (technical skills and interpreting scientific information), scribe (listening and communication), and blogger (communication and writing). Instructors and peer mentors act as facilitators. The students take responsibility for developing theories and solving problems. Students discover facts and concepts promoting long-term learning.[14]

Since its introduction, the CDC has increased the "C or better" pass rate in chemistry from 61 to 85 percent for CHEM 101 and from 73 to 80 percent for CHEM 102. At the same time, more students are also earning As and Bs. All this has occurred while the standards for earning each grade have also been raised. The number of chemistry and biochemistry majors grew after the CDC opened, with majors increasing in each area by 70 and 42 percent, respectively.

A final footnote to this story is offered here as a word of caution, because culture change is hard as hell and sustaining change is just as difficult. After Bill LaCourse developed the CDC, he led it for four years, during which time we saw great improvement in student grades and persistence. After he became chair and then dean, the personnel in charge of the center changed over time. For a while, the approach to CHEM 101 and the CDC began to slip back toward the "traditional pedagogical style," and student grades began to slip again before we became aware of this backsliding and could take corrective action. As we say, "success is never final." When we enact change on campus, we have to assume that our progress is neither complete nor necessarily permanent. Progress can be undermined in a heartbeat, intentionally or unintentionally. We must be vigilant. The arc of history bends toward justice—but only if we work toward it and then make sure our progress is sustained.

A Culture of Innovation

By 2005, we had seen success with the Meyerhoff Scholars Program, our NSF-funded ADVANCE program, an entrepreneurship program funded by the Kauffman Foundation, the CDC, the Shriver Center, and the creation of a research park, bwtech@UMBC. We had data that demonstrated how we had accomplished the goals we had set out with each of these efforts.

Culture change does not happen all at once. It can be almost imperceptible at times. One person gets it, then another, and then another. And then one day you sense that it has happened and that the tipping point has been crossed. These successes had altered our beliefs as a community about what is possible. They had altered our values. We had embraced inclusive excellence, student success, and innovation. Our faculty looked in the mirror and began asking, "How can I change my course to better support student learning?"

To be sure, UMBC is not the only campus that is innovating or redesigning courses, particularly in STEM. As noted, Bill LaCourse was informed by a movement that pioneered new pedagogical approaches in chemistry education and that was, in turn, part of a broader movement to redesign STEM courses. Carl Wieman, Nobel Prize winner, has led efforts to reform science education at the University of Colorado and the University of British Columbia, as well as through the National Academies' Board on Science Education and the White House Office of Science and Technology Policy. In their book *Making Scientists: Six Principles for Effective College Teaching*, Gregory Light and Marina Macari discuss "Northwestern University's Gateway Science Workshop, where the seminar room is infused with a sense of discovery usually confined to the research lab."[15] There are many specific examples one could cite.

We can also point to programs, both at the national level and at our university, that are spearheading change in the way we think about course design:

- The Association of American Universities Undergraduate STEM Education Initiative is a coalition of universities pledged to redesign STEM courses on their campuses. Project sites include the University of Colorado Boulder, the University of Arizona, Brown University, the University of

Pennsylvania, Washington University in St. Louis, Michigan State University, and the University of North Carolina at Chapel Hill.[16]

- The Business Higher Education Forum's National Higher Education and Workforce Initiative provides examples of university-industry partnerships to enhance undergraduate STEM education, especially in data science and analytics, cybersecurity, risk management, and social and mobile technologies.[17]

- The Alfred P. Sloan Foundation provided seed funding to institutions in order to start a movement nationally to create Professional Science Masters programs.[18]

- Transforming Postsecondary Education in Mathematics (TPSE) is working with campuses that are innovating in undergraduate mathematics programs and courses to better support students in quantitative coursework. TPSE grew directly out of a recommendation in PCAST's *To Engage and Excel*, calling for experimentation in college mathematics education.[19]

- The Kauffman Foundation Entrepreneurship Grants program funded UMBC, as well as Arizona State University, Brown University, Carnegie Mellon University, Georgetown University, New York University, Purdue University, Syracuse University, and the University of Wisconsin–Madison.

- UMBC's BreakingGround participants are engaged in national associations of like-minded people on other campuses, whose work also supports campus community engagement.

Here in our state, the USM, of which UMBC is one campus, established the Maryland Course Redesign Initiative under Chancellor Brit Kirwan, which provides grants to faculty in USM institutions for course redesign. At its outset, this program cited the 2006 Spellings Commission on the Future of Higher Education for its inspiration. That commission wrote in its final report, "We urge states and institutions to establish course redesign programs using technology-based, learner-centered principles drawing upon the innovative work already being done by organizations such as the National Center for Academic Transformation." The USM initiated the first system-wide initiative adhering to this recommendation. Each USM institution redesigned at least one pilot course during a three-year period starting in 2006.[20]

What stands out for UMBC in this larger national context is that so many faculty members across many departments would innovate in their course design. Our FDC, led by director Linda Hodges, has been one source of inspiration and support. The FDC consults with faculty who seek help with course design and provides classroom observation and feedback. The FDC also offers workshop and book discussions on teaching and learning and provides support for pedagogical innovation and research. Further, the center administers the Hrabowski Innovation Fund. Endowed by awards from the Carnegie Corporation and the Heinz Foundation and funds raised at the twentieth anniversary of my time as president, this fund, like the Entrepreneurship Grant, provides small grants to faculty members to support their work in course design innovation.[21]

But even without this formal institutional effort, faculty are innovating on their own. In this environment, BreakingGround emerged organically from a conversation, and faculty began to innovate in their courses. This was a grassroots, bottom-up movement that we later agreed to support with a BreakingGround grants program. Similar to that of the Hrabowski Innovation Fund, the BreakingGround program awards grants to faculty to support the infusion of civic engagement in their courses. Meanwhile, some faculty have redesigned their courses in response to the incentives of formal programs, but others are innovating in their classrooms because they have seen a better way and are working to realize it on a supportive campus.

Course Redesign

Let's take a look at some of the work at UMBC.[22]

CASTLE

Following the successful launch of the CDC, the CNMS established a larger dedicated active learning space in 2008, the CNMS Active Science Teaching and Learning Environment (CASTLE). Employing the lessons learned from the CDC experience, the CASTLE classroom was specifically designed to provide the benefits of active learning to many more students enrolled in foundational courses across the natural sciences and including mathematics, biology, and physics.

CASTLE is a ninety-three-student classroom with moveable tables, computers, wall-mounted whiteboards, and monitors that serves as a flexible and interdisciplinary platform for innovative courses. The instructor's station has the latest interactive instructional software linked to eight wall-mounted LED monitors. Its construction was funded through institutional funds supplemented by grants from the Science Applications International Corporation, HHMI, and the NSF. The space has been successfully utilized by twenty or more foundational science and mathematics courses. The deployment of CASTLE at this large scale had its challenges, including efficient class scheduling that provided an effective return on investment, balancing demands for the space among departments, meeting multiuser storage needs, updating software, and keeping the space secure and clean. But these are good problems to have.[23]

Sarah Leupen, lecturer in biological sciences, has used CASTLE for redesigned courses based on the pedagogical model known as TBL, which CASTLE supports. CASTLE opened the year she arrived, and she was delighted to have both the space and departmental support needed to innovate—especially since the campus she came from had not been supportive of course innovation. She initially drew support from the FDC, where she met other faculty who introduced her to TBL, which she adapted to her course. She describes her work as follows: "I'm a certified trainer/consultant in a teaching strategy called 'Team-Based Learning' that incorporates a lot of best practices; it's a type of flipped-classroom strategy in which students prepare with basic content knowledge outside of class and then after assuring that they are truly prepared, they work though increasingly complex application problems, in permanent teams, during class time."[24]

National Academies' Summer Institutes
on Scientific Teaching

Jeff Leips, professor of biology, was happily focused on winning grants and pursuing his research agenda. While he had little interest in changing the way he taught his courses, what attracted him to UMBC was our commitment to cutting-edge research without compromising the quality of our teaching mission. But in 2004, Jo Handelsman founded the Summer Institutes on Scientific Teaching at the University of Wisconsin, and Jeff's faculty colleague, Philip Sokolove, encouraged Jeff to attend with him. Handelsman had been inspired by the 2003 National Academies report *Bio2010: Transforming Undergraduate Education for Future Research Biologists*, which urged biology faculty to rethink their courses using the latest research into how students learn and to incorporate teaching practices whose effectiveness had been established by evidence.[25]

"It opened my eyes to the different ways students learn," Leips later said of the three-day workshop he attended. Subsequently, to make them more student centered, he redesigned his biology courses around the concept of TBL that he had learned about at the workshop. He also decided that, rather than cram as many concepts as possible into a course, he would focus on the most important concepts and find ways to engage the students more deeply with those fundamentals. Leips found that he had to invest a lot of time into the redesign process, which was a sacrifice for his research and service activities. He also needed resources to do it right. But ultimately, he found that he had more fun teaching and, as a result, became much better at it. And, most importantly, the resulting benefits to his students were quite evident and tangible.

When Leips attended the 2004 workshop, the department had paid his expenses on the expectation that he would share his ideas with others as he implemented them. One of the colleagues he worked with on TBL was Sarah Leupen. When Leips received the USM Board of Regents Award for Teaching in 2014, Philip Farabaugh, chair of the Biological Sciences Department, said, "Jeff Leips has managed to lead a revolution in our department's approach to teaching." The revolution, he continued, has "led us to be a much more student-centered teaching community."

Flipped Classrooms, Flipped Learning

TBL incorporated what is now known as the "flipped classroom" into its approach before that term was invented. As this strategy has become more popular at UMBC, many other UMBC faculty have adapted flipped classroom pedagogy to redesign their courses. This approach is designed to provide students with their first exposure to course content through online resources while devoting class time more effectively to collaborative and individual problem-solving. This "flips" the classroom, replacing traditional homework with class activities and traditional class instruction with online materials.

Chuck Eggleton, Neil Rothman, and Anne Spence in the Mechanical Engineering Department have used flipped classrooms in fluid mechanics, machine design, and engineering mathematics, respectively. Tara Carpenter and Tiffany Gierasch in the Department of Chemistry and Biochemistry use a modified flipped classroom approach in the Introductory Chemistry and Organic Chemistry sequences, respectively. Online class preparation involves students taking quizzes on reading materials and solving problems that are then used as springboards for more in-depth classroom activities.

Anne Spence, who now teaches at Baylor, used a flipped classroom model in her engineering mathematics course. Students watched two eight- to ten-minute videos of short lectures prior to class, and Spence then used class time for solving problems related to the material presented in the videos. She reported that while some students prefer a more "passive" approach to learning, nine out of ten eventually appreciate the benefits of the more active problem-centered approach—a signal that students are taking increasing responsibility for their own learning. A similar effect was observed with students in the CDC.

Taryn Bayles has enhanced student learning in her chemical engineering classes by using the concept of "learning by teaching." Bayles challenges junior chemical engineering majors in her class to teach fundamental concepts in heat and mass transfer in high school classrooms. By doing so, they learn that they must do more than just complete problems for homework; they have to understand deeply and then explain fundamental concepts—which takes their learning to another level.

Maryland Course Redesign Initiative

The Maryland Course Redesign Initiative has provided competitive grants to faculty at USM institutions for course redesign across disciplines. At UMBC, the first USM-funded redesign initiatives began in 2007 with the redesign of our Introductory Psychology courses, PSYC 100 and 200. English Composition and Organic Chemistry were next, followed by Precalculus and Introductory Sociology. These redesigns are informed by several approaches identified by the National Center for Academic Transformation as best practice and utilize, to varying degrees, web-based teaching tools and various forms of active and collaborative learning.

When Eileen O'Brien came to UMBC, her department chair, Carlo DiClemente, assigned her to teach Introduction to Psychology (PSYC 100). As she looked into UMBC's experience with this course, she quickly realized that she would need to reinvent it. "It was a disaster," she said. Colleagues advised, "Don't put a freshman in PSYC 100, they won't make it." As was the case with introductory classes in the natural sciences, the course had been taught to "high standards" as a mark of "rigor." But, as a consequence, there was a bimodal distribution when it came to success of students: there were those who did well and those who really didn't and gave up.

O'Brien believed that the students in these courses, the "consumers" of the learning experience, were providing a lot of useful information about the effectiveness of the "product," and she decided, in her words, to "blow it up." The USM course redesign program gave her the opportunity to do just that. She attended several USM meetings and workshops before moving ahead to apply for a USM redesign grant, and when she was awarded the grant, she sought to develop a course that supported students better in learning the material. She wanted to reach each student through individual-level interaction that would enhance general learning and mastery of key topics.

The process she used illuminates both the promise and challenge of redesign. Many instructors, faced with large classes with many struggling students, preferred not to teach PSCY 100 and also had little interest in or understanding of course redesign. To overcome this, O'Brien convened a faculty steering committee charged with the task of redesigning PSYC 100, and she gave a presentation on the PSYC 100 redesign at a departmental retreat to make sure that all of the department's faculty were informed and able to provide input and feedback.

The key to success in this redesign was its focus on making the course topical. The steering committee identified the topics and structured the course so that everyone in the department could be involved. During one semester, O'Brien had faculty come to the course one by one to give a presentation on their research as it related to a given topic being covered in the class. This worked for everyone. Student interest climbed, and students began to better connect with faculty, even asking to work in their labs.

Meanwhile, Sally Shivnan, senior lecturer and associate director of the Writing and Rhetoric Division in the English Department, also became involved in reshaping an introductory class, English

Composition. She had not been contemplating a redesign of her course, but when she saw an announcement that the USM was providing grants to faculty to do that, she brought together a group of colleagues who taught the class to talk about what they might do. They agreed that they could think more deliberately and intentionally about their teaching and how students learned and so applied for a grant. They got it.

Instead of presuming that they knew what to do, this group of colleagues first set out to gather evidence about the various ways that faculty provided feedback to students on their writing and what might work better. For example, they found that faculty spent a great deal of time providing handwritten comments to students on their assignments but had little sense of how well students learned from that feedback. They launched a comparative experiment in which comments were provided face-to-face to some students and in writing to others. This experiment revealed that in-person feedback was much more effective.

With that information, Sally and colleagues began thinking about the ways they might redesign English Composition to increase interaction between faculty and students. "Not Your Grandfather's Comp Class," a *Chronicle of Higher Education* article that later described the redesign, characterized the transformation in approach this way:

> Previously, the classes, of 24 students each, met twice a week in a classroom for 75-minute sessions. The instruction was lecture-based, with time allotted for small-group activities. Now each section, of two dozen students, meets as a group only once a week. On the other day of class, a dozen students gather in the university's new writing lab, where they work on short assignments or revision, guided by a trained undergraduate writing tutor. Meanwhile, the other 12 meet four at a time with their instructor. The schedule rotates so all students have a regular small-group meeting every other week.

The redesign also included the use of new software that lets students comment on each other's writing as peers, allows instructors to quickly insert standard comments on assignments, and provides videos on subjects related to writing and composition. "But so far, the most popular innovations, among students and instructors alike, is low-tech." It's the personal feedback.[26]

As with all redesign efforts, there are challenges. With as many as thirty faculty teaching English Composition, not all are completely on board with the new approach. Some come from other campuses where they have taught, or were taught, differently and are not familiar with our new approach. It is time intensive to get faculty ready to teach, but it is worth it.

Hrabowski Innovation Fund

In 2011, the Carnegie Corporation of New York awarded me its Academic Leadership Award, which came with $500,000. I donated the award to UMBC so we could create the Hrabowski Innovation Fund, which would provide grants to faculty for innovations in teaching and learning, course redesign, curriculum development, or other projects designed to improve student learning. In 2013, the Heinz Foundation presented me with the Heinz Award (Human Condition), which came with $250,000; this was also added to the fund. In honor of my twentieth anniversary as president, the university held a Celebration of Leadership + Innovation that raised $3 million, which we also added to the endowment.

Under the direction of the provost, the FDC administers biannual competitions for funding from the Hrabowski Innovation Fund. Faculty can apply for Seed Awards of up to $3,500 that support course design; Adaption Awards of up to $10,000 to support the adaptation of existing successful innovations into other courses, programs, or disciplines; or Implementation and Research Awards of $3,500–$25,000 to implement a course redesign. Initially, grants were awarded for twelve months, but evaluation of the results prompted us to extend the grant award period to two years in order to close the loop on assessment of learning outcomes. Those receiving Implementation Awards receive the title of "UMBC Innovation Fellow" and are required to make sure that their approach and its results are communicated broadly, both to campus leadership and to faculty across the disciplines. Proposals must define a project or a problem to be investigated, outline how the project will potentially impact student success, describe how the project is informed by existing research, weigh the feasibility of the project, and outline plans for assessment and additional fundraising.[27]

The fund awarded its first grants in 2013, and they have funded ten seed grants, three adaptation projects, and twelve implementation and research projects in total. The work has covered everything from developing a "Math Gym" that provides walk-in tutoring for students on mathematical skills, to developing an interdisciplinary course entitled "Designing and Developing Effective Mobile Applications" led by a team from visual arts and computer science, to the "Baltimore Metropolitan Area Study on Race, Inequality and the City: A Graduate Student Survey Research and Training Program."[28]

A great example of course redesign supported by the Hrabowski Innovation Fund is "Playing the Past," a course taught by Anne Rubin (history) and Marc Olano (computer science and electrical engineering) that combines the study of history with game development. Through the course, history and game development students collaborate to conceptualize and build a game that is simultaneously fun and instructive, using Civil War Baltimore as its platform. This experiment had its challenges. For one thing, Anne Rubin says, since she is not a "gamer," it took her significantly out of her personal comfort zone. For another, grading in a team environment was complicated given the very different fields and expectations of the faculty team. Yet the students enjoyed the class. The project led students to marshal evidence, analyze and think, write, and create for a public audience. They liked "creating" a game that many people, internal and external, can see and play as opposed to writing a paper that only the professor will see.

Another example is "Quantitative Reasoning: Measurement and Skills Lab," developed by a team led by Bill LaCourse, now dean of the CNMS, and including Tara Carpenter (chemistry), Lili Cui (physics), Sarah Leupen (biological sciences), Andy Miller (geography and environmental systems), Nagaraj Neerchal (mathematics and statistics), and Anne Spence (mechanical engineering). This foundational skills laboratory course for first-year STEM majors focuses on quantitative reasoning using measurement, inherent to all scientific fields of study. The course is delivered through problem-based learning and emphasizes interdisciplinary aspects of the tools and skills of measurement across UMBC's three colleges. The course features two-week sessions focused on physics, engineering, biology, chemistry, and environmental studies, followed by group and student projects.

Faculty Development Center and Mythology

Ancient studies is a field that sometimes feels like it is perpetually in crisis. In the early 1990s, the USM Board of Regents came close to abolishing both the Theater and Ancient Studies Departments at UMBC. I asked the board, "Would Yale get rid of its Classics Department? Shouldn't middle-class students have the same opportunity to study the Classics as those who attended privileged universities?" The head of the Greek Orthodox Church in Baltimore City wrote a letter demanding that we keep ancient studies. The board meeting considering these potential cuts was, by coincidence, held on our campus, so members of our Theater Department took advantage of this to interrupt the meeting, walking in carrying a coffin to symbolize "the death of theater." The departments were saved, but while they lived to see another day, the message underlying the threat was clear: if you're not relevant, you're gone. So, the question for the classics was and is, how do we keep it alive in the minds of young people?

When Timothy Phin arrived at UMBC, he was tasked with teaching Classical Mythology. As Eileen O'Brien found with PSYC 100, Mythology wasn't working. It had been taught as a lecture course, and the faculty teaching it focused on memorization. The students were not reading Homer or Ovid; they were reading a predigested summary of the myths and mythological characters. The class used Scantrons for test taking.

Phin believed that this approach to Mythology missed the point of teaching it. "I want them to have these texts that have been part of Western Civilization for thousands of years. They are so instrumental in our lives. The way we speak. The rules of rhetoric. Ideas of rage, ideas of passion, ideas of fear, ideas of why war is necessary. All of these are in these classical texts if students will just read a few pages, right?"

So, Phin's goal for course redesign was very simple: "How do I get them to read?" First, he tried all manner of incentives, such as special prizes and games. These didn't work. Then, he sat down with Linda Hodges, director of the FDC, and had a detailed discussion with her about the problems, goals, and options. For Mythology, they decided, they would try hybridization. Working with Hodges, Phin reasoned that he needed to build a learning scaffold for the students. Except for a small percentage of students, most could not just open the *Iliad* and start reading. Most of them would open the *Iliad*, see lots of Greek names, and have no way to move forward. John Fritz introduced Phin to a technology called Voice Thread, which allowed him to create a multimodal presentation of a text that engages students through text, images, and voice.

This has not been a quick fix. Phin says that it has taken about four years to get the scaffolding where he wants it. However, he has seen significant progress. Students are reading more and becoming more involved in class discussion and online groups. Phin now says, "My class is a big draw. I have the students, so my goals are to keep them and make them lifelong students of Homer, Aeschylus, and Euripides. Keep them in the throes with all this wonder, all this value that should be treasured."

A final word about this story highlights a truth about an institution like UMBC: because of our size and role in our state, we may be forced by circumstances to innovate when others are not. At the University of Maryland, College Park, for example, Mythology is a lecture class of three hundred students with a professor and five teaching assistants. The course is taught using a traditional lecture approach, because it can be. At UMBC, Mythology is a one-hundred-student course with a professor and no teaching assistants. "I can't individually reach 100 students by myself even though I want to," says Phin. "Not possible." So, he is innovating by changing the delivery of course content instead. The number of students majoring in ancient studies has recently increased to thirty, about the same as at College Park, which is a far larger campus.

Our Ancient Studies Department has just experienced a complete transition in its faculty. There had been four tenured faculty in the department, the last of whom had been hired in 1978. There were no new hires until 2010. Since then, all of the original faculty members have retired, and a new group of five faculty members have joined the department. Now, all of the faculty, except the chair, rotate through all of the courses, including the language courses. This creates an environment that continually refreshes courses, as faculty bring different ideas and approaches to each course as they rotate. And this naturally creates opportunities for conversations about teaching and learning that do not happen in siloed departments.

Challenges

Challenges remain. Even with the swirl of course redesign and curriculum innovation, we have faculty who do not appreciate, or see the need for, new approaches to teaching and learning. There are some departments in which few or no faculty members have redesigned their courses in a meaningful way. Occasionally, new hires will come in to teach a redesigned course and, without understanding the new approaches that have been carefully developed and implemented, revert to a more traditional approach to pedagogy. Progress cannot be taken for granted. Leadership from the president to the provost, from the deans to the department chairs, must continually monitor for backsliding and work to move others forward.

Nevertheless, from the institutional level to the individual class-room our university has embraced innovation under its current leadership. Our community as it is currently constituted sees innovation as a shared value that is prized and rewarded. But change cannot be sustained unless it is institutionalized and adopted broadly by faculty, staff, and students throughout the university. Without this deeper planting of seeds, disruptive events, such as a new administration, could cause such change to gradually disappear. Therefore, as we hope we have demonstrated in this chapter, it is critical to view culture change and permanent innovation as not just being about the president and the provost. For change to be sustainable it must be the work, the vision, and a shared value of the entire campus community.

10

The New American College

In a visionary article in the *Chronicle of Higher Education* in March 1994, Ernest Boyer observed that our nation's universities had included service as a mission from the 1860s through the 1960s. "But what about today?" he asked. "I'm concerned that in recent years, higher education's historic commitment to service seems to have diminished. I'm troubled that many now view the campus as a place where professors get tenured and students get credentialed. The overall efforts of the academy are not considered to be at the vital center of the nation's work. And what I find most disturbing is the growing feeling in this country that higher education is a *private* benefit, *not* a public good."

Boyer called for a "New American College," one that "celebrates teaching and selectively supports research, while also taking special pride in its capacity to connect thought to action, theory to practice." He argued that the academy should connect its work to today's problems, for example, the plight of the American city, with such challenging issues as crime and economic opportunity. Our faculty should relate what they discover to the problems of the world. Research should not just discover "knowledge for knowledge's sake." Rather, scholarship should synthesize, communicate, and apply knowledge. "Students," Boyer argued, "urgently need to connect what they learn with how they live."[1]

Based on the notion that student learning can be enhanced through engaged, experiential learning and broader connections, UMBC has developed an assortment of service-learning programs and implemented two initiatives that have infused entrepreneurship and community engagement into existing courses. With a grant from the Kauffman Foundation, we have incorporated entrepreneurship and entrepreneurial activities into more than seventy courses across all our colleges. Similarly, based on the notion that students can learn the skills and habits of "empowered citizenship," UMBC's BreakingGround has "developed courses in which students can invest themselves in making practical, innovative contributions to the common good." The Alex. Brown Center for Entrepreneurship and BreakingGround both also support programs outside the classroom to engage students in entrepreneurial activity, democratic participation, and community engagement.

Service Learning

John Martello arrived at UMBC in the fall of 1974 full of idealistic ambition to tackle one of the nation's most pressing problems, the development of urban youth. He had just completed his bachelor's degree at Pennsylvania State University and enrolled at UMBC as a doctoral student in community clinical psychology, an integrative program combining research and clinical practice, to focus on the complex interplay of psychosocial problems with community, mental health, and physical health. After completing his master's degree at UMBC in 1976, he began part-time work on his dissertation, focusing on the development of black youth in nearby Baltimore City.[2]

Upon his arrival at UMBC, Martello also accepted a position in which he would establish and direct a Cooperative Education Program at UMBC. Seeded with a federal grant, the program was located in UMBC's Division of Student Affairs and connected students with employers through internships that they held while students at UMBC. As Martello later recalled, "The program grew, established relationships with local businesses and public agencies, and placed an increasing number of students in paid, full-time positions related to their fields of study."

Martello believed that experiential learning could enhance learning in the classroom in a complementary manner, a notion that he spread among the faculty as he developed his program. However, acceptance of experiential learning, through service or work, as a legitimate curricular tool by faculty would be a long-term challenge requiring change in academic culture over time. Martello related that "back in the 70s and 80s, the feeling of our faculty was that education is best which occurs in the classroom." While many faculty members could appreciate the idea of "academically-targeted, part-time internships" related to majors, many were "uncomfortable with the idea of vocationally-driven, full-time co-op positions."

Students enjoyed the experience and were able to earn money as well, yet the program still existed on the periphery of the academic mission of the university, and students were not realizing the benefits that would derive from better integration of the program with their academic work. Adding to the marginalization of the fledgling program, it bounced around UMBC's organizational structure several times. In 1979, the campus administration transferred the co-op program to the Division of Academic Affairs, creating an opportunity for better linkages for students between their academic programs and placements. In 1982, the program was moved once more to a newly created Office of Professional Practice that would include both co-op and internship placements.

The program finally reached critical mass in 1989 after fifteen years of growth. Martello, who had completed his PhD in 1984 and was hired as an affiliate faculty member in psychology and a program administrator, renamed his office the Center for Learning through Work and Service. From 1974 to 1995, the number of UMBC students placed in co-ops and internships grew from 8 to more than 1,000. This was a stunning success in terms of numbers, yet even then the academic culture as it related to co-ops and internships had not shifted significantly.

Martello brought into the new center an initiative working with juvenile offenders that included a service-learning component—an opportunity for students to engage in active, engaged learning through community service. The CHOICE Intensive Advocacy Program had been the brainchild of Mark Shriver, who had originally established it in 1987 as an independent organization. Shriver designed the program to offer a supervised, community-based pathway for juvenile offenders, providing an alternative (or "choice") to the existing juvenile justice system, which focused on detention. While based on a sound idea, Shriver's organization struggled to grow initially in the African American community of Cherry Hill in 1987 and 1988. Shriver had secured initial funding for CHOICE from the Joseph P. Kennedy Foundation, founded by his grandfather. He had launched the organization. He had moved to the neighborhood and made contacts. And yet, participation and persistence were not reaching levels that Shriver sought and would be needed for organizational effectiveness and sustainability.

Shriver believed that he needed something more. In 1988, he discussed the initial development and trajectory of CHOICE with George Zitnay, his mentor, who was executive director of the Joseph P. Kennedy Foundation. Zitnay offered that the program might be strengthened by attaching it to a university that could provide an organizational structure and home, as well as other resources, including student volunteers and faculty researchers. Both Sargent Shriver, Mark's father, and George Zitnay called Adam Yarmolinsky, provost at the University of Maryland, Baltimore County, about Mark's project in Cherry Hill. Adam, who had once worked for the elder Shriver in the Office of Economic Opportunity (OEO), was intrigued. He and Mark met to discuss CHOICE, how it had been established, its development to date, and where it might go.

Yarmolinsky believed there was promise in the CHOICE program and, moreover, knew just the person at UMBC to help Mark.

He connected him to John Martello, a young assistant professor in psychology on his campus who was interested in many of the same social issues that he and Sargent Shriver had worked on at the OEO from 1964 to 1966. Mark called John, and they discussed Mark's program. Mark asked John if there might be a way for UMBC to provide tutors and mentors for CHOICE participants, and even if there might be a way to affiliate the program with UMBC. Martello told him of his deep interest in both working with urban youth and providing service-learning experiences to UMBC students and said that there could be an opportunity to bring their interests together. Martello suggested that they meet and talk further. Things did work out, and in January 1989 Shriver and Martello brought the CHOICE program to UMBC.

To reap the benefits of this providential happenstance by landing the program, Martello had needed help, as there were significant internal and external hurdles that had to be cleared to bring CHOICE to UMBC. Internally, Martello needed support from university leadership. While UMBC had a corporate internship program for its students, the university had never had a service-learning program, and, in fact, such programs were rare at American colleges at the time. The backing of leadership from Adam Yarmolinsky was crucial, particularly as word of the program spread and significant concern among faculty and staff emerged about bringing juvenile offenders to campus.

Externally, there was also skepticism in the black community that a predominantly white university in the suburbs could be seriously interested and useful in helping juvenile offenders who were overwhelmingly black and poor. Indeed, community leaders in Cherry Hill were quite reluctant at first to trust their children to UMBC. Having spent ten years in inner-city Baltimore at Coppin State, I had enough credibility in that community to ask them to give the university a chance to show what we could do. So, I joined Martello at a community meeting in Cherry Hill to convince community leaders that if UMBC took on the CHOICE program, it would not do so lightly. I told the gathering that our university would make a significant, long-term commitment to help the youth who participated in the program. I argued that the university was not in this just to do research but to provide an important service. This engagement—and leadership commitment—was critical to community acceptance and to the long-term success of the program.

The CHOICE program was administered by caseworkers (called Choice Fellows today) who worked with program participants out in the community. While they were university employees, they did not feel much attachment to our institution in the program's early days. The program's "College Night," by contrast, relied on our undergraduate volunteers for its work and provided a deeper connection between our campus and the program. Two nights per week, CHOICE participants came to UMBC and other Baltimore-area campuses by van for tutoring, a meal, and a recreational activity. The tutors were undergraduates who committed to providing one-on-one tutoring for a CHOICE participant each of those two nights per week for a semester. Being a tutor was similar to being an intern in terms of commitment, but what made it service learning was both training and opportunities for students to engage in framing and reflection.

The Shriver Center

While the process for moving the CHOICE program to UMBC was underway, Martello had the opportunity to meet Sargent and Eunice Shriver at their home in Potomac, Maryland. He was very much impressed with Sargent Shriver's connections to and interest in Baltimore and Maryland, as well as his lifetime commitment to tackling the nation's most pressing social problems. It dawned on Martello that a "Shriver Center" at UMBC could build on those interests, honor the Shrivers for a lifetime commitment to social justice, bring together all of UMBC's service and experiential learning programs in one place, and lend a bit of the luster of the Kennedy dynasty to a young and ambitious university.

Martello broached the subject with the Shrivers. Sargent Shriver was captivated by the concept of a university-based center focused on service. He agreed that Martello should develop and present a proposal. Martello went to work on a plan that would convert UMBC's Center for Learning through Work and Service, an umbrella for the university's internship and service-learning programs, into the Shriver Center, which would provide vehicles for directing the intellectual resources of UMBC's faculty and the altruism of its students toward improving life for residents in big cities like Baltimore, through civic engagement, community development, criminal justice reform, and other approaches to major issues in urban life.

The next step would be to gain approval from both the university administration and the Shrivers. With Martello's proposal on the table, Sargent Shriver, Michael Hooker, Adam Yarmolinsky, and I talked about the possibility of creating a Shriver Center, but we were making little progress on the proposal other than to request further revisions from Martello. To break the impasse and move the discussion forward, Shriver asked Martello, "What would the press release for the opening of the Shriver Center look like?"

Martello went back to the drawing board. While he thought about Shriver's assignment, though, the proposal development process took a new turn. UMBC had recently joined the "Campus Compact," a new national coalition of college and university presidents committed to campus-based civic engagement. A meeting of the presidents of the founding campuses was scheduled for the near future in Washington, DC. Michael Hooker could not attend, so he asked John Martello if he would like to go in his place. He did.

The two principal speakers at the meeting were Senator Edward "Ted" Kennedy, Eunice Shriver's brother, and Ernest Boyer, who had written a report on "Higher Learning in the Nation's Service" with Fred Hechinger in 1981. At the end of their talks, Martello introduced himself to each of the two speakers. He told Senator Kennedy that he was working with the Shrivers on campus-based civic engagement, and he told Boyer that his speech had been very inspirational—so inspirational, in fact, that Martello thought it would be great if Ernest Boyer could be enlisted to draft the "press release" that Sargent Shriver had requested. It turned out that Shriver knew Ernest Boyer, and another critical connection was made.

Boyer was, at the time, working with the Abell Foundation in Baltimore, and on one of his trips to the city he stopped at UMBC to meet with Martello to discuss the proposed Shriver Center. Coming out of this discussion, Boyer agreed to help and drafted what would eventually become, after further revision, the Shriver Center's original vision statement:

- The Shriver Center seeks to focus, in an integrated way, the resources of the colleges and universities of Greater Baltimore on pressing urban issues of the region.
- The Shriver Center will engage faculty, students, and the community in the strengthening of existing service and learning programs and in developing new initiatives to improve the quality of urban life.
- The Shriver Center, while focusing its efforts on Greater Baltimore, will also work to renew the academy itself, helping students deepen their sense of civic responsibility and discover the relationship of formal learning to contemporary issues.
- The Shriver Center, through its programs, will seek to broaden the meaning of scholarship to include research, teaching, and the application of knowledge.
- The Shriver Center will seek to lead the nation in ensuring that higher education more effectively relates the work of the faculty and students to urgent social issues, advancing the common good through applied projects and public advocacy.

This statement of what the Shriver Center would undertake moved Sargent Shriver and me. We agreed to establish the Shriver Center, officially launching it on December 14, 1993, to honor the lives and work of Sargent and Eunice Kennedy Shriver.[3] The Shriver Center pulled together under one organizational umbrella the CHOICE program, UMBC's Community Service and Learning Program, and UMBC's Center for Learning through Work and Service, as well as other programs. In 1993, the Shriver Peaceworker Program was transferred from Georgetown University to the Shriver Center as well. Peaceworkers are returned Peace Corps volunteers who, as graduate students, participate in a "two year social change leadership program integrating three key components: graduate study, community service leadership, and ethical reflection."[4]

Established simultaneously with the Shriver Center, and sharing its mission and vision, was the Shriver Center Higher Education Consortium, which included the ten higher education institutions in the Baltimore metropolitan area.[5] The president of each member institution signed a memorandum of understanding supporting the consortium. Some of the institutions, such as Loyola College, participated in the College Night component of the CHOICE program. In 1994, the Shriver Center received a Learn and Serve America grant from the Corporation for National Service (CNS), recently created under the Clinton administration. This grant provided the funds that established service-learning programs across the institutions in the Shriver Consortium. The funds provided for capacity building, faculty course development in service learning, and opportunities to engage students.

The CNS funding provided UMBC with its first opportunity to provide faculty grants for course redesign. Faculty at UMBC and other institutions across the Shriver Consortium applied for grants that would support them in incorporating experiential service learning into their classes. At UMBC, a core group of faculty who were deeply committed to service learning worked to infuse service learning into existing classes. While some of these courses were sustained over time, in many instances faculty grantees developed new, special topics courses that were often only taught once. The outcomes for UMBC were mixed. On the one hand, we gained some experience with using grant funding for course redesign that would provide important context for future efforts in this area. On the other, the lack of staying power for new courses suggested that, in future efforts, we would need a new approach to course redesign.

Entrepreneurship

Craig Weidemann, then UMBC's executive vice president and now at Penn State, viewed engaged scholarship and experiential learning as fruitful for researchers, students, and society and also a potential special niche for UMBC. When Alex. Brown & Sons gave us a $250,000 gift for a program centered on entrepreneurship,[6] Weidemann felt that this was a great fit for an engaged campus. He used the grant to establish a new Alex. Brown Center for Entrepreneurship and served as its first director until he hired Vivian Armor for that position.[7]

In its earliest days, the new center brought UMBC alumni back to campus to teach a few courses on entrepreneurship each semester. The further development of the center—which would facilitate collaborations between UMBC faculty and staff on the one hand and entrepreneurs, businesses, government agencies, and nonprofits in the Baltimore-Washington corridor on the other— had not yet fully formed. At that time, the center remained siloed, a bit invisible to the rest of the campus, and it had no connection to UMBC's research park, bwtech@UMBC.

But this small beginning provided UMBC an opportunity. I had begun talking with Carl Schramm, president of the Ewing Marion Kauffman Foundation, about our campus. (Carl lived in Baltimore, where his wife was an attorney, but commuted weekly to the Kansas City headquarters of the foundation, so I had had a chance to get to know him.) Learning from me that UMBC had recently established a new entrepreneurship center, Carl invited us to submit an application for funding under a new Kauffman program that would provide grants to universities to pursue programs that incorporated entrepreneurship into their curricula.

In 2003 a small team, made up of Vivian Armor, Greg Simmons

from corporate relations, and Pat McDermott from the Office of the Provost, formed to develop a proposal that would focus on "exposure to the ideas, education about the field, and experience in the practice of entrepreneurship." If successful, the grant would allow UMBC to hire faculty fellows, conduct summer workshops, and assist faculty in the development of classes that "infused" entrepreneurship directly into the student learning experience.

The Kauffman Foundation did not fund our first proposal. Their comments on our proposal suggested that the campus culture and infrastructure at UMBC were not "ready" for an initiative designed to promote entrepreneurship. There were two significant issues that appeared to be the main, and seemingly insurmountable, obstacles. First, while we now had the Alex. Brown Center, we did not have a business school, as did all of the other universities the Kauffman Foundation funded to focus on entrepreneurship. We are surrounded, in Maryland, by other public universities with business schools: the University of Maryland, College Park; Towson University; the University of Baltimore; and Morgan State University. To avoid program duplication, the state of Maryland prevented us from creating a business program, and that was a key challenge in moving our proposal to a funded project. Second, as a young public university, UMBC did not at that time have the fundraising infrastructure of other institutions that would have allowed us to raise millions of dollars in additional matching funds to complement the Kauffman grant. Unfortunately, this was something we could not promise.

As was also to be the case with our first and unsuccessful application to the NSF for an ADVANCE grant to address the underrepresentation of women in our science and engineering faculty, the process of writing a proposal for the Kauffman Foundation stimulated deeper conversations on our campus about how we might develop an entrepreneurship program and what it would mean for the campus. In 2003, the proposal team had met with each department chair on campus to ask two questions: (1) what would entrepreneurship mean in the context of your discipline, and (2) what would your department propose to do as part of a funded entrepreneurship program. Over the next two years, the proposal team continued their conversations on campus about entrepreneurship —essentially beginning the work it had proposed but without the benefit of the Kauffman funding.

These conversations started a robust dialogue on campus about what entrepreneurship meant or could mean. Several UMBC faculty advocated for a program consisting of courses that either addressed entrepreneurship from an academic perspective or included activities that facilitated the development of innovative ideas, a business pitch, or even a start-up. Other UMBC faculty were less comfortable with the idea of an entrepreneurship program. They either had reservations about applied learning as a pedagogical approach or saw "entrepreneurship" as a code word for the "corporatization" of the university, part of what they saw as a larger trend of cutting costs, declining state appropriations, increasing emphasis on "training" for jobs rather than liberal education, and forming corporate partnerships. Most simply said they had little exposure to the subject and had no idea how they would teach it.

Despite these reservations, the conversations captured the imagination of a core group of respected faculty members who gave the effort a measure of legitimacy, helped reframe conversations to enable broader buy-in for an initiative, and grew momentum. In addition to Vivian, Greg, and Pat, the team now included Sheldon Caplis, vice president for advancement, and several senior faculty who were "early adopters" of entrepreneurship, having infused their courses with entrepreneurial content or been entrepreneurs themselves. These senior faculty included Bill LaCourse, professor in chemistry, who had his own small business, ran his research laboratory like a company, and would later redesign Introduction to Chemistry; Kriste Lindenmayer, professor and chair of history, who would be one of the five founders of UMBC's BreakingGround initiative that focuses on community engagement and social entrepreneurship; and Uri Tasch, professor of mechanical engineering, who was working on the development of a diagnostic tool that could identify lameness in cattle, a costly condition, before a farmer could detect it through observation.

Because UMBC lacked a business school, the proposal team reached out to and obtained buy-in across the campus, an activity that reshaped what entrepreneurship meant at UMBC and turned what had been a liability into a significant asset. Bill, Kris, and Uri —representing senior faculty from each of UMBC's three colleges— helped lead further outreach to the campus community, holding further conversations in departments across their colleges. As they did so, they discovered that it was important to speak the language of each particular college culture in order to have a meaningful discussion about entrepreneurship that would resonate across the faculty. The key was to help others see entrepreneurship as creativity, the development of ideas through critical thinking that could be used not just for commercial applications but also for social innovation and change.

Once it was made clear that entrepreneurship at UMBC embraced both economic entrepreneurship and social entrepreneurship and spanned all disciplines and interdisciplines, it gained significantly greater traction and acceptance on campus. Eventually, a broader definition of what entrepreneurship means at UMBC emerged, one that is now encapsulated in the Alex. Brown Center's mission statement on entrepreneurship on its website: "UMBC believes that entrepreneurship is the ability of an individual to identify a goal, provide the leadership and mobilize the assets necessary to reach that goal. As such, individuals taking the risk to push the envelope in science and technology, break ground in the creative arts or craft new solutions to society's problems are all entrepreneurs."[8] This description also makes clear that an entrepreneur is someone who is passionate, expert, and working to engage others to adopt novel ideas—this could include faculty and students with many diverse interests and experiences.

In 2005, the Kauffman Foundation invited UMBC to submit a second proposal. They noted that several of the institutions funded in the first round had neither fully followed through on their proposed plans nor raised the promised matching funds, so UMBC's lack of a business school or fully developed fundraising infrastructure were no longer considered liabilities. In response to this invitation, and drawing upon the conversations they had engaged in for the previous two years, the entrepreneurship team crafted a much stronger proposal, noting practices already underway, underscoring the wide acceptance of the concept across schools and departments, and proposing a diverse set of activities that included both commercial and social entrepreneurship.

This time, the Kauffman Foundation funded the proposal. The keys to our success were a well-developed understanding of the way the program would work within our campus culture to achieve its goals; our evolving, broader definition of entrepreneurship; and the focus on faculty buy-in, an element that has been critical to the adoption and sustainability of so many initiatives at UMBC. Another key aspect of the new proposal was that entrepreneurship would be infused into *existing* courses, and this would prove an important feature of the program. We had learned from our experience with service learning—funded by the Corporation for National Service—that existing courses infused with service learning were far more likely to be sustained than newly created courses, which were often taught once or twice and then disappeared from the schedule of courses. Under the entrepreneurship grant, we required that faculty be tenured or tenure-track, obtain approval from their chair on the proposed work, and redesign existing courses or guarantee that a new course would be offered at least twice over three years.

In addition to the development of entrepreneurship-infused courses, the new program had two other elements: faculty fellows and summer institutes. The first three faculty fellows, serving from 2008 to 2010, were LaCourse, Lindenmayer, and Tasch. They continued to provide leadership within their colleges and helped by demonstrating, in practical ways, how infusing entrepreneurship into a course could enhance both teaching and learning on the one hand and innovation on the other. Summer institutes on the subject of entrepreneurship were organized for faculty in each of UMBC's colleges. Not only did these institutes provide space and time to learn about new pedagogical approaches, to begin to experiment, and to work on course development or redevelopment, but they also allowed each college to engage in entrepreneurship in a manner that was consistent with each college's distinct culture. Faculty who participated in the summer institutes would then go on to implement their plans for courses infused with entrepreneurship during the following academic year.

The results were impressive. By 2016, over seventy courses across all our colleges had been infused and redesigned with an entrepreneurial emphasis. Once our faculty had created a critical mass of courses, the next logical step was to create an academic minor in entrepreneurship, something our students had been asking for. The Alex. Brown Center and the Kauffman Fellows developed and guided the proposal for a minor through our campus shared governance structures, and the entrepreneurship minor was first offered in 2011, with four students declaring it.

Today, UMBC offers a wide range of entrepreneurship courses and experiences across its colleges and divisions. Two core courses required for the minor are Introduction to Entrepreneurship and The Entrepreneurial Mindset. Other courses include the kind one might ordinarily associate with such a minor, such as Entrepreneurial Marketing and Entrepreneurial Finance, but they also include courses like Innovation, Problem Solving, and the Social-Preneur; Design Thinking for the Social Entrepreneur; and Civic Agency and Social Entrepreneurship. As seen in the box below, the courses range across information technology; engineering; natural sciences; management, finance, economics, and statistics; history, social sciences, and public policy; and the arts.

The story of entrepreneurship at UMBC is one in which the concept proceeded from an idea, through a landscape of pockets of acceptance and resistance, to a successful destination with adoption, course infusion, and the creation of a minor. We believe that this

UMBC Courses Infused with Entrepreneurship

Information Technology
Database Application Development
Data Mining Techniques and Application
Markup and Scripting Languages
Special Topics in IS: 3D Printing for Entrepreneurship
Social Media: Networking and Mobility
Desktop Publishing and the Web

Engineering
Survey of Sensors and Instrumentation
Introduction to Mechanical Engineering Design with CAD
Mechanical Engineering Systems Design Capstone
Vibrations and Controls Laboratory
Global Engineering
Special Topics in Mechanical Engineering: Medical Device Development
Creativity, Innovation, and Invention
Social Bases of Public and Community Health

Natural Sciences
Microbial Systems and Synthetic Biology
Advanced Topics in Cell Biology
Analytical Chemistry

Management, Finance, Economics, and Statistics
The Practice of Management
Human Resource Management
Introduction to Statistical Consulting

Principles of Microeconomics
Financial Management
The Economics of Innovation and Technology
Health Economics
Portfolio Analysis and Management
Venture Capital and Capital Markets
International Finance

History, Social Sciences, and Public Policy
Themes in World History; Entrepreneurship in the Early Modern World
American Entrepreneurs from Columbus to Jobs
Service Learning in Public History
Creating Food System Justice
Studies in Feminist Activism
Problem Solving in the Urban Black Community
Technology and the Future of Aging

Arts
Preserving Places, Making Spaces in Baltimore
Space and Place in Public Art and Urbanism
Digital Darkroom
Social Entrepreneurship in Place
Introduction to Animation
Applied Curatorial Enterprise and Social Innovation for Museum Practice
Careers in Music
Auditioning and the Business of Acting

is of great benefit to our students, who now have an opportunity to develop skills that were not previously available to them. The Alex. Brown Center now hosts a speaker series and CEO chats that connect our students to entrepreneurs in the Baltimore-Washington area. It has also created an "Entre-space"—"a place on campus for students to come together, work on projects and network with each other."

The Alex. Brown Center has also established two competitions to help students further develop and refine their entrepreneurial skills. UMBC's Idea Competition, held every fall and open to all undergraduates and graduate students, is "designed to challenge you to think about problems and opportunities facing society." It provides students who have innovative ideas an opportunity to develop them into a competitive proposal. Ideas can focus on almost anything: products or services, commercial applications of a UMBC research project, innovations to address social or environmental concerns, ideas that generate artistic value, or campus innovations. Teams of one to four students develop proposals that define the problem or opportunity and then describe their idea for addressing it. While not required, students can post a video to YouTube to "pitch" their idea to the campus. Prizes are awarded for Best Idea ($750), Second Place Idea ($500), Third Place Idea ($250), and Best Pitch ($250).[9]

The Cangialosi Business Innovation Competition, held annually in the spring semester, is an opportunity for UMBC undergraduate and graduate students to experience the process of planning the creation of a start-up business by developing and submitting a business plan, three to five pages in length. The competition pairs each team with a mentor from the business community who provides guidance and feedback. The top qualifiers in the competition present their ideas to a panel of judges. First prize is $3,000, second is $2,000, and third is $1,000. The winners are offered free membership in Betamore, a nonprofit founded in 2012 by Greg Cangialosi, Mike Brenner, and Sean Lane to advance entrepreneurship to the benefit of the city of Baltimore. Betamore has a physical presence—a coworking space, incubator, and campus for technology entrepreneurship—as well as outreach into the larger community. The winners also receive free legal services, advice on accounting and fundraising, and pitch practice with Betamore Angels.[10]

Entrepreneurship at UMBC now extends beyond the classroom and student competitions to incorporate the development of new businesses and business partnerships. UMBC's new strategic plan envisions the tighter integration of the Alex. Brown Center (under the provost), technology commercialization (under the vice president for research), and our research park, bwtech@UMBC (under the vice president for institutional advancement). Our goal is to institutionalize collaboration that currently exists informally, align and pool existing resources to make the whole greater than the sum of its parts, and make strategic investments that lead to research-driven economic development activity in the research park and beyond. For example, about one hundred UMBC students hold internships with companies in our research park each academic year. This opportunity could be more formally coordinated with our entrepreneurship program.

Breaking Ground

The success of UMBC's many innovations has created a culture in which community members can come together, have conversations, and develop initiatives of their own. A powerful example of this "empowered university" is a grassroots "movement" within UMBC known as BreakingGround.[11] I use a number of quotes from David Hoffman, a leader in this movement, in the text below because they beautifully describe both the BreakingGround initiative and the campus culture it has grown out of and now affects. Moreover, the language of an organic, democratic, empowered movement on our campus provides us an opportunity to think more deeply about how we engage with students to promote both civic agency and leadership.[12]

BreakingGround emerged from a meeting of "five people, with different roles on campus, sitting in a room, having a frank conversation that departed from the usual scripts."[13] They were David Hoffman, then from Student Affairs and now director of our Center for Democracy and Civic Life; Michele Wolff, director of the Shriver Center; Kriste Lindenmeyer, professor of history and a Kauffman Fellow; Delana Gregg, then assistant director of the Sondheim Public Affairs Scholars Program and now assistant director of UMBC's Learning Resources Center; and Yasmine Karimian, then president of our Student Government Association.

As their conversation evolved, the group realized they had a common approach to supporting students and colleagues. They quickly "recognized a common philosophy of democratic engagement linking their separate programs and learning spaces." For them, this philosophy focused on the notion "that individuals and collaborative groups are powerful agents of meaningful change, and that students deserve genuine respect as agents of their own lives and as partners in building community."[14]

The group decided to work together to advance their existing work in civic agency and community engagement, by creating a "movement" on campus—a "broadly-inclusive, campus-wide organizing process built in part on insights and contributions from undergraduates who had experienced extraordinary growth as civic agents"—that would extend their ideas and approaches to others.[15] They then held further discussions on campus: "Those initial conversations worked well because they embodied the ideals the original group was seeking to advance: full participation by people collaborating to envision and create the future of their (campus) community."[16]

These conversations "snowballed" into a movement. The organizing group was careful not to immediately turn this movement into a "program" and did not even give it a name for two years; in 2012 they began to call their collective work "BreakingGround." While there are advantages to establishing a "program," such as a recognizable name and identity, programmatic goals, an institutional location, dedicated staff, and a budget, there can also be disadvantages, such as the creation of hierarchy, centralization, and "siloing." All of these disadvantages have the potential to work against an effort to promote wide adoption of practices that support civic agency and community engagement.[17] What the initial group of five collectively imagined and created in BreakingGround, says David Hoffman, is instead "a very unusual initiative in higher education, in that it embodies the holistic, organic, democratic ethos it is designed to foster."[18] "We want people at UMBC to view Breaking Ground as our collective work and culture, not as a separate entity with a mind of its own. . . . BreakingGround never takes action, hosts events, sends invitations, or sponsors programs, people and groups do."[19]

What makes BreakingGround so interesting in the context of this book is its relationship to UMBC as an "empowered university." BreakingGround is deeply rooted in UMBC's culture of collaboration, based on the notion of empowered, democratic, participatory process. "In this work," writes Hoffman, "our collective, institutional past has been among our greatest resources. We have no shortage of stories embodying UMBC's ethos of deep engagement in living democracy."[20] Indeed, BreakingGround is informed by and builds on the notion of "empowerment" that has been central to our work, including our cooperative education programs, the Shriver Center, the Meyerhoff Scholars Program, the Kauffman entrepreneurship initiative, the Chemistry Discovery Center, team-based learning, and our ADVANCE program, which has supported the success of women faculty in the natural sciences. Empowerment is central. The primary goal of BreakingGround is "to foster an inclusive *culture* of civic agency."[21]

BreakingGround was initiated to enable deeper experiences based on the notion that, drawing on their talents, personal experiences, and academic work, students could develop their own ideas about how they would address real and challenging problems, often the ones that people thought could not be overcome, and then work to bring about real change on campus and sometimes off campus in the community. As David Hoffman related in a discussion with us, most colleges expose their students to civic engagement through experiences that are often circumscribed and perhaps even contrived. Students step into volunteer roles, and then they return to their program of study. Students step into a voting booth on Election Day, and then they step back out. These can be important acts of citizenship, but they have the quality of isolated occurrences rather than deeply felt agency and authentic engagement. BreakingGround recognized that students had a creative capacity that could be liberated and that, in combination, students and faculty could produce genuine change, whether on campus or off.[22]

The central idea in BreakingGround is to move learning beyond the "usual" activities, designed by others, including their faculty. "Designed activities are both useful and inevitable in higher education: they create occasions for learning and partition experiences into controllable increments of time, task, and topic; and they enable us to gauge progress, manage outcomes, and measure and acknowledge achievement."[23] However, these designed activities can sometimes feel "unreal" and even "disempowering" because they are not the authentic, creative work of students that enables their civic agency. Real experiences, with both deeper learning and rewarding effort, are arrived at when students are involved in the process "as agents rather than as objects."[24]

Hoffman has described the BreakingGround approach as one in which students sense that they are deeply engaged and can effect real change in two ways:

1. One was by causing visible, meaningful changes in people and situations. Among their transformative experiences were participating in program and budget decisions and then seeing their consequences; launching a new organization and having it embraced by UMBC staff and students;

and engaging in conversations with peers, faculty members, and administrators that altered the mindset or behavior of the other participants. Observing the changes they had made, the students drew the inference that we were actually present in a world that could be altered through their actions and experiences themselves as newly visible and alive. Inspired and empowered, they approached subsequent opportunities to make a meaningful difference with new eagerness and confidence, feeding what became a virtuous cycle of experience, reflection, and growth.

2. The students also drew profound inferences about their agency and capacity to make a difference from authentic interactions that departed from the usual scripts. Many of these conversations occurred outside the context of any experience designed to foster democratic engagement. For the students, simply being seen and appreciated when they did not expect to be, and transcending the constraints of agency-inhibiting roles to achieve a mutual and genuine presence with others, inspired a greatly expanded sense of efficacy.[25]

Some of these changes might be practical in nature. For example, the Student Government Association had initiated a program called "ProveIt!" that provides small grants to winning proposals from students to address a problem they identified on campus. "ProveIt! is a campus change competition in which students are challenged to create a novel and innovative project, service, or event on the UMBC campus that not only serves to better the community, but also to show that students truly do have the power to take ownership of their surroundings."[26]

BreakingGround is a prime example of UMBC's shared, empowered leadership. David Hoffman notes, "I've had the freedom to find partners across UMBC, in various roles, and work with them in ways that would have been impossible if we had been constrained by bureaucratic silos and hierarchies."[27] Indeed, the work is directed not "from above" but by a BreakingGround Working Group. "Provost Rous has been an active partner in this work, and his approach has been to think with the BreakingGround working group, challenge us, and ask how he can help, rather than to dictate the outcomes or methods."[28]

Similar to the manner in which we infused entrepreneurship into our courses, BreakingGround has been extended into UMBC's academics through two programs funded by the Office of the Provost that award grants for curricular innovations and community projects with civic agency at their core. As of fall 2018, these programs have provided forty-two grants for the creation or redesign of courses that foster civic agency and thirty-one community program grants producing social contributions beyond episodic service, as well as more than 280 stories and reflections shared on the BreakingGround blog.

The impact of BreakingGround cannot be fully quantified. Just as the Meyerhoff program has led to other efforts on our campus, so does BreakingGround have profound "cultural ripples extend[ing] well beyond its funding streams" out into the curriculum, student affairs, and our community.[29] "Harry Boyte has called Breaking-Ground 'a window into a remarkable, ongoing process of engagement at UMBC, which has made the university a model for hundreds of colleges and universities across the country. . . . Students have been agents of constructive change.'"[30]

Echoing the voice of Ernest Boyer from an earlier generation, in early 2012 the National Task Force on Civic Learning and Democratic Engagement produced *A Crucible Moment: College Learning and Democracy's Future*, and the US Department of Education issued *Advancing Civic Learning and Engagement in Democracy: A Roadmap and Call to Action*. These reports urge colleges and universities to regard civic education and engagement as "essential parts of the academic mission." BreakingGround seeks to be at the forefront of this "vibrant, new movement toward increased campus and community engagement—a movement that is now gaining ground nationally."[31]

An Example of Experiential Learning

Tyson King-Meadows, associate dean in our College of Arts, Humanities, and Social Sciences and associate professor of political science, teaches Problem Solving in the Urban Black Community. This course, infused with both entrepreneurship and civic engagement, is a terrific example of how we can use experiential learning to amplify what is taught in the classroom. "The course," according to its description, "utilizes the principles of social entrepreneurship to examine the nature and causes of sociopolitical and economic problems within urban black communities as well as to examine the various remedies proposed to address such problems."[32]

King-Meadows challenges his students to contest the notion of what "the problem" is. Instead of taking at face value the accepted notion of the problem, King-Meadows encourages his students to imagine and consider what the problem might be if they see it through another lens. He also trains students to approach policy making from a holistic point of view, one that brings together the perspectives of history, cultural and social structures, race relations, economics, and politics. For example, as an exercise within the course, students work collaboratively on group policy projects. They begin by undertaking a "SWOT" analysis—delineating strengths, weaknesses, opportunities, and threats. They then work on developing policy from the "inside out" rather than from the "outside in," allowing the specifics of the case to drive their thinking about what's possible rather than applying preconceived or ideological notions. In this way, they are supported in innovative thinking about problems and solutions that leads to entrepreneurship in a social and political context. Through this and other activities, King-Meadows instills a "can-do mentality" in his students. They are to reduce their use of the word "can't," he says. "UMBC is about can."[33]

11

Difficult Conversations

It was as if childbirth was like "having the flu."[1]

In the 1990s, women faculty at UMBC began to share how their experiences as women in the male-dominated fields of science and engineering affected their career advancement. Women in the natural sciences and engineering made it clear that major obstacles to their career success at that time were the way childbirth was handled, the arbitrariness with which parental leave was made available, and the impact of having a child on the tenure clock. These conversations revealed significant differences across departments in the way parental leave was handled at UMBC. While some departments collegially offered parental leave when a woman gave birth or adopted a child, other departments treated childbirth and adoption as if they were just another illness.

Some women faculty turned to the Office of Human Resources to learn about parental leave options available to them. They were often met with a long pause and then told, "Go talk to your chair." The institutional parental leave policy applied to staff but not to faculty. Talking to one's chair, though, was generally not an option for many, as pregnancy was perceived as "a women's issue" that had no place in a research lab. Many women felt that the best option was a well-timed pregnancy with a summer delivery, though that was never a sure thing.

As this conversation developed on our campus, women scientists and engineers across the country were likewise discussing their concerns about the advancement of women faculty in their careers. Indeed, a major report was about to change the national conversation. As internal and external dialogues converged, the opportunity to set a new course emerged that would allow us to meaningfully address the underrepresentation of women in the natural science and engineering faculty.

Women in Science and Engineering

In August 1994, sixteen of the seventeen tenured women faculty in science at the Massachusetts Institute of Technology asked the dean of science, Bob Birgeneau, "for an initiative to improve the status of women in the School of Science." Birgeneau convened a committee to study the status of women in the science faculty in 1995, and that committee delivered a final report in 1999 that proved to be a watershed for MIT, whose leadership took the report seriously. The MIT study reported the following:

> The committee discovered that junior women faculty feel well supported within their departments and most do not believe that gender bias will impact their careers. Junior women faculty believe, however, that family-work conflicts may impact their careers differently from those of their male colleagues. In contrast to junior women, many tenured women faculty feel marginalized and excluded from a significant role in their departments. Marginalization increases as women progress through their careers at MIT. Examination of data revealed that marginalization was often accompanied by differences in salary, space, awards, resources, and response to outside offers between men and women faculty, with women receiving less despite professional accomplishments equal to those of their male colleagues. An important finding was that this pattern repeats itself in successive generations of women faculty. The committee found that, as of 1994, the percent of women faculty in the School of Science

(8%) had not changed significantly for at least ten and probably twenty years.

MIT president Chuck Vest wrote in a preamble to the report that he had believed that gender discrimination was part reality and part perception, but that now he understood "that reality is by far the greater part of the balance." He went on to argue, "Our remarkably diverse student body must be matched by an equally diverse faculty. Through our institutional commitment and policies we must redouble our efforts to make this a reality."[2]

Along with climate studies at other research universities, the MIT report had a powerful impact nationally. Together, for example, these informed reports from the National Academies on the status of women in science and engineering.[3] They also led to conversations and turning points on many campuses as women faculty in the sciences and engineering drew inspiration from them and organized to support action.

At UMBC, concerns about the status of women faculty in the sciences and engineering had been percolating for some time. Women faculty on our campus had been talking among themselves already and felt that their experiences and our institutional values were not yet aligned. Following the release of MIT's report, they sought an initiative to increase the representation of women among the faculty in STEM departments and, in so doing, establish UMBC as a leader in this area. They then organized to spur action on our campus similar to that at MIT. Explicitly drawing on the example of the Meyerhoff Scholars Program, they challenged the university to do for them what it had accomplished for high-achieving African American students in the natural sciences and engineering in terms of recruitment, retention, and success.

This challenge turned into a collegial, though challenging, project for the university that has involved many serious, and even ongoing, conversations. The questions posed by our women faculty colleagues were simple yet powerful: Had we looked at the data on women faculty in the sciences as a place to begin an exploration of the problem? Are we meeting our goals? Could we use mentoring and a strong sense of community, powerful components of the Meyerhoff program, to recruit, retain, and advance women faculty in STEM? What can we do together?

In response to conversations happening on our campus and the MIT report, Provost Art Johnson established a two-year Provost's Ad Hoc Committee for Gender Equity in Science, Mathematics, Information Technology, and Engineering in August 1999. The committee gathered both quantitative and qualitative information and issued a report in June 2001. In their report, the committee found substantial underrepresentation of women in STEM faculty. Data from 2001 showed that there were twenty-seven women faculty in the natural sciences and engineering, of whom five were full professors, ten were associate professors, and twelve were tenure-track assistant professors. These twenty-seven women represented 17 percent of our faculty members in these fields. There seemed to be some gender equity at UMBC with regard to work space and salary, yet the qualitative portion of the report documented that women faced substantial structural challenges for career advancement.[4]

In their interviews with all but one of the women STEM faculty employed at UMBC at that time, the Ad Hoc Committee discovered the following:[5]

1. Women in departments where they were alone or one of a few felt deeply isolated unless they were able to make contacts in other departments.

2. The tone of the department chair is crucial to climate issues within departments. Women in departments where the chair was unaware or nonsupportive of gender issues felt unsupported.

3. Women faculty at all ranks felt that there was too much service expected of them and that service was not rewarded. There was also a real concern that one could not refuse service requests.

4. Wide variations in department policy and practices are not

> monitored by any central administrative review. The lack of
> clear policy undercuts women's ability to use policy without
> a negative career impact.

The last of these referred to a lack of clear guidelines for both tenure and promotion and for parental leave.

As the Ad Hoc Committee worked, women faculty in science
and engineering began to realize that by formally organizing they
could both support each other and collectively advocate for improved conditions for women. In fall 2000, Lynne Zimmerman
and Phyllis Robinson, both faculty in biological sciences, decided to
invite all the women faculty in science and engineering for tea and
cookies. This small gathering led to the creation of the Women in
Science and Engineering (WISE) faculty group, which met monthly
to provide what one member called "a network of women in STEM
to provide information, support, advice, wisdom, resources, en-
couragement, allies, and champions."[6]

The formation of WISE satisfied an important need for community by bringing together women who represented small numbers in their departments but a larger group when assembled from
across STEM departments. One event that has cemented bonds for
the group has been the annual WISE picnic. Everyone is invited to
bring their families. When WISE first held this event, it was great
for community building because most women in STEM did not yet
really know each other. WISE has also played a more formal role
within the university. WISE has organized workshops on a range
of topics, including hiring, promotion, tenure, scientific writing,
grant writing, and creating a teaching portfolio. WISE members
also meet with women faculty candidates from across departments
when they visit campus, a step that would prove critically important to recruiting women to UMBC.

ADVANCE Grant

In 2001, Rita Colwell, the first woman to serve as National
Science Foundation director, oversaw the creation of the NSF's

ADVANCE program in response to the MIT report. The goal of the ADVANCE program, which includes Fellows, Leadership, and Institutional Transformation grants, "is to increase the representation and advancement of women in academic science and engineering careers, thereby contributing to the development of a more diverse science and engineering workforce. ADVANCE encourages institutions of higher education and the broader science, technology, engineering and mathematics (STEM) community, including professional societies and other STEM-related not-for-profit organizations, to address various aspects of STEM academic culture and institutional structure that may differentially affect women faculty and academic administrators."[7]

The NSF's new ADVANCE initiative was perfectly timed for us. We had taken the critical first step, that hard look in the mirror in which we identified and substantiated the problems women faculty members faced in the sciences and engineering here at UMBC. After the Ad Hoc Committee's final report, we created the UMBC's Priorities for Women's Advancement, Retention, and Development (UPWARD) Committee, a formal group, to continue our work to advance women faculty in science and engineering. Members of UPWARD met on a monthly basis, and eventually their work led to our first ADVANCE Institutional Transformation proposal. Meanwhile, WISE complemented UPWARD by bringing speakers to campus, including Rita Colwell, who helped keep the larger UMBC community attuned to issues of gender equality in STEM.

Working together, WISE members and the women on the UPWARD Committee challenged us to question our anecdotal impressions and look at the quantitative data, as we had done previously to understand the situation of African American undergraduates in science. Personally, I had assumed we had made progress in advancing women in the faculty and that many were now doing well at UMBC. I had seen many women working in our science departments and laboratories. However, it turned out that most of those women were not tenure-track faculty, but technicians, graduate students, or lecturers. The numbers of women among the professoriate were really quite low. The data definitively identified the challenges women in STEM faculty faced at UMBC. The findings startled many men, including me.

We knew that to improve conditions for women faculty in science and engineering would require significant institutional culture change. To enact long-term, sustainable change, an institution has to identify and substantiate the problem, signal to campus the support for change of senior leadership, and authorize and empower the affected constituency within the institution to raise the issue and act. We had already begun this work through the partnership between WISE and the UPWARD Committee. Given the NSF's newly created ADVANCE Program, it was an optimal time for us to seek out substantial funding to support our culture change efforts.

Our first attempt to secure an ADVANCE Institutional Transformation grant, in 2001, was unsuccessful. It was "a rather naïve proposal," recalls one of its authors. In 2003, we decided to try again, and our second proposal succeeded. In that year, the NSF made nine grants to institutions out of seventy-two applications received. UMBC's award was for $3.2 million for the period from September 2003 to February 2010. Obtaining outside funding has played an important role in facilitating culture change and innovation at UMBC, and, once again, receiving a grant was a game changer. It elevated UMBC as one of just seventeen institutions with an ADVANCE grant in the first two rounds of the program.

One of the important differences between our first and second proposals was that I took a more formal step and insisted on serving as the principal investigator (PI). Serving as PI on the ADVANCE grant allowed me to communicate the importance of this work to both the university and the NSF, sending a message that we were serious about the work and also thoughtful about how to approach it. As we crafted our proposal, I had a conversation with NSF leadership about what it meant to me to be committed as a PI on our proposal: It meant that the project had the highest level of institutional commitment and that we would expect results. I also observed that I was joining the project as PI to signal the importance of men being deeply involved. "Just as whites should be interested in the issues of people of color in STEM, men should be interested in the issues of women in STEM," I told them. "This is not a women's issue, it is an American issue."

I was joined on the second Institutional Transformation grant proposal by four co-PIs, women and men and a mix of senior faculty and administrators symbolically communicating the importance of the work across the campus. The co-PIs were Lynn Zimmerman, professor of biological sciences; Govind Rao, professor and chair of chemical and biochemical engineering, Janet Rutledge, associate dean of the graduate school, and Marilyn E. Demorest, professor of psychology and vice provost for faculty affairs. Jack Prostko, founding director of UMBC's Faculty Development Center, and Phyllis Robinson, associate professor of biological sciences, served as faculty associates.

Preparing for Change

We knew that we wanted the ADVANCE grant to radically transform the culture of our institution. We had no illusions about how momentous our task would be, as it would not be enough to simply change policy or create incentives for short-term behavior change. We had to change institutional culture so that these would become deeply and authentically embedded in the institution's values and mission. To meet our first objective, to create a culture of inclusion, we needed a concrete strategy for deep institutional buy-in and support. We had to engage at the department level to address issues related to faculty hiring, promotion, and climate. We also needed a course of action that leveraged existing policies and enacted new ones, provided targeted resources to support change, and engaged in effective assessment and monitoring of outcomes.

Change can sometimes feel overwhelming, especially when it requires us to question our long-standing beliefs and assumptions. I wanted people on campus—particularly male faculty in the sciences—to not react defensively but be open-minded and willing to engage with this important issue. So, I modeled the behavior I wanted to see in others by communicating that I, too, had a lot to learn about the challenges women were facing. I asked questions and participated actively in the conversations that would identify the problem and look for solutions. I believed that if I acted in this manner, then it would signal to others on campus that it was okay to accept that we all had something to learn, that we could all grow beyond our assumptions. It also allowed me to connect this issue to the larger institutional and national agenda—that by advancing women in the sciences and engineering we were not only advancing these fields at UMBC but also advancing the mission of our entire institution.

But we still had to build critical mass for change across the campus. We needed male full professors in science and engineering to support the effort. We knew that younger men in these fields often expressed concerns similar to those of women faculty. For example, they argued that the university could better support faculty in balancing family and work and better support junior faculty as they navigated the promotion and tenure process. We also needed to work with department chairs and faculty search committee chairs. We began by assuming that we all were generally people of goodwill who, when provided with compelling evidence, would better understand the problem and work together to address it.

One of our next steps, then, was to explore together as a community what implicit bias is and the ways it affects the professional careers of women in STEM. To be sure, as on any campus, we had instances of explicit bias. However, we also had to address the challenges and consequences of implicit bias, the often-overlooked ways our taken-for-granted everyday assumptions, lack of information, or limited exposure to an issue impact the climate and culture of our institution.

To understand the nature of implicit bias, the ADVANCE program administered a climate survey that asked respondents whether they believed there were problems related to bias in their departments. The survey results indicated that while many of our senior male professors thought there were no significant issues regarding the inclusion of women in the STEM faculty, both junior women and men faculty believed there was a significant problem that needed to be addressed. Many women said their male colleagues were reasonable people, but they just never questioned their own assumptions or the status quo.

So, it was important, once again, to change the conversation, beginning with the evidence. When provided with empirical evidence about the number of women faculty and the barriers to their success, some of the more senior male faculty members changed their perspectives and became more supportive of the need for change. It was helpful that junior male faculty were able to articulate the problems faced by women faculty and how they, too, faced similar issues, for example, with regard to parental leave.

In sum, all that we had learned through data gathering and conversations gave us a more revealing portrait of who we were and informed the options available for programmatic interventions to recruit, retain, and advance women.

Policies and Programs

The NSF awarded UMBC an ADVANCE Institutional Transformation grant for $3.2 million over five years. We immediately began establishing an overarching framework for recruiting, retaining, and advancing women in STEM faculty at UMBC. Building on the earlier work of UPWARD and WISE, we identified the following three goals as crucial to the success of our ADVANCE program and the creation of a culture of inclusion by educating and engaging the campus broadly in ongoing discussions addressing issues of gender (and also racial) diversity in STEM fields:[8]

1. Develop, revise, and institutionalize policies, practices, and resources that (i) support recruitment, selection, and hiring of women faculty and (ii) provide clear and supported

pathways for advancement of these women, including women of color.

2. Provide a community of support for women faculty at UMBC.
3. Establish a system of targeted mentoring programs that support the transition of women into leadership positions at the university.

We achieved these goals by implementing policies and programmatic initiatives to support the recruitment, retention, and advancement of women faculty in science and engineering.

Recruitment
Improving the Faculty Search Process

Lasting change does not begin and end with enacting or changing policies. Changes in policy and procedures represent the end of the beginning. In 1998, then provost Art Johnson issued a policy mandating that every department on campus planning a faculty search had to draft a faculty diversity recruitment plan as part of their search process. The ADVANCE team noted that while these plans often produced more diversity in our applicant pools, we nevertheless struggled to hire female or minority candidates. Now, our ADVANCE initiative allowed us to expand this policy, embedding it into a multifaceted recruitment and outreach program. This approach would more fully align policy change with the goals of changing institutional culture and producing more diverse faculty hires. First, these faculty diversity recruitment plans became more robust and required search committees to specifically delineate their active recruitment and outreach strategies to attract a more diverse applicant pool. Second, while the institution provided resources for targeted recruitments, we required the deans to also be accountable by reviewing and providing feedback on the composition of both search committees and candidate pools. Third, ADVANCE developed mandatory Implicit Bias Awareness meetings and workshops for deans and chairs, as well as mandatory training for search committee chairs on issues related to bias and broadening the pool of candidates. Fourth, we provided support for newly hired women faculty.[9]

Some faculty were skeptical about the potential effectiveness of the ADVANCE program's new approaches to recruitment and hiring. One department chair articulated his belief that the lack of women faculty in his department was not a consequence of bias, but rather that the opportunities to recruit, interview, and make an offer to a woman were slim because there were so few women in the field. But he was open-minded enough to participate in the training and surprised at the results. "The training led us to take new approaches to our search effort," he recalled later. "We not only got more women in the candidate pool but we also got a more qualified group of excellent faculty candidates. For our next two hires, we made offers to women. The first turned us down, but we got the second. It turned out I was wrong in my assumption and I was glad to be shown that I was wrong."

A turning point was a performance by the Center for Research on Learning and Teaching Players, a theater group from the University of Michigan. Their performance, *Navigating Departmental Politics*, simulated a search committee meeting. It demonstrated both how women were typically treated and how implicit and explicit bias emerged in collective decision-making. It was a memorable event, being both humorous and revealing, and it drove home key points that the participants would not forget. I was struck by how the performance, masterfully executed by the actors, allowed for the creation of a safe space for discussion of difficult issues and self-reflection among the dinner participants. I hosted a dinner for faculty afterward that provided a forum in which people from different backgrounds and perspectives could interact in a meaningful dialogue about gender.

Additionally, search committees began to see WISE as a resource they could draw on for their interview efforts. One search in particular brought this home to us. During a visit to campus to interview, a woman candidate who was eventually offered a position met only with faculty members of the department, which, at the time, was composed solely of men. In rejecting the offer, she made it clear that she was concerned about being the only woman in the department. When I heard this, I asked department leadership, "Why didn't you have her talk to Catherine Fenselau?" They responded, "She isn't in our department." They were thinking inside the box. We needed to be more creative. Going forward, we worked with the WISE group to offer women who came to campus for interviews the opportunity to meet with other women faculty if they wanted to, even if they were in other departments. It made all the difference. People do not just want jobs; they want to work in an environment where they will feel comfortable, supported, and not isolated.

Research Assistant Support

Revising and enacting our hiring policies and procedures accomplished much, but we also had to create programmatic initiatives that signaled during candidate recruitment our institutional commitment to professional development of new women faculty. We developed ways to support new hires as well as current faculty. For new hires, the ADVANCE Research Assistantship (RA) Program provided support for newly hired tenure-track, assistant professors in the STEM fields to help them establish their research programs. The RA award, which is a full-time position, included tuition and health insurance for a graduate student who would work with the new hire. To apply, a chair provided a letter of support for the newly hired faculty member that included their commitment to initiate a Faculty Development Plan and identify a UMBC faculty/peer mentor.

During the course of our ADVANCE grant, we supported thirteen RAs, five in the biological sciences, two in geography and environmental systems, two in chemical and biochemical engineering, and one each in chemistry and biochemistry, physics, mechanical engineering, and mathematics and statistics. One of the first recipients of RA support under this program was Hua Lu, then newly hired as assistant professor in biological sciences. Dr. Lu employed an RA in her lab during her second year of employment. She has recently been promoted to full professor.

Faculty Horizons

The ADVANCE Program also supported the Faculty Horizons Program, an annual, national conference that supported pathways into the professoriate. This program staged two-and-a-half-day workshops during the summer that focused on providing women in STEM with the knowledge they need to navigate transition points in their academic careers. Faculty Horizons allowed our ADVANCE program to have broader impacts by engaging women scientists and engineers from across the country in these professional development activities. Topics covered included how to secure your first faculty position, successful negotiating techniques, grant writing, tenure and promotion, mentoring, career-life balance, and time management. In consultation with experts in the field and UMBC Meyerhoff alumnae, Faculty Horizons also integrated issues of particular concern to STEM women faculty of color. Held annually from 2004 to 2008, the workshop had 322 participants—302 women and 142 underrepresented minorities—that included senior graduate students, postdoctoral fellows, and new faculty hires. Our department chairs also attended Faculty Horizons, providing an opportunity to dispel their misconceptions about the lack of diversity in the science and engineering talent pool. While this effort was discontinued when grant funding ended, ADVANCE and WISE have continued to offer programs on similar topics for women students, postdoctoral fellows, and faculty at UMBC.

Retention

Of course, recruiting and hiring women are just the first steps. Once women join our faculty and are members of our community, we want them to stay, thrive, and advance in their careers. We have offered support toward these ends through a range of policies, information, and assistance.

Mentoring

The participation of the president and provost in the project provided it more weight than it would have had otherwise. The provost and I facilitated many of the meetings and workshops on the hiring and promotion of women faculty. There were instances in which participants were unhappy that attendance at meetings was mandatory, but requiring the involvement of everyone signaled the importance of the issue. One of these instances occurred when we sought to engage in difficult conversations around the unevenness of mentoring faculty across departments. I held a meeting with department chairs about the issue. While some departments clearly valued mentoring and their chairs were supportive in the meeting, some chairs said, in effect, "What is this warm and fuzzy stuff about mentoring?" and "If faculty need hand-holding, we don't want to tenure them." Departments that had that kind of attitude generally had more cases of junior faculty not reaching their potential. The inconsistency in the way departments approached these issues was unacceptable, and it left many faculty members, especially women, deeply concerned about the development of their careers as UMBC faculty.

Under ADVANCE we created a series of mechanisms to formalize mentoring for newly hired women faculty. We required chairs to develop an individualized Faculty Development Plan for each new hire, outlining a set of clearly defined expectations for tenure and promotion for the new faculty member. This plan established a relationship between the new hire and the chair during the earliest stages of the faculty member's career and identified major milestones that must be met to have a successful third-year review and tenure decision. The plan also detailed transition resources available to the faculty member along with mentoring opportunities with senior faculty. This policy was developed under ADVANCE and has now been incorporated into the written tenure and promotion guidelines required by the provost from all departments.[10]

We also knew that it was important to provide women STEM faculty with mentoring opportunities within their field of expertise in the larger scientific community. As a result, ADVANCE created the Eminent Scholar Mentoring Program, which facilitated a mentoring relationship between each UMBC STEM woman faculty member and a prominent researcher in their field at another research university. This was designed to enhance their success as they advanced through the ranks of academia. Over the course of this two-year formal mentoring program, ADVANCE provides funding for the mentor to visit UMBC, give a distinguished departmental seminar, and spend a substantial amount of time with the identified mentee during the visit, thus beginning the mentoring relationship. In the subsequent year, funding is provided for the UMBC faculty member to visit the mentor's home institution and give a seminar, as well as continue the mentoring relationship. Regular contact was expected (e.g., at least one time per semester) between the mentor and the mentee. Remarkably, in the entire history of this program, no external mentor (most of whom have been women) has received or requested any additional compensation. Moreover, the NSF recognizes our Eminent Scholar Mentoring Program as a best practice from our ADVANCE Institutional Transformation grant. Other ADVANCE institutions have learned about our work through the annual NSF ADVANCE workshop and have since replicated this initiative.[11]

ADVANCE and WISE sponsored opportunities for informal mentoring as well. ADVANCE hosted "Luncheons for Newly Hired Women Faculty" to facilitate more informal mentoring for women. We invited all STEM women assistant professors who have not yet completed their third-year reviews and those who were new to UMBC to attend these once-a-semester lunches. At these lunches, the director of the Faculty Development Center and the ADVANCE program director held an informal discussion where the women discussed career-life balance issues and any barriers or challenges they were experiencing. This informal atmosphere encouraged women to talk with each other and establish networks for themselves early on to guard against isolation within departments for new STEM women faculty. We worked closely with the WISE group, whose activities expanded to support a formal Faculty ADVANCEment Workshop Series. The monthly workshops, open to all STEM faculty members, focused on understanding the tenure process, promotion to full professor, effective teaching, resource negotiation, grant writing, contract review, departmental politics, career-life balance, effective communication, and laboratory and project management.

Transparent Promotion and Tenure Guidelines

We also discovered inconsistencies among departments regarding promotion and tenure. In some departments, like History, the expectations for promotion and tenure—in terms of research, publishing, teaching, and service—were clear, in writing, and available to junior faculty. In many of the STEM departments, however, the promotion and tenure process was opaque. In some instances, these departments did not have written guidelines. One might get a glimpse of what the expectations were if one knew the chair or senior faculty in the department well. This allowed the process to be informal and subjective rather than transparent and fair and represented a potential breeding ground for bias. Women and minorities were often at a disadvantage. As a consequence, the provost worked with our faculty senate to create a new policy that required every department to develop clear, specific guidelines for promotion and tenure and to articulate the expectations for promotion.

Family Support Plan

The unbalanced way that we handled parental leave across departments was yet another barrier to women's advancement. The

Ad Hoc Committee had already earlier interviewed women and men faculty and found that UMBC did not have a consistent approach to handling childbirth, adoption, and family leave, which impeded the career advancement of women STEM faculty. While some departments collegially offered parental leave when a woman gave birth or adopted a child, other departments did not. One of the tangible outcomes of the Ad Hoc Committee's pre-ADVANCE grant work was the development of a Family and Medical Leave Policy. This policy prescribed the amount of time faculty could take following childbirth or adoption, was available to both men and women, and was also designed to be supportive of UMBC's LGBTQ (lesbian, gay, bisexual, transgender, queer) faculty—understanding that families should be defined in an inclusive manner. The ADVANCE program later enhanced the policy by creating a comprehensive Family Support Plan to assist with such family needs as caring for the faculty member's newborn child, caring for a child placed with the faculty member for adoption or foster care, caring for a faculty member's child or other family member with a serious health condition, and eldercare. Working together, the faculty member and department chair develop an individualized plan that allows the faculty member to reduce or otherwise modify their workload, especially teaching duties, during the semester in which leave is taken. This plan also includes an automatic one-year extension of the tenure review.

Moreover, before ADVANCE, UMBC's family leave policy was neither well known nor widely used in STEM departments. In fact, none of the STEM women faculty had ever requested use of family leave, medical leave, or any other type of faculty support plan. ADVANCE worked to educate current and potential faculty, as well as department chairs, about UMBC's Family Support Plan and the types of leave and support options available. As a result, our program developed the first campus-wide Family Support brochure. The brochure is available to current faculty and department chairs and is given to all prospective faculty during their campus interview.[12]

The adoption of the expanded policy in 2004 appeared to have an impact. The next spring at UMBC, five female faculty gave birth. The policy has supported UMBC faculty in their relationships and facilitated family life. By 2010, much higher proportions of UMBC faculty in STEM were married or in domestic partnerships than their peers were nationally, and much higher proportions also had children. Under the NSF-funded ADVANCE years, approximately 25 percent of the forty-five STEM women faculty have initiated or made use of a variety of leave and support options. UMBC ADVANCE continues to assist faculty in evaluating the types of support plans available and exploring the options most important to them.

A family support policy was so clearly needed and successful at UMBC that, in 2013, the University System of Maryland adopted a new parental and family leave policy that was based on UMBC's policy and put into effect on all of the system's campuses. The USM's institutionalization of the Family Support Plan also included a minimum assured period of eight weeks paid parental leave.[13] In 2015, the Association for Women in Science held a panel on family and parental leave, at which it emerged from the conversation that most institutions, even those with ADVANCE grants, had still not tackled this issue.

Advancement
Moving through the Faculty Ranks

Recent analysis of the impact of the UMBC Family Support Plan shows that 54 percent of our women associate professors in STEM have used the UMBC Family Support Plan at some point in their academic career at UMBC. Additional analysis, however, reveals that women in STEM faculty who have used a Family Support Plan still do not progress from associate to full professor at the same rate as their male colleagues. Women, who often carry significant caregiving responsibilities throughout their career, are at higher risk of experiencing "productivity gaps," which inevitably stall their progression to senior faculty ranks. Support from federal grants and contracts, coupled with high publication rates, is strongly associated with career advancement in the sciences and social sciences at Carnegie-ranked research institutions. Overall, tenured faculty in the sciences who were direct recipients of federal monetary support are 44 percent more likely to advance to full professor at all types of institutions, and 60 percent more likely to advance at research-intensive institutions. And yet, several studies have confirmed that women are less likely than men to apply for federal funding, and those with children were 26 percent less likely to do so than women who were married without children, and 19 percent less likely than single women without children to have their work even partially funded by federal grants and contracts.[14]

To address this problem, in 2013 we successfully applied for funding from the NSF's Early-Concept Grants for Exploratory Research program, to pilot "'On Ramps' to Full Professor: Institutional Support for Post–Family Leave Faculty Research Reintegration."[15] We sought to provide carefully calibrated support in the form of course releases, research graduate student support, domestic and international travel grants, and research and grant writing support to help accelerate research productivity. We invited women associate professors who had used a family support plan, at any point during their career, to apply for this support by submitting a research acceleration plan and a letter of support from their chair. The eight recipients of these research acceleration grants have written funded grant proposals, published journal manuscripts and books, presented at conferences, chaired conference sessions, and served on review panels. We are currently assessing the outcomes of this pilot to determine whether we should institutionalize it.

Under the same NSF grant, we have also established the UMBC Career-Life Balance (CLB) initiative, which has included education and awareness activities that promote CLB policies to the UMBC campus community, with a plan toward wide dissemination throughout the USM. CLB has also included seminars and productivity-based workshops that serve large groups of faculty, postdocs, and graduate students.[16] A major outcome of this initiative has been the creation of parental leave fellowships for graduate assistants, one of very few such policies at research universities nationwide. During the fellowship period, the graduate assistant retains his or her full stipend and benefits, provides no service to the university, and maintains enrollment as a full-time student.

Leadership Development

Women are underrepresented not only in STEM fields but also in leadership positions in STEM and in higher education more generally. Our ADVANCE program sought to address this through the ADVANCE Leadership Cohort Program. This program component has provided women who were already tenured STEM faculty or midlevel administrators with the knowledge and skills they need to advance into university leadership positions. Using a cohort model, the program has focused on intentional career advancement, and participants have explored such questions as what positions do women hold now, what positions in leadership do they want to attain, what is needed to get there, and what would a path to that position look like for themselves.[17]

To date, four cohorts of four to five women each have completed the program. The women have participated in a variety of activities, including behind-closed-doors meetings with senior leaders at UMBC and external women leaders in STEM. They have visited five campuses and met with women presidents, asking, "What is power, how do you get it, keep it, and use it?" They have also shared and discussed readings on leadership, worked with a career coach to review their curriculum vitae, and engaged in career mapping exercises.

Participants in the ADVANCE Leadership Cohort program have since formed the ADVANCE Leadership Alliance, which is charged with serving as an advisory board for future leadership cohorts and continuing leadership training to systematically transform the culture of the university. This remarkable program has led many talented women to take senior leadership positions at UMBC, benefiting our campus with strong leaders committed to diversity who know the institution well. Alumnae of the program have become vice provosts, deans, chairs, and center directors at UMBC and other institutions.

Lessons Learned, Outcomes, and Challenges

With the ADVANCE grant's programmatic initiatives and policy interventions, as well as buy-in from campus, we have made significant progress in advancing women in STEM faculty positions. As discussed in the next chapter, we have now institutionalized and expanded many of the grant-funded activities, policies, and procedures to also support efforts to recruit, retain, and advance underrepresented minority faculty.

We have learned from our experiences with ADVANCE that, in order to change behavior and culture across a campus, forging a partnership between campus leadership and the faculty at the grassroots level is very powerful. Sustainable institutional transformation cannot occur unless there is leadership from the president, provost, and other administrators in combination with leadership from the constituencies directly impacted by the problem. Support and buy-in from allies and champions also enable this broader and deeper change.

As we form a campus-wide partnership, we must be honest with ourselves, take that hard look in the mirror, and not only identify and name the problems but also be committed to working together to develop policies and programmatic initiatives to address them. If existing policies and programs are working, use them; if not, be prepared to adapt them or create new ones. Also, although money can help, change is possible without a lot of resources; it just takes fostering a collective commitment to shared goals and vision. This is not always easy, but it can be achieved through forging meaningful partnerships. Patience is important. The process of change takes sustained effort over a long period of time. Remember that change is often incremental; start small, celebrate success, and grow further.

Fifteen years after our ADVANCE award, we have many successes to celebrate. We have significantly increased the representation of women in STEM faculty overall. The number of women tenure-track faculty in STEM has increased 63.3 percent from fall 2003 (N = 30) to fall 2018 (N = 49), compared to a 13.5 percent increase in men tenure-track faculty (from N = 133 to 151 in the same period). As of 2018, 24.5 percent of all UMBC STEM faculty are women. Additionally, with the support offered through ADVANCE, the numbers of STEM women at the assistant, associate, and full professor ranks have increased substantially—assistant professors by 31 percent (from N = 13 in fall 2003 to N = 17 in fall 2018), associate professors by 67 percent (from N = 12 in fall 2003 to N = 20 in fall 2018), and full professors by 140 percent (from N = 5 in fall 2003 to N = 12 in fall 2018).[18] The impact of the work cannot just be measured in numbers, nor do the numbers tell the entire story. Members of our ADVANCE community have shared our story through presentations at conferences across the country. They have also worked with other universities to help them with ADVANCE grant proposals. For example, Pat McDermott, vice provost for faculty affairs, assisted Jackson State University in their successful effort.

It is also critical that we remain vigilant. Change can be undone without constant focus on and assessment of progress toward our goals. We are proud of what our ADVANCE grant accomplished, but there is a cautionary tale to be told. When the ADVANCE grant ended in 2010, we had a collective sense of "mission accomplished," that the culture had been transformed by the effort and that our successes would continue into the future as a matter of course. We were wrong. As soon as we took our eye off the ball, we slipped—the percentage of women faculty hired in science and engineering decreased. In 2011, we once again looked in the mirror, assessed whether we were living out our values, and committed new institutional funds to the program to replace the expended grant funding. We also signaled to the university the importance of the initiative by placing the work under the purview of the Office of the Provost. The provost created the ADVANCE Executive Committee, a group of tenured women and men allies in science and engineering to provide advice and counsel on the policies and programmatic initiatives necessary to sustain and expand the work of ADVANCE. As we discuss in the next chapter, we intertwined our institutionalized ADVANCE program with a renewed commitment to diversifying the faculty even more broadly.

12

Looking in the Mirror

As a healthy campus, we must look in the mirror and be honest with ourselves.[1]

At UMBC, we celebrate our accomplishments. We also acknowledge the work that remains to be done. When it comes to inclusive excellence, we are a national model for educating African American undergraduates in STEM fields who go on to earn research doctorates. When it comes to women in our science and engineering faculty, our ADVANCE grant and our hard work have allowed us to make significant progress. When it comes to increasing the racial and ethnic diversity of our faculty, however, we can only say that we are slightly ahead of our peer institutions and still have much to do.

This is not because we have not paid attention to the issue. On the contrary, the issue has been with us since our campus opened fifty years ago, and, over and over again, we have developed and implemented programs and plans to increase the representation of minority—particularly black and Hispanic—faculty. But until recently, these programs had not been deeply effective. They focused on processes that changed behavior in the short run and produced marginal results. They did not change the culture that would support sustained progress in the long run.

This fundamental difference between changing behavior and

changing culture is often difficult to grasp and even more difficult to act on. But it makes all the difference. We are now applying the lessons we have learned from ADVANCE about the way culture change enables and sustains progress to our campus-wide work on faculty diversity.

Shifting the Paradigm

I was appointed acting president of UMBC in 1992 and then inaugurated as the fifth president of UMBC in 1993. As a new president and, moreover, as an African American president, I had to use my political capital carefully. At the time, I focused foremost on advancing student diversity through the Meyerhoff program, which would demonstrate that African American undergraduates could achieve at the highest levels at UMBC if supported. This was tangible, doable, socially important, and externally funded, and we had buy-in from enough key white faculty in the natural sciences for the project to have reasonable prospects for success. It was the right focus at the time, and we kept that focus until we had "proof of concept," which then provided the additional political capital I could use for other innovations, including diversifying the faculty.

In the meantime, the effort to support faculty diversity defaulted to the bureaucratic, almost soulless, affirmative action exercise in place for two decades in one form or another. Each year we produced a thick binder that provided our affirmative action policies, identified numerical goals, included examples of hiring paperwork, described discrimination complaint processes, and outlined the audit process. None of this really changed behavior, culture, or outcomes. Most search committees saw this as "checking the box," or acted in a way that could be so interpreted.

So, starting in 1993, the number of black full-time, tenure-track (FT/TT) faculty hovered between twenty and twenty-three for almost two decades. At that time, UMBC had twenty-one black FT/TT faculty (four full professors, eight associate professors, and nine assistant professors). In 2011, we also had twenty-one (four full, twelve associate, and five assistant). Since the size of UMBC's over-all faculty increased during that period, we actually experienced a decline in black representation from 6.6 to 5.4 percent of the FT/TT faculty.

What was confounding, though, was that we did hire at least ten black faculty between 1994 and 2003, and five of them remain on our faculty today. But we also lost ten during that period, five of the newer hires and five faculty who had been with us for some time. This raised a flag: hiring was essential but not sufficient; we had to retain and promote new faculty once they came here, a tough lesson we were also learning at that time as we implemented our ADVANCE program. And that required a change in tactics and deeper conversations about fairness, values, and perceptions of who can succeed.

UMBC's Department of Modern Languages, Linguistics and Intercultural Communication (MLLI) was one department that had pioneered changes in its culture and hiring on its own. Angela Moorjani, MLLI chair from 1986 to 1988, led their effort to increase diversity and inclusion in the faculty. The department had hired Stanley McCray as its first black faculty member in 1981, and he would remain with the department until his retirement in 2012. While Moorjani was chair, the department hired three more. Omar Ka came on board in 1987 and is still teaching. Moorjani also hired two black women who were with the department for a shorter time, but, with four African American faculty for a time, MLLI represented a real example of the kind of breakthrough a department could achieve.

To export this success, Angela gave several workshops on hiring people of color, inviting chairs and faculty from departments across the university. She had a more open approach to looking at criteria for hiring beyond the traditional ones. She argued that it was not enough to just look at resumes; search committees needed to look holistically at what the person could bring to the department. It was not enough to look at just the research; they needed to look at how the person could open the minds of the students and other faculty. It was not enough to consider what the person could do on day one; they had to think about what someone would be capable of if given support. She asserted that most whites who held doctorates were way ahead of doctorates from underrepresented groups because they had received much more coaching along the way. Often the underrepresented candidate did not receive the coaching and needed the coaching and mentoring now to catch up, and would catch up if given the support and opportunity.

Dr. Moorjani was challenging our thinking about how to hire faculty, but the example of Moorjani and MLLI was the exception and not the rule in the late 1980s and early 1990s. As a campus we were changing the culture around student success for black undergraduates in STEM fields during this period, but we had not yet extended culture change to faculty hiring across departments. Moorjani had started the necessary conversations; the other elements needed for broader change and faculty buy-in did not come together until a decade later, when our ADVANCE grant provided an opportunity to more deeply examine and change our policies and practices to support the recruitment, retention, and advancement of women faculty in STEM. Prior to the ADVANCE grant, we had developed many plans for increasing racial and ethnic diversity over the years, many of which looked great on paper, but we had not yet had the difficult conversations, we had not yet formed a partnership between university and grassroots faculty leadership, and we had not yet developed the network of allies and champions that are needed for real change and more robust results.

In 2010, the Black Faculty Committee of the College of Arts, Humanities, and Social Sciences (CAHSS) wrote a position paper documenting UMBC's low numbers of black faculty members and describing the obstacles to increasing diversity among our faculty.[2] They detailed how the numbers of black faculty were low in absolute terms and relative to the percentage of black students in the undergraduate population. They expressed their deep concern that bias, isolation, and excessive service contributed to these low numbers. Members of the committee shared their strong view that these factors, particularly isolation and excessive service, also lowered the morale of existing black faculty and increased the likelihood that they would leave UMBC for other institutions should an opportunity present itself, as they often did. Collectively, the committee repeatedly underscored the urgent need for an immediate and highly visible demonstration of commitment by the UMBC administration to address these issues.

The paper led to the same kind of partnership between university leadership and grassroots faculty leadership that had successfully promoted our work to increase the number of women in our STEM faculty. The provost and vice provost for faculty affairs read the position paper and met with the Black Faculty Committee to discuss the committee's concerns and potential action. The conversation led to a shared understanding that we needed a highly visible campus-wide initiative to recruit, retain, and advance faculty members from underrepresented minority groups. As a result of this new partnership, the Office of the Provost would (1) launch a campus-wide Faculty Diversity Initiative; (2) create the Executive Committee on the Recruitment, Retention, and Advancement of Underrepresented Minority Faculty,[3] composed of tenured faculty who would provide advice and counsel to the provost on the policies and programmatic initiatives needed to support our faculty diversity efforts; (3) hire a full-time program coordinator to support these initiatives and the new Executive Committee; (4) work with the Executive Committee to develop models for a potential postdoctoral and/or bridge program to facilitate recruitment; and (5) work with the Executive Committee to create and implement a comprehensive outreach and visibility campaign.

The Black Faculty Committee also asked us to focus our next annual campus retreat on the issue of faculty diversity in order to send the strong message to the campus that our university leadership recognized the critical importance of both understanding the issue and acting to address it in a substantive way. We talked about the issue at the retreat, which included panel discussions of faculty diversity, especially as it related to the paucity of black faculty.

I took this occasion, as well as at our Fall Opening Meeting that followed the retreat, to reinforce to the campus—especially our faculty—my own strong commitment to recruiting and retaining faculty from underrepresented groups. One of the key lessons we had learned from launching both the Meyerhoff program and ADVANCE was the importance of having these difficult conversations, discussing the evidence, and beginning the work through a dialogue about both the issues and the ways we could address them. The retreat offered an important opportunity to bring our faculty members directly into the conversation. I knew that we needed buy-in from faculty about addressing the issue and developing a shared understanding that increasing the ethnic and racial diversity of our faculty, just like increasing the representation of women faculty in STEM, would benefit UMBC as a whole.

To keep the momentum going, two months later I hosted a reception for UMBC's black faculty and our university leadership. Among those attending were the provost, the academic deans, and the vice provost for faculty affairs. I offered welcoming remarks, during which I reaffirmed my commitment. Elliot Hirshman, who was then our provost, formally announced the formation of the Executive Committee and the launching of the Postdoctoral Fellowship for Faculty Diversity, which would be an important recruiting tool for us. He also identified and discussed important challenges like isolation and retention. The deans introduced each of the black faculty in their college, noting their research and accomplishments. This has since become an annual event. The provost's office reports progress, and each dean talks about what their college is doing to recruit and advance underrepresented minority faculty.

Dimensions of the Problem

As a nation we are at a crossroads. Our challenges at UMBC reflect a larger national, systemic problem with minority underrepresentation in the faculty. While students on campuses nationwide have become increasingly diverse, the professoriate has remained primarily white, at about 75 percent for FT/TT faculty at four-year colleges and universities. Asian Americans represent another 10 percent of such faculty. The representation of African Americans, Hispanics, Native Americans, Alaskan Natives, Pacific Islanders, and other underrepresented racial and ethnic minorities in the professoriate is abysmal. They collectively represent 9.4 percent of full-time faculty nationally, a low number when we realize that they constitute 30 percent of the US population, 28 percent of undergraduates at public four-year institutions, and 24 percent of undergraduates at private, nonprofit four-year colleges and universities. This is deep and pervasive underrepresentation.[4]

The problem is more challenging in some fields than others. Noting that activists at the University of Missouri–Columbia demanded, in 2015, an increase in the percentage of faculty and staff who are black to 10 percent by 2017/18, Diyi Li and Corey Koedel, faculty at that institution, analyzed the demographics of 4,000 tenure-track faculty at forty selective public institutions during the 2015/16 academic year to understand the nuances of minority underrepresentation in the faculty. They found that blacks and Hispanics are indeed underrepresented generally, but that this underrepresentation is primarily driven by severe underrepresentation in STEM fields: "black faculty account for just 0.7–2.9 percent of faculty in biology, chemistry, and economics; but 8.8–15.1 percent of faculty in educational leadership/policy, English, and sociology."[5]

A national effort to address this underrepresentation is overdue. A National Academies report, *Expanding Underrepresented Minority Participation: American's Science and Technology at the Crossroads*, recommended in 2011 that the National Science Foundation establish an ADVANCE-like program for increasing the participation and success of underrepresented minority faculty in STEM fields as it does for the success of women.[6] In the meantime, we essentially pioneered this work in our self-funded expansion of ADVANCE to address the recruitment, retention, and advancement of underrepresented minority faculty.

So, within this national context, how does UMBC stack up relative to our student population? Our FT/TT faculty in the fall of 2018 was 67 percent white, 19 percent Asian, 7 percent black, 4 percent Hispanic, and 3 percent other. Blacks and Hispanics are underrepresented in our FT/TT faculty when compared to our undergraduate population, which in the fall of 2018 was 40 percent white, 22 percent Asian, 18 percent black, 8 percent Hispanic, 5 percent two or more races, and 7 percent other.

According to the *Chronicle of Higher Education*, we are slightly ahead of our peer institutions that are "high-activity research universities." Overall, underrepresented minorities constitute 9.7 percent of our faculty compared to 8.4 percent for our peers. We are slightly ahead for black faculty (6.4% vs. 4%), but slightly below our peers for Hispanics (3.3% vs. 4%).[7] Our black and Hispanic faculty, however, are less likely to be full professors and more likely to be assistant or associate professors than minority faculty at other high-activity research universities. Our black and Hispanic faculty are skewed away from STEM fields in a manner similar to national patterns. Among black and Hispanic FT/TT faculty, 75 percent are in arts, humanities, and social sciences, and just 25 percent are in the natural sciences and engineering. The data here make it clear that while we might pride ourselves on being slightly ahead of the game on faculty diversity relative to our peer institutions, we are still short of the mark when it comes to minority representation in our faculty by other standards. We still have work to do.

Shared Action and Assessment in Implementation

As leaders we often find ourselves in situations where there is a moral imperative to act, yet we see uncertainty and risk surrounding the possible ways to move forward. While we—both university leaders and grassroots leaders—agreed about next steps at this stage, we struggled in the early stages to find the right approach to the problem. For example, one of our initial efforts focused on an incentive hiring program in which we offered departments funding they could use for an additional hire if they identified a qualified underrepresented minority candidate during the regular search process. We quickly realized that this was not the best approach because it did not change the culture in a way that supported inclusion and it still left many new hires feeling isolated in their professional lives, leading to problems with retention.

The ADVANCE program had transformed our culture, elevating and creating the space within which we could, as a healthy campus, take that hard look in the mirror, be honest, and change course as appropriate. What helped us as we struggled was that we collected and shared data and partnered with the affected constituencies to understand the issues and chart a course to address the underrepresentation of our faculty. We shared the recruitment and attrition data with the Executive Committee, as we still do at each of its fall meetings, and we had those necessary difficult conversations about our approaches and progress. The data showed that the incentive program was not working as we had hoped and planned. So, we discontinued the program and took a different approach that focused on the recruitment process. The Office of the Provost began to work directly with the deans, who were now given the responsibility of leading efforts to recruit and retain diverse faculty members. The deans of our three colleges began, in turn, to hold implicit bias workshops that would change not just short-term behavior but the overall culture, which could more profoundly alter both the way we hire and the way we support and retain diverse faculty.

Also, during the early years of our Faculty Diversity Initiative we partnered with our Office of Institutional Advancement to develop a brand and marketing approach to our outreach efforts. We created the slogan "We're Changing Minds, Come Join Us." We featured this slogan prominently on our first-ever Faculty Diversity Brochure, which showcased our faculty's scholarship on diversity and inclusion; community-based faculty groups, including WISE and the Black Faculty Committee; and our programmatic initiatives. We also launched a companion Faculty Diversity website that serves as a public platform for external and internal audiences and gives visibility to UMBC's ongoing diversity initiatives. The website includes links for applying for all of UMBC's faculty openings, highlights the research and accomplishments of our diverse community of scholars, showcases specific programs linked to diversity recruitment and retention, and provides information about UMBC's community-based faculty groups.[8]

At the same time, the Office of the Provost began funding delegations of UMBC faculty to attend the Southern Regional Education Board's (SREB) Institute on Teaching and Mentoring annual conference to recruit for our faculty openings. The SREB conference is the largest gathering of early-career minority PhD scholars in the country, and their explicit goal is to prepare students from underrepresented backgrounds for the professoriate. This venue allows us to actively recruit potential future faculty and to heighten the national visibility of UMBC among academic communities of color. UMBC also has access to the SREB doctoral scholars database, which is used in our diversity recruitment activities.

The Postdoctoral Fellowship for Faculty Diversity was perhaps our largest undertaking at this point in time. As one way to challenge the notion that departments "can't find minority candidates," in 2011 we created a Postdoctoral Fellowship for Faculty Diversity that includes a pathway to a faculty position at UMBC. This program brings talented, diverse young postdoctoral fellows to our campus, targeting, but not restricted to, members of groups that have historically been underrepresented in the professoriate. All fellows must have a commitment to diversity in the academy.[9]

The program also serves as a way to introduce potential future faculty to UMBC, particularly in competitive fields. As a campus, we conduct an open national search for these postdoctoral fellows. The two-year fellowship provides each fellow with opportunities to teach one course per year, conduct research, and create a track record to build on, the goal being preparation for a tenure-track faculty position. Each fellow has a mentor and is provided with a typical support package of a stipend, health benefits, funding for conference travel, office space, and the normal library and other campus privileges of faculty. In the first two cohorts of the fellowship, 2011–13 and 2013–15, we hosted five fellows, and we hired one fellow to a tenure-track position at UMBC.

Internal and external events once again converged in early 2015, leading us to hold further difficult conversations about our work in diversifying the faculty. Internally, during both the fall 2014 and spring 2015 Executive Committee meetings, members demonstrated, using the recruitment data, that our candidate pools were not becoming more diverse despite our recent efforts, a fact reflected in the very small numbers of black or Hispanic faculty hired between 2011 and 2015. As an institution, we also did not hire any of the three fellows from our second cohort of Postdoctoral Fellows for Faculty Diversity. As we struggled with this, we recognized that one of the missing components was that we had not sufficiently garnered buy-in from majority group faculty to join us in taking collective ownership of this work as we had done under ADVANCE.

Meanwhile, externally, in the wake of several shooting deaths of unarmed black men in Florida and Missouri, a growing national discussion about race relations reemerged. That conversation came to Baltimore in April 2015, when Freddie Gray died from injuries he sustained while in police custody. A group from the Black Faculty Committee asked to meet with me and the provost to talk about the situation in Baltimore. This discussion led to the teach-in we held on campus about race relations in Baltimore. It also refocused our attention on how to support underrepresented minority students and our work to increase the racial and ethnic diversity of the faculty. Tyson King-Meadows, an African American in the political science department and cochair of the Executive Committee, asked what more we could do to extend the work of ADVANCE to hiring underrepresented minorities as well as women. King-Meadows did not mince words when he told me, the provost, and the vice provost for faculty affairs, "We are mediocre when it comes to minority faculty representation. When did we at UMBC ever want to be mediocre?" It was true. And it was time for us to change again.

Historically, as an institution in Maryland, much of the focus on diversity had addressed issues about representation of blacks in the student population and our faculty. In the intervening years, Maryland and also our campus had become much more multicultural. We have growing numbers of Asian American and Hispanic students and faculty who have been grappling with issues important to their communities. These have included the push for the Maryland DREAM Act, which was enacted by the Maryland General Assembly and signed by the governor in December 2012. Our LGBTQ colleagues likewise had concerns. Some of these were addressed when voters approved the referendum legalizing same-sex marriage in Maryland on November 6, 2012. Hispanic, Asian American, and LGBTQ faculty each met with the provost to share that, as with our black faculty, they had concerns about faculty recruitment, retention, advancement, bias in the workplace, and visibility. Eventually, these faculty have followed the example set by WISE and the Black Faculty Committee and have organized their own community-based groups to provide each other support and advocate for their professional success and the well-being of UMBC's students.[10]

Our work in creating a campus that embraces and supports LGBTQ faculty, students, and staff is particularly instructive. For most of our history, LGBTQ members of our community had made the decision not to be out at UMBC. Fortunately, the conversation and climate on campus are changing. Now, LGBTQ staff and faculty are far more comfortable, and UMBC even has a page on the official UMBC website—the UMBC OutList—providing names and photos of LGBTQ faculty and staff who are out at UMBC. The website notes, "UMBC's OutList represents faculty and staff members who self-identify as Lesbian, Gay, Bisexual, Transgender or Queer and have chosen to be included on this virtual space. The OutList promotes greater visibility of the LGBTQ community and reflects the commitment to diversity and inclusivity at UMBC."[11] This Out-

List benefits not only our faculty and staff but also our students, because now they are able to find role models and mentors.

As a campus, we are now moving on to also talk more openly about transgender issues, with discussions of gender and gender identities. The recent tragic suicide of a transgender staff member brought forth deeper discussions than we have ever had before. The LGBTQ Faculty/Staff Association asked for a meeting with me and other senior leaders to have an open conversation about challenges affecting our faculty, staff, and students who are members of the LGBTQ community. Many felt that this conversation was so important, difficult as it was, that they came out by attending and participating in the meeting. As one follow-up to the meeting, I personally asked that leaders in the LGBTQ Faculty/Staff Association join the President's Council for a meeting and provide LGBTQ awareness training to enhance sensitivity and inclusion and keep the conversation going.

All of our conversations with our community-based faculty groups were inclusive, engaged, and ultimately productive discussions. We agreed that we had more work to do to continue to reshape faculty culture and improve our hiring outcomes. We also had a growing sense that we could draw more deeply on what had worked in the ADVANCE program to support the hiring of diverse faculty. So, based on the recommendations of the Executive Committee, we then developed an expanded faculty diversity initiative. In the past four years we have institutionalized for underrepresented minority faculty many of the best practices from ADVANCE: we extended the Eminent Scholar Mentoring Program for newly hired faculty from underrepresented groups, and we adapted the faculty diversity recruitment plans. We also strengthened the Postdoctoral Fellowship for Faculty Diversity and expanded our focus on the search process through the acquisition of Interfolio Faculty Search, the revision of our search processes and protocols, and the creation of the faculty-led Committee on Strategies and Tactics to Recruit to Improve Diversity and Excellence (STRIDE), which provides peer education to search committees on how to conduct searches that center on diversity and inclusion.

Our Collective Acknowledgment of the Imperative

While we (administration leaders, the Executive Committee, and members of the community-based faculty groups) were working together to continue to evolve our program, we were also mindful that—as with ADVANCE—we had to include the entire campus community in the conversation and work. In my State of the University Address in August 2015, I made a point of saying, "With one of the most diverse student bodies of any institution of higher education in the United States, we will continue to focus on attracting faculty from underrepresented groups, particularly African Americans and Hispanics. Our Executive Committee on the Recruitment, Retention, and Advancement of Underrepresented Faculty is working closely with the provost and deans to lead this effort."[12]

Similarly, in the fall of 2015, Provost Philip Rous and Professor Tyson King-Meadows, cochairs of the Executive Committee, made both the problem and the importance of working on it as a community clear to our campus. Rous and King-Meadows noted that UMBC has deservedly established a national reputation for the diversity of our student body and our commitment to educating and supporting students from all backgrounds, but they did not mince words when they underscored the incongruence between the diversity of our student body and that of our faculty body. They acknowledged our progress but reasserted that we must do much better in recruiting and retaining underrepresented minority faculty. The cochairs were explicit about the reasons for this work: we must recruit and maintain a diverse and inclusive professoriate because UMBC cannot reach its full potential as a leading public research university without the benefit of a full range of diverse perspectives and backgrounds driving our educational mission, research, scholarship, creative activity, and civic engagement; the vibrancy of the intellectual and social life of the UMBC community is enriched when minds from diverse backgrounds work, learn, create, and engage with one another in respectful and insightful ways.[13] It is, of course, also the right thing to do for reasons of equity.

As it happened, the timing of these conversations dovetailed with the development of "Our UMBC: A Strategic Plan for Advancing Excellence." This multiyear process to write a strategic plan was deliberately designed to be inclusive and engage a wide range of stakeholders from across our campus. It presented a terrific opportunity for us to weave our faculty diversity work into this strategic plan, which likewise focused on institutional goals and activities with measurable metrics to advance excellence.

Our collective acknowledgment of this imperative is reflected in our new strategic plan, which identifies diversifying our faculty as a critical step toward advancing all aspects of our mission. Diversity and inclusion were two foundational principles that undergirded all aspects of our strategic plan. We clearly articulated their centrality across a range of objectives.

As part of the effort to enhance the student experience by increasing the cultural and global competencies of all students, the plan says we must "increase significantly the diversity of tenure-track faculty" by aggressively recruiting and retaining underrepresented minority faculty, particularly at the junior and midcareer ranks, with the goal of increasing the diversity of UMBC faculty to mirror the diversity of UMBC's student population.

To achieve a diverse and inclusive faculty, a university must create shared values around the importance of diversity and inclusion, expand and diversify the pool of qualified candidates, hire more women and minorities from those diverse pools, and create an inclusive climate that supports retention and advancement of diverse members once they join the faculty. We have shaped the culture and established our goals. Now we must deliver on the work, which requires sustained effort around recruitment, retention, and advancement of underrepresented minority faculty. In the sections that follow we share some of the policies and programmatic interventions from our expanded faculty diversity initiatives.

Recruitment
Improving the Faculty Search Process

Just as we had under ADVANCE, we revisited our faculty search processes and procedures to advance our diversity hiring. We took a fresh look at our Diversity Hiring Recruitment Plans that we require of each search committee before a search is authorized by the provost. In these plans, the search committee must outline their specific recruitment, advertising, and outreach activities to assemble a diverse pool. The majority of these plans had simply documented where a department would place the job advertisement (i.e., the *Chronicle of Higher Education*, disciplinary venues, listservs) or the conferences at which they would recruit. We realized that this was insufficient, so we adopted an approach that would be broader than a single search and make connections with prospective faculty for the long run through a more active, network-building outreach strategy.

The provost called this "faculty-field networking," in which departments engage in continuous and active recruitment. We would continue to attend and network at such diversity-targeted conferences as the SREB, the Society for the Advancement of Chicanos and Native Americans in Science, the Annual Biomedical Research Conference for Minority Students, the Annual Ford Foundation Fellows Meeting, and the Grace Hopper Celebration of Women in Computing Institute. We also expected UMBC faculty attending their disciplinary conferences to take and share information related to UMBC's faculty openings, including the Postdoctoral Fellowship for Faculty Diversity. We wanted all faculty to expand their networks and develop relationships with future prospective faculty in the field by visiting poster sessions and talks. We also directed search committees to do more to activate their own professional networks to share the job listing, so that for each search all faculty members, not simply one person, had the shared responsibility to distribute and actively recruit for the position. Departments are now using social media to stay connected with alumni and cost-effectively share job openings. As part of this social media strategy, we filmed a faculty recruitment video featuring a diverse range of newly hired faculty sharing why they chose to come to UMBC. Simultaneously, the provost and I began encouraging our departments to engage more with their alumni as part of a "hiring our own" approach. We are a top producer of underrepresented minorities who go on to earn PhDs in the natural sciences and engineering. Many go on to obtain faculty positions at prestigious universities. The question was, why not here at UMBC?

As part of a broader institutional strategy to craft job advertisements that are welcoming and inclusive and move beyond the traditional description of the job duties, we now ask search committees and departments to draft a job advertisement for review by the college and the Office of the Provost. We encourage search committees to think deliberately about whether or not their language is broad and inclusive, thereby producing a more diverse and interesting applicant pool. For example, in the History Department, looking for a Civil War historian produces a less diverse pool than searching for a professor of nineteenth-century US history. Search committees should demonstrate the commitment of the department, the college, and the institution to diversity and inclusive excellence throughout the ad. In STEM fields like mathematics and statistics, where there is not a research focus on diversity per se, this might include sharing information about the Meyerhoff Scholars Program and opportunities to mentor diverse undergraduates. The point here is for departments to think intentionally about how diversity and inclusive excellence is a central aspect of the work they do. We also signal our commitment to diversity and increase our insights about applicants for our faculty positions by requesting of all applicants a statement of commitment to inclusive excellence in higher education as part of their application materials. These statements are just as important as the research and teaching statements.

Finally, we have asked search committees and deans to place a stronger emphasis on ensuring fair, consistent, and transparent criteria and review processes. As part of the Diversity Hiring Recruitment Plan, search committees now describe their interview protocols and how they will evaluate applicants. We require committees to provide all candidates for on-campus interviews with contact information for UMBC's community-based faculty groups, allowing them to meet informally or have a phone conversation with them during their interview or later. The Office of the Provost charges each dean with ensuring that these plans are implemented as outlined. As an important component of this work, each dean leads an annual Implicit Bias and Expectation Setting workshop for all search committee and department chairs, another intervention developed under ADVANCE. Earlier in our work, the provost required implicit bias training for all search committee chairs. As discussed in the previous chapter, this training focuses on minimizing the impact of both gender and racial bias on faculty hiring. The dean provides participants with best practices for broadening a search and recruiting a diverse candidate pool and the development of transparent guidelines to ensure that search committees are consistently and fairly applied in the evaluation of each candidate.

In 2014, to bolster our faculty diversity recruitment initiative, we acquired Interfolio Faculty Search, an online interface that allows us to receive and review applications online. This software has revolutionized our data analytics through Interfolio's Equal Employment Opportunity questionnaire, which all applicants are prompted to voluntarily complete upon the submission of their application. This questionnaire collects gender, race, ethnicity, veteran, and disability status information from applicants. With Interfolio, for the first time ever, we had reliable data on the diversity of our applicant pools that could be disaggregated at the institutional, college, department, and search levels. In other words, we could now quantitatively measure our progress and make decisions based on data. Each dean monitors the diversity of the applicant pool for each faculty search at various stages in the search process, including the application close date, long list, short list, and on-campus interview list. The dean compares the diversity of these various pools with that of the PhD holders in a specific field as defined by the NSF's Annual Survey of Earned Doctorates. This review is one way for deans to ensure that search committees actually follow through with their Diversity Hiring Recruitment Plans and allows us to address issues during the search rather than after. In addition to monitoring the diversity of job applicant pools for faculty positions, Interfolio Faculty Search's online review and evaluation features increase transparency in the search committee's review of candidates.

STRIDE

Even with these changes, we needed more. We had to partner with all of our faculty, just as we had done under ADVANCE. At a fall 2013 meeting of the Executive Committee, members shared their concern that the majority of our faculty diversity initiative work was led by senior administrators (president, provost, vice provost for faculty affairs, and the deans) and underrepresented minority faculty, whether through the URM Executive Committee or the community-based faculty groups. They once again noted the excessive service burden and the cultural taxation that faculty of color face related to diversity work and argued that the burden had to be more widely shared. Our faculty peers from majority groups had to step up. This would require meaningful culture change and deeper work at the departmental level.

As a result of this conversation, the provost led a series of information-gathering visits to institutions across the country to learn about their approaches to faculty diversity. One such visit was to the University of Michigan in fall 2014. There we learned about STRIDE, which uses a peer education model in which highly respected faculty provide advice and counsel to deans, departments, and search committees on implicit bias and ways to recruit and ultimately hire a more diverse faculty. In spring 2014 we invited two Michigan STRIDE fellows to UMBC to conduct a workshop for senior administrators and select faculty. Following this visit, in spring 2015 the Executive Committee recommended to the provost that UMBC create its own STRIDE Committee to reach our faculty peers and help them engage in this work. The Executive Committee also voted that the program coordinator for faculty diversity serve as the director of UMBC STRIDE.[14]

Over the summer of 2015, the vice provost for faculty affairs, director of STRIDE, and deans worked together to identify the inaugural STRIDE fellows. Based on the recommendation of the Executive Committee, we looked for faculty who were well respected, were from "majority" groups, and already had a demonstrated commitment to diversity and inclusive excellence. Significantly, we were not looking for research expertise, just commitment. The Executive Committee wanted to send a strong message that regardless of one's teaching and research agenda at UMBC, we all have a shared role to engage in this work. After identifying four fellows, the provost sent invitations, and all agreed to participate. Our inaugural committee consisted of Chris Murphy, a white male full professor and then chair of psychology, who had successfully mentored and converted a postdoctoral fellow for faculty diversity; Kevin Omland, a white male full professor of biological sciences, who has a demonstrated track record of mentoring undergraduates and graduates from underrepresented backgrounds; Wayne Lutters, a white male associate professor of information systems, who was engaged with our ADVANCE work and our Center for Women in Technology undergraduate program; and Susan McDonough, a white female associate professor of history, who served as the inaugural president of UMBC's LGBTQ Faculty/Staff Association.

In fall 2015, the fellows traveled to the University of Michigan to meet with its STRIDE team and participate in a live STRIDE training. Following this visit, the STRIDE fellows spent the next year meeting biweekly to review UMBC's recruitment and retention data and to read and discuss literature on implicit bias and best practices, and they also invited faculty with expertise on diversity and inclusion in higher education to behind-closed-doors meetings to discuss the issues and strategize on how to implement the STRIDE approach. STRIDE also met with each community-based faculty group to learn more about their concerns and receive advice and guidance on the best approach to engaging with our faculty peers.

As part of the launching of UMBC STRIDE, we once again hosted the University of Michigan's Center for Research on Learning and Teaching (CRLT) Players on our campus to perform *Navigating Departmental Politics*.[15] This time, the performance focused on the dynamics of a search committee deliberating applicants and demonstrated the ways in which gender, racial, ethnic, ability, and rank-related implicit biases can derail the search process. As they did for ADVANCE, having the CRLT Players provided another opportunity to bring the entire campus community together to discuss and highlight the importance of recruiting and retaining a diverse faculty and to introduce the new STRIDE initiative. Many institutions do not have the level of commitment to faculty diversity on the part of the president and provost that we have at UMBC. I gave remarks after the performance and then participated in the facilitated discussion to reinforce how important I felt this work is to our institution. Afterward, the CRLT Players artistic director said that this was the first time that a president had participated so meaningfully in one of their performances.

Following this performance, STRIDE fellows began its direct work with their faculty peers. UMBC STRIDE developed a series of focused conversations around the recruitment process: Developing an Effective Diversity Hiring Recruitment Plan, Creating Shared Evaluation Criteria, Best Practices for Reviewing Applications, and Best Practices for Inclusive Interviewing. They have also developed a retention-focused conversation on inclusive mentoring. These focused conversations are open to the entire campus, are highly engaging, and focus on how to operationalize a search to increase the diversity of the applicant pool and the likelihood that we will hire diverse colleagues. Most importantly, STRIDE fellows position themselves not as experts but as a peer resource. Upon invitation, STRIDE fellows provide targeted consultations to search committees to work on specific aspects of their search, whether that be developing an active recruitment strategy, an inclusive job ad, shared evaluation criteria, or an interview strategy. In the 2017/18 academic year, STRIDE facilitated twenty-one such consultations. Using Interfolio EEO data, we are able to see an increase in the diversity of the applicant pool of those search committees that have worked directly with STRIDE. Entering its fourth year, STRIDE has expanded to six fellows and is now disseminating its work through conferences and publications.

Postdoctoral Fellows for Faculty Diversity Program

We were disappointed that none of our postdoctoral fellows from our second cohort (2013–15) converted to faculty positions at UMBC. The Executive Committee suggested that deans talk to their department chairs to increase their understanding of the way the Postdoctoral Fellowship for Faculty Diversity could be used as part of their broader diversity recruitment strategy. That is, they could take active measures to recruit applicants in their field and, if awarded a fellowship, to mentor them well and convert them to faculty members. As part of these efforts, we recognized that we needed to strengthen our applicant review and selection process and do more to support the postdocs during their fellowships and after. To that end, we worked with the dean of the CAHSS, where all but one of the postdocs thus far had been hosted, to develop a comprehensive internal selection process that we shared with departments. This document provided deadlines, evaluation metrics, and protocols for departments, deans, and the selection committee to use when reviewing applications, interviewing, and selecting finalists. We use the evaluation criteria to assess applicants based on scholarly promise and departmental readiness to support a postdoctoral fellow based on (1) programmatic fit (needs and goals of department(s)/program(s)), (2) availability of an appropriate mentor(s), (3) departmental and programmatic commitment to program purpose and goals, and (4) proposed plans for office space and for inclusion of fellow into departmental/programmatic culture and activities.

We also developed a comprehensive onboarding process for departments (chairs, mentors, and administrative support staff) and the postdoctoral fellows to ensure that the fellows' transition to campus is welcoming and seamless. Relatedly, the URM Executive Committee required that the postdocs and their mentors develop Faculty Development Plans each semester that outline the fellow's research, teaching, and professional development goals with benchmarks and timetables. At the end of each semester, the mentors and postdocs individually complete a progress report. This new reporting mechanism has been so helpful in supporting new postdocs that some departments, such as psychology, have adopted some of the principles to mentor new assistant professors. Finally, working with the dean of the CAHSS, we developed and implemented a conversion policy that details how departments can convert a postdoc to a tenure-track assistant professor position within their department. Conversions typically happen during the second year, but the policy allows for early conversion as well. As a result of our implementation of these changes to the postdoctoral fellowship, we successfully converted all three fellows for cohort 3 (2015–17) to tenure-track positions at UMBC, and in 2017 we welcomed seven new fellows in cohort 4, our largest group of fellows to date.

CNMS Pre-Professoriate Program

To date, all but one of the postdoctoral fellows for faculty diversity have been hosted by our CAHSS. The dean of our College of Natural and Mathematical Sciences, Bill LaCourse, along with Executive Committee members from the natural sciences, recognized that this model did not work well in laboratory sciences. As a result, in 2016 the dean and the provost partnered to pilot the CNMS Pre-Professoriate Fellows Program. Modeled on the principles of the Postdoctoral Fellowship for Faculty Diversity, the CNMS Pre-Professoriate Program is an open search within a specific department. Fellows, who might have already completed a postdoctoral fellowship, are hired as a research assistant professor and receive a starting stipend of $50,000, health benefits, $5,000 for conference travel and preparation of scholarly work, up to $5,000 in instrument services, up to $10,000 for supplies/consumables, lab space, office space with computer, library access, and other privileges at the university. During the two-year term of appointment, most of the fellow's time is devoted to pursuing research. In addition, the fellow teaches one course (one semester only) per year. Highly experienced research and teaching mentors meet with the fellow regularly to provide guidance on developing a pedagogically sound teaching philosophy and plan and improving the skills needed to pursue an academic research career, including proposal and manuscript writing and technical presentation skills. Fellows also participate in professional development opportunities across the campus. At the end of the two-year fellowship, there is also a conversion process to a tenure-track position at UMBC. In 2017, the Department of Biological Sciences piloted the first search and hired a Hispanic male fellow. From this same pool of applicants, they also identified a female African American assistant professor and then hired her. In 2018, the Departments of Biological Sciences, Chemistry and Biochemistry, and Physics all participated in searches for a Pre-Professoriate fellow.[16]

Retention and Advancement
Eminent Scholar

The Executive Committee had already expanded the Eminent Scholar Mentoring Program developed under ADVANCE for women assistant professors to all newly hired assistant professors from underrepresented minority groups. After studying the impact of the program, in 2015, they saw how effective this program was and advised the provost to provide this opportunity to all newly hired assistant professors at UMBC regardless of their background. The institutionalization of this program is an example of how everyone benefits from a practice originally implemented for a specific group. Now, all newly hired assistant professors are automatically provided $3,000 in their start-up funds to support participation in this program. Working with their department chair and dean, the new junior faculty member identifies a prospective outside mentor, and then the dean of the college sends an invitation to the mentor explaining the program purpose and introducing our faculty member.

Although the Eminent Scholar Mentoring Program is implemented by each college, the Office of the Provost provides oversight by requesting that the junior faculty member submit a report at the conclusion of the formal mentor relationship. This report includes information about the activities during the Eminent Scholar mentor's visit to our campus and our junior faculty members' visit to the mentor's campus. We also ask the mentee to describe the benefits of their participation in this program and specify plans for future interactions with the mentor beyond the formal two-year funded period. These reports are an invaluable source of information because they provide us with concrete data on the impact of the program in helping our assistant professors establish themselves within their fields beyond UMBC. From these reports we have learned that the mentors have provided feedback on grants, given career-life balance advice, conducted experiments at their facilities, nominated our faculty to serve on panels or give keynote lectures, collaborated on research, and introduced our faculty to colleagues in the field. Finally, while the Eminent Scholar Mentoring Program helps with the retention of our faculty once hired, as with all of our retention initiatives, it is an excellent recruitment tool when trying to persuade a candidate to accept our offer.

Community-Based Faculty Groups

We are acutely aware that social and academic isolation remains a critical factor in determining whether a faculty member joins us and stays at UMBC. In many departments, we are still trying to hire our first underrepresented minority faculty member. It is extremely important that we support and provide a source of community to these faculty. Just as WISE provided a support group for women in science and engineering departments who might be the "only one," community-based faculty affinity groups have organized to support other minority faculty across departments. In addition to WISE, we have the CAHSS Black Faculty Committee, the Latino-Hispanic Faculty Association, the Asian / Asian American Faculty Association, and the LGBTQ Faculty/Staff Association, as well as the CAHSS Women's Faculty Network. In addition to meeting with prospective UMBC faculty during their interviews, these groups provide members with peer mentoring, research collaborations, professional development opportunities, and support during the promotion and tenure process; organize symposia, teaching circles, and writing groups; and also advocate for UMBC students. As you can see, these groups provide a supportive network for their members that is invaluable and should be fostered on any campus.[17]

Faculty ADVANCEment Workshops

As we did under our ADVANCE grant, the Office of the Provost hosts Faculty ADVANCEment Workshops on a range of issues related to faculty career success. Two workshops we hold every year are on the tenure process and the process of promotion to full professor. The provost and I believe that we must signal the importance of promoting transparency in these processes so that everyone is informed about the steps they need to take to be successful. The provost attends both workshops, offers welcoming remarks, and shares his perspective on these processes. The vice provost for faculty affairs then provides an institutional overview of all of the review committees and steps associated with tenure and/or promotion. The deans also attend, offering their expectations and advice on the process. A panel of newly tenured and/or promoted faculty share their experiences, tips, and advice having just gone through the process. Additionally, we host workshops on other topics our faculty propose. Recently, we have conducted workshops entitled Curating Your Digital Footprint, Developing Your Research, and Tips for Effective and Efficient Teaching, as well as one on the Eminent Scholar Mentoring Program.

External Professional Development Resources

Since 2016, the Office of the Provost has sponsored the participation of women and underrepresented minority faculty, especially assistant professors who have already had their third-year contract renewal, in the National Center for Faculty Development and Diversity's (NCFDD) Faculty Success Program. The NCFDD is a national organization that provides mentoring and professional development resources, particularly for the advancement of underrepresented faculty in the academy. The Faculty Success Program is a twelve-week intensive virtual writing boot camp that helps tenured and tenure-track faculty "to improve research productivity through intense accountability, coaching, and peer support and to propel their work-life balance and personal growth to a whole new level."[18] Our faculty members who have participated in this program have told us that it helped them build realistic schedules, helped them achieve a better balance between work and wellness, and showed them how to build accountability into activities like research. Overall, all of our participants have shared that this program has helped them feel less overwhelmed by the demands of research, teaching, and service.

Because of the success of this program, in 2017 the CAHSS Black Faculty Committee recommended to the provost that UMBC secure an institutional membership to the NCFDD, so that all of our faculty, postdocs, and graduate students can take advantage of these external mentoring and career development resources. Soon after, we obtained an institutional membership. These groups now have access to Monday Motivator newsletters, opportunities to participate in fourteen-day writing challenges, a core curriculum that covers ten key skills for success, webinars with guest experts, and also a dissertation success curriculum. And, as with other programmatic initiatives, our NCFDD institutional membership likewise serves as a recruitment tool.

Expanding On-Ramps to Full Professor

Beyond ensuring that our faculty are retained and stay at UMBC, we are also committed to ensuring that all of our faculty have the opportunity to reach their full career potential. We want all of our faculty to become full professors and even consider leadership positions. Our Family Support Plan, discussed in the previous chapter, has been a game changer in helping our junior faculty achieve tenure while balancing the demands of work and family. From looking at our time-in-rank data, however, we noticed that women faculty, across all colleges, were staying in the rank of associate professor much longer than their male counterparts. We discovered that women still faced invisible gender barriers, often in the form of disproportionate familial caregiving responsibilities. These barriers led to "productivity gaps" in their research agenda, which have the cumulative effect of stalling their progression to full professor. Our underrepresented minority faculty have told us that they too experience productivity gaps. They identify excessive service burdens, often in the form of a disproportionate amount of mentoring our students of color and also isolation, which can often preclude their inclusion in research collaborations.

In 2015, we received funding from the NSF's Early-Concept Grants for Exploratory Research program, to pilot "'On Ramps' to Full Professor: Institutional Support for Post–Family Leave Faculty

Research Reintegration." We identified a group of post-tenure women STEM associate professors who had utilized the Family Support Plan at any point during their careers to apply for research acceleration grants in the form of course releases, research graduate student support, domestic and international travel grants, or research and grant writing support to help accelerate research productivity. Eight women received awards, and we are tracking the progress of the women in the three years since the award. As with other ADVANCE initiatives, we are currently studying this program's impact for a potential expansion to support the career advancement of our underrepresented minority faculty.

Success Is Never Final

What would it take to make UMBC a "destination" for underrepresented minority faculty and not just another campus? The recruitment process is not just about outreach, broadening the pool, and hiring. It importantly also involves visible, robust, and multifaceted approaches that create an environment in which faculty of all backgrounds are included, valued, and thriving. The richness of such a climate pays dividends by creating a place that other faculty will seek to be a part of, giving us opportunities to recruit, retain, and advance a diverse teaching and research faculty. The benefits accrue to our students and also the larger Baltimore-Washington region.

This is not easy work. We do have to continually look in the mirror, have difficult conversations, and have the courage to act. University leaders, furthermore, cannot do this alone or in a top-down fashion. The whole campus must be engaged in the effort. At UMBC, we have instituted what Susan Sturm has called "integrated responsibility for diversifying the whole structure."[19] That is, instead of having an office of diversity or an office of minority affairs and, with it, a vice president or vice provost for diversity, we have integrated the responsibility for encouraging, enacting, and sustaining diversity into the mission of each of our administrative offices.

Where does one start? Conversations, listening, weighing evidence, being honest with oneself, creating buy-in from stakeholders, developing allies, and changing the culture. It requires sustained effort over a long period of time. However, the benefits of this work, hard as it may be, far outweigh the costs of inaction.

13

Success Is Never Final

"Whatever we wear, wherever we go, yes means yes, and no means no!"

I could hear the students chanting as they climbed the stairs. The chants grew louder as they reached the tenth floor and then turned toward the president's conference room. I had been informed that the crowd at the protest across campus had spontaneously decided to march to the Administration Building and confront me.

"What do you want to do?" I was asked. "Should we lock the building?"

"Let them come," I said. "I'll invite them to my conference room and talk with them."

What had prompted this protest and confrontation was a lawsuit filed in federal court that alleged that UMBC and others had mishandled cases of sexual assault. Now, students packed the conference room, with more overflowing into the hallways. As I entered, I thought back to the only other time we had had such a scene in my thirty years at UMBC. That time, in my first month at UMBC, the protest had been about race. The takeover of the tenth floor would last five days because the chancellor and the protestors would not talk to each other. Could things be different this time if we stayed true to our values? What if we listened respectfully and began having those difficult conversations that had been central to other efforts to move our campus forward?

Listening Respectfully

Because higher education matters and sexual assault can upend students' lives, our universities must be safe places for all members of our community. We have to redesign courses, improve teaching and learning, support students academically, and provide opportunities for experiential learning. We must create an inclusive campus, diversify the faculty, and work to ensure that our students graduate. We must also embrace a campus culture that is respectful in every way. And that respect must be extended to all persons regardless of sex, gender, gender identity or expression, or sexual orientation. That respect must include opportunities to participate fully in the life of the campus. It certainly must include feeling safe and actually being physically safe.

In 2011, through what has come to be known as the "Dear Colleague Letter," the US Department of Education issued new guidance on the implementation of Title IX, the way universities respond to reports of sexual harassment and sexual violence, the way we conduct Title IX investigations, the obligations of faculty and staff to report incidents, and the appropriate supports and resources that should be available for students on their campuses.[1] More than that, the Obama administration in 2014, under the leadership of Vice President Joe Biden, pressed us all in the higher education community to confront fully the plague of sexual assault on our campuses. As did other institutions, UMBC responded and took action. Over the next several years, we shifted our Title IX adjudication processes from student judicial review to a review process overseen by faculty and staff. We added a new Title IX coordinator and then hired additional attorneys to work as civil rights investigators. We revised our policies and procedures in accordance with the applicable federal, state, and local laws and regulations, as well as University System of Maryland policies, so that they reflected what we believed was best practice and consistent with our campus culture. We trained hundreds of faculty and staff.

When it came to policy, process, and staffing, we had been taking necessary steps and were meeting the compliance requirements. We thought we were also making positive changes to make our campus safer and ensure that our Title IX processes were fair. But we had not done everything we needed to. That was clear now from the situation in front of us.

The long-overdue #MeToo movement is empowering individuals to speak out on sexual assault. Many have brought to light individual cases of sexual harassment and sexual assault that have raised our awareness and emboldened others, providing them the courage and strength to speak out about their experiences. These conversations are difficult. For those who have experienced the trauma of sexual assault, it is often deeply painful to revisit the trauma, to speak about it, and to make what many consider a very private matter public. And yet, the movement has created a space for these conversations, which are necessary to reshape our culture in the long run, so that survivors are empowered to report sexual assaults and we can work to reduce the incidence of sexual harassment and sexual violence in the future.

We were now having that difficult conversation in my conference room. The students read a statement and a list of demands. I sat and listened attentively, knowing not only that all the eyes in the room were on me but also that, in this era of smartphones and social media, the confrontation now happening in my conference room was being "live-streamed" for all the world to see. One misstep would be costly not only for me personally but also for the institution.

Now more than ever, in a room of students who were confused, were angry, or simply didn't trust the university (meaning me, because the buck stops with me), I needed to be authentic, humble, thoughtful, and responsive. Looking into the faces of my students, I knew two things: first, these were young, intelligent thinkers who were fighting for a just cause but had been led to believe that the university had done something wrong; second, most of the students were remarkably respectful and trying to understand the issues. Only a couple of people in the room crossed the line between civility and rudeness. After the meeting broke up, some of the students apologized for the rudeness of some students. But others came up to me and asked, "We know you, why would you do us like this?"

When confronted in this way, our first response is naturally "fight or flight," to be defensive and combative or to give in. Some leaders avoid facing such a situation by simply refusing to meet with protestors; others make promises that defuse the immediate situation, even though they may not be the best actions for the long run. But responses such as these in the heat of the moment do not really make conflict go away. Indeed, they often deepen the conflict. In such a moment, it is best to embrace the conflict, to "own it" as it were. By doing so respectfully and interactively, we shift from "conflict" to "conversation." This is perhaps a painful conversation, but nonetheless one that offers the hope that something good will come of it, that the work will follow, and that issues will be addressed.

So, I took a deep breath. I told the students around me that I was proud of them for caring about these issues, the university, and one another. I told them I was impressed by their courage to speak truth to power. I apologized, saying that I had thought we had been doing all we could to address sexual assault but that we had not done enough. "Whenever you have more than a hundred students in your conference room, clearly something isn't right." At a minimum, I continued, we had not been communicating to students what we were doing, and perhaps there were other things we could and should be doing differently. The list of demands included practical suggestions that we would consider implementing. Perhaps there were even more suggestions for us to consider as well if we provided opportunities for everyone on campus to speak. I told them that I was listening, that the administration and our campus leaders were listening. Indeed, I mentioned that I had already met for several hours the day before with "We Believe You," a survivors group on campus, and others and that we would have a town hall—a "listening session"—that would provide an opportunity for anyone to speak later in the week.

Engaging Productively

No matter how healthy our campuses are, we are always just one event—for example, a lawsuit—away from protests and crisis. They happen. What defines us is not whether crises happen but how we respond to them. Indeed, the same is true of both crises and opportunities. We began this book with a discussion of how we responded when presented with national media exposure in the wake of an unexpected basketball victory. We came together as a campus—leaders, staff, faculty, students, and alumni—to communicate who we were as an institution and why people should also pay attention to what we deliver for students academically. Now, we had to come together again. We had lost trust, and we needed to rebuild it by talking with people and also providing productive ways to include and involve members of our community in the work. How do we do that?

First, listen. Do not turn the students away. Be calm, bring a thick skin, be respectful, and listen. Welcome students with humility. Authentically praise them for caring about the community and its members. Assert that the safety and well-being of our students is our highest priority and that students should call us on it when we are not successful. Then, listen to what they say. Be honest and transparent in your response. Tell them that this is a good first conversation and that, together, we must take the time and create the space for people to talk more, to give voice to their experiences, to identify and name the problem, and to begin to explore what changes could address their concerns and benefit the entire campus.

Second, look in the mirror and be honest about what you see. Be clear about what the problem is and in naming the problem. Gather information, data, and evidence about the problem and potential solutions. Bring in an outside group for an external review, if that would be helpful for evidence gathering and a candid, objective statement of the problem and issues. Be transparent about that information so that all stakeholders on campus understand the issue in its many dimensions. Engage those stakeholders as the campus struggles together, weighs facts, and discusses possible courses of action.

Third, have the difficult conversations. Here's the challenge: information is leaked, people have opinions, and social media amplifies accusations without pausing for evidence and reason. However, evidence and reason have to prevail. By having conversations in town halls, with groups, and with individuals, we can gradually ground discussions so that we all agree on the same set of facts and the same set of potential future actions. It will often take time to get there. There will be people who are oppositional and will need more time to let go of conflict. But it is worth it for the long run to invest the time in these conversations so that conflict is channeled into constructive work.

Fourth, involve people in the work. Identify those among staff, faculty, and students who are willing to be allies. I don't mean this cynically. I don't mean that these are allies in a "fight." These are allies who can help shape the agenda, provide honest feedback, champion the effort, engage in and even lead the work, and bring others into it. When you are meeting with various groups, look for those who are analytical or innovative, have the courage to compromise, or are willing to work with the administration to develop and implement solutions. This is critically important. The president may be the initial target of a protest and, ultimately, responsible for the campus, but for real progress to happen the whole campus community has to own and work on a problem—particularly one as challenging as sexual assault—if there is to be lasting change for the better.

Fifth, stick with it for the long run. Positive outcomes are rarely achieved overnight. It takes hard, sustained work. It takes "grit." It takes knowing that things will be okay when the whole campus is involved and we are committed to change.

Conversely, there are things that presidents and other campus leaders should not do. Do not hide from students or turn them away. Do not promise things you will not follow through on. Do not compromise on matters that are legally nonnegotiable, like privacy and confidentiality. Do not scapegoat. Many protests demand that people be fired. It is important that we do not indulge that impulse. Just as we approach problems with evidence, reason, and fairness, we also approach personnel decisions with the same measure of evidence, reason, and fairness. Do not in the heat of the moment read the negative emails, text messages, social media, and media accounts because they will only pull you down at a time when you need all the energy you can muster. Instruct your staff to just bring you messages when there is something positive or constructive that will help you move forward.

Balancing Considerations

I might have avoided the protest, the confrontation in my conference room, and the painful conversation that ensued had I immediately acceded to demands made over the weekend that I fire several of our colleagues, but there are some things that are nonnegotiable, including personnel decisions. After we received the lawsuit on a Friday, we began to see reactions to it on social media that same day. It was clear that many were coalescing around the narrative in the lawsuit. I began talking with my senior leadership team, and we agreed that it made sense to call a meeting of our student leaders. This would be an opportunity for us to ask them why so many students assumed that the lawsuit was based on valid claims, why they were so angry, and why so many jumped to the conclusion that a letter from the administration to campus noting that we had held Title IX training was just part of a "cover-up." It would also be an opportunity for students to offer suggestions. That Sunday, I met with leaders from the Student Government Association, the Graduate Student Association, the We Believe You campus survivors group, the Pan-Hellenic Council, student-athletes, and residential students. They made a number of suggestions and demands at the Sunday meeting that were later also included in the list of demands presented by protestors on Monday. One of the demands was that I immediately fire several colleagues involved in the Title IX process. The students wanted to see immediate action, and if I had agreed to do that, there would not have been a protest on Monday. However, I made it clear that no one would be made a scapegoat and that we would not make impulsive personnel decisions, particularly if they would be based on claims that were not true.

Several presidents contacted me after the protest, trying to make me feel better, saying that it was clear to them that I had the trust of students broadly because even in the midst of this intense anger no one called for me to resign. That didn't make me feel much better, because the students instead called for us to make rash and unfair personnel decisions about our colleagues. Presidents need to be prepared for that moment when some group on campus demands that someone should be fired. In some cases, that will be the appropriate action. In other cases, though, it won't. And so I said to the students when they demanded action that we do not make personnel decisions that way. But the students were not yet willing to trust me or yield. They believed they had the right to know everything. And so the protest the next day went forward.

At my lowest point in the midst of all of this, I was very discouraged that more students did not trust me and trust that we were doing the right thing. In this moment, it was quite difficult to keep silent about confidential information that students did not have about the cases in the lawsuit and the news. However, confidentiality is critical to protect people involved in these cases, and we have a legal obligation to respect that. It became clear to me that we had not done what was necessary to educate the broad student body on Title IX processes and what we were all expected to do to ensure fair investigations. Without that education, they did not

272 THE EMPOWERED UNIVERSITY

understand that we could not simply expel students from campus because they had been accused, but that due process required that sanctions, like expulsion, could only be implemented if the accused were found responsible. An instructive example for institutions was the infamous Duke lacrosse case. In that instance, three Duke lacrosse players were accused of rape and arrested. Later, when they were exonerated, the players sued Duke for its actions during the incident and won a reported $60 million in damages.

There is a delicate balance between ensuring that our responses to reports of sexual assault are trauma informed and ensuring that they are also informed by due process considerations for all of the individuals involved. After the protest, our student newspaper, the *Retriever*, discovered information related to one of the cases referenced in the lawsuit and published it. University administrators had already been aware of this information but, because of our adherence to requirements for privacy and confidentiality, had not been in a position to speak about it publicly. The article was published the day of the listening session. Despite the campus now having this new information related to the university's proactive actions, we were still being criticized for protecting students who had been accused to the detriment of those who had come forward to report sexual assault, as many students had not yet read the article. The typically private balancing act that the university is tasked with when a report of sexual violence is made was now taking place in a public forum. Once students finally saw the new information, they understood the situation better. Prior to that, they had questioned our commitment to supporting survivors and creating a safe place in which students can learn and thrive. At the core, they questioned our values.

Communicating Clearly

Communication is central to the health of a campus, whether it is in the midst of a conflict or crisis or not. In this particular instance, we, as campus leaders, had believed that we were making significant progress in improving our Title IX policies and processes. We assumed that the work we were doing and the training offered to staff, faculty, and students would be enough to let students know we were taking this matter very seriously. But we should have been more proactive and transparent. Those who are not involved in a process do not know the details of the work. In the absence of information, they can and will fill the void with conjecture or misinformation. It was our job to make sure there was no void to be filled.

One lesson that we have learned is that it is not enough to invite someone to participate in a single session or training. We have to make sure they attend, and we have to ensure that the information is shared on an ongoing basis. Currently, incoming first-year undergraduate, graduate, and transfer students have the opportunity to take online training related to issues of sexual assault, prior to the start of the fall and spring semesters. This online training has been strongly encouraged but is not mandatory. During summer and winter orientation, both students and parents participate in an in-person session, hosted collaboratively by representatives from the Title IX Office, University Police, Student Conduct, and Student Affairs. During these in-person sessions, students are provided with an overview of the university's sexual misconduct policy and procedures, as well as what constitutes prohibited conduct, the definition of consent, the impact of alcohol and drug use related to sexual activity, and safe and positive options for bystander intervention. A one-time training related to these issues, over the course of a student's career with the university, is not enough. We are currently at a place where we must move beyond compliance and seek to be more aligned with best practices as they relate to educating our students and our entire campus community. The training and education must be more in-depth to deepen understanding of the processes and procedures in place to address, prevent, and remedy incidents of sexual violence and discrimination.

Ironically, on the very day that the federal lawsuit was filed we were holding our fourth annual full-day training on Title IX provided by two national experts from an outside law firm. The juxtaposition of that scene (with 125 faculty and staff deeply involved in discussions about our Title IX processes) to the scene a few days later (with 125 students angry about our handling of and response to sexual assault cases) was jarring and spoke volumes. At the training, staff talked about the progress we have been making in handling sexual assault cases. At the protest, students condemned us for inadequate handling of sexual assault cases. Further, we sent a letter to the entire campus the day the lawsuit was filed. We noted that we had held training that very day. I received positive messages from several staff and faculty about the letter, noting that it was a model that other campus leaders should follow. During the protest, I learned that others had found the letter insulting, even arguing that the training had been staged deliberately as part of a larger "cover-up."

We were not communicating well. Whether we were right or wrong, we had to admit that everything was not right when there were such deeply held, diametrically opposed views. Communicating to and with the campus, listening in town halls, engaging with groups and organizations, talking with those who wanted to understand and work productively on solutions—these are the central features of the work that is needed to heal the divide, bridge the deep differences, and find a common path forward.

We spent a challenging week improving our communication to restore trust and lay the groundwork for collective action. This began by listening: After the lawsuit was filed on a Friday, a campus survivors group met with me for several hours over that weekend. I listened to their experiences, concerns, and suggestions. On Monday, student protestors confronted me in my office, presenting a list of demands. I listened further and said we would be taking constructive steps. On Thursday, we held a campus listening session, during which students and staff spoke about their experiences for two hours. The session was both painful and powerful, helping us to understand better the problem of sexual assault, how our campus handles Title IX cases, and what we might do differently.

During this week, we met with a broad range of campus groups and individuals, including leaders from the We Believe You campus survivors group, student government, and the Pan-Hellenic Council. I met with the head of the Women's Center, the chair of the Gender, Women's, and Sexuality Studies Department, the head of the WISE group, and senior campus leaders for diversity. After the listening session, I then announced the appointment of a team to continue the work we had begun. That Friday, I was joined at a meeting of the USM Board of Regents by leaders from UMBC's student government, the Graduate Student Association, the campus survivors group, and the Women's Center. We all spoke about how we were working together to find a way to move forward.

It had been a challenging week, but we were in a different place at the end of the week than we were at the beginning. We had begun the work of healing the campus and improving both climate and safety.

Acting Together

While the protest was sparked by a lawsuit, it brought forth emotions held just below the surface for a long time. The silver lining for us was that we as a campus began to realize that our society's "rape culture" has had an even deeper hold on our campuses than we had understood, and we soon agreed on next steps. The students I met with suggested a listening session where survivors could talk. I was not to respond but just listen, so I sat on the stage with other campus leaders as students gave voice to their experiences and ideas. It was the second most painful moment of this period but was handled masterfully by the president of the Student Government Association and the vice president of the survivors group, with the help of leaders from other student groups, including athletics and Greek life. They had determined the guiding principles for the event, including the time limit for how long individuals could talk. Students and staff spoke. Tears flowed. Hearts and minds were opened.

While we would not make impulsive personnel decisions, we had practical steps that we could begin to take immediately:

1. Require mandatory training of all faculty, staff, and students about sexual assault prevention, reporting, and Title IX obligations.
2. Seek advice from colleagues on campus who are substantive experts on gender, sexual assault, mental health, and related issues (e.g., faculty in the Department of Gender and Women's Studies, staff in UMBC's Women's Center and Counseling Center, student affairs professionals).
3. Work with students to identify a third party—an external group—to evaluate our processes, identify what is working well and what isn't, and make recommendations for improvements we should implement.
4. Organize a walk-around on campus with students to identify those places, such as walkways near woods, that are potentially dangerous and could be made safer through additional lighting and other improvements.
5. Change our campus ID cards to include information on what to do in an emergency.
6. Improve our signage with regard to these issues around campus.
7. Address the deeply felt need for twenty-four-hour service for health and counseling needs.
8. Work with nearby hospitals to improve our ability to respond to sexual assault.

Success is never final. The moment we believe we have arrived is the moment we begin going backward. We know we can always be better, so all of this is work we must and will engage in. Moreover, both the good times and the challenging times provide opportunities to reaffirm who we are and what we envision for the future. In all of this work, a realistic but positive attitude is critical.

A Great Challenge

We have talked throughout this book about how we have worked to create an "empowered university," one in which we, as a campus community, develop a shared culture, enable broad leadership, and support students and colleagues. We have related stories that illustrate how we have taken a hard look in the mirror, asked how we can be or do better, gathered and analyzed data, held those important (and sometimes difficult) conversations, established a shared sense of both the problems and the possibilities, and enabled colleagues to take the lead in developing and implementing new, innovative practices that work.

We have embraced shared governance and shared leadership. Many people talk about shared governance; we have worked to make this concept a reality. Further, we have developed pathways and opportunities for our colleagues with experience in shared governance to move into campus administrative positions. Many articulate a campus vision; we have also aimed to be a place where people who share our academic and community values thrive and take leadership roles. We have worked to develop leaders at all levels of our campus, through training programs and through practice.

Our efforts have led to considerable success, and we are very proud of our alumni and the impact of their contributions to our society. We have produced graduates who teach in economically disadvantaged schools in Baltimore City; go on to earn the PhD or the MD-PhD and then secure positions at institutions from Duke to Johns Hopkins, from Penn to Harvard; or become leaders, like the director of the Johns Hopkins Applied Physics Laboratory, the president of Clemson University, the new speaker of the Maryland House of Delegates, and the US surgeon general.

We are also very proud of our colleagues, and just as they have engaged deeply in the advancement of our campus, we have worked hard to support their success in order to "empower" our university and to provide an environment in which they could reach their own professional goals. As we have succeeded in our work, other institutions that have understood our success have begun to recruit away an increasing number of our colleagues. Some years ago, the chair of our mathematics department was hired to chair that department at Carnegie Mellon. Similarly, our chair of information science joined Rochester Institute of Technology as dean of computing and information science, before accepting a similar position at Penn State. Our first woman dean of engineering recently moved to Virginia Tech to become the dean of engineering there. Our vice president for research went on to become provost at American University. One of our premier historians has just accepted a full professorship at MIT.

We acknowledge that we often do not have the resources to keep some of our colleagues when their professional aspirations take them on the path to great positions elsewhere. It is our obligation to also point out this loss of talent from UMBC and the state to our friends in the Maryland General Assembly. As George LaNoue has argued in his book *Improbable Excellence*, we must work to obtain the equitable funding per student we need from the state of Maryland to recruit and retain great faculty and administrators who, in turn, inspire our students and keep us on the cutting edge of teaching and research. We have been encouraged by the efforts of the current governor and the assembly to increase our operating budget per student. We have experienced much of our success by leveraging state appropriations and the substantial capital investment the state has made in our campus.

While some colleagues will choose to pursue great opportunities elsewhere, we can continue to be successful in recruiting and retaining our very best colleagues who embrace our culture, share our fundamental values, and support our mission. So, just as we are very proud of our alumni for their contributions after leaving UMBC, we are also proud when our colleagues receive opportunities and do the same. We are delighted to prepare those who go on to leadership positions on our campus or at other institutions. We are playing our part in preparing the next, diverse generation of leaders in academia who embrace inclusive excellence. It's a great challenge to have.

Notes

Preface

1. Eric Weiner, *The Geography of Bliss: One Grump's Search for the Happiest Places in the World* (New York: Twelve, 2008), 3.

Chapter 1. And Then We Did It

1. https://twitter.com/sethdavishoops/status/974821766546812928.
2. https://twitter.com/bleachrpreachr/status/974839365951160321.
3. https://twitter.com/jonheyman/status/974841873515864065.
4. https://ftw.usatoday.com/2018/03/virginia-umbc-university-maryland-baltimore-county-upset-march-madness-ncaa-tourament-twitter-funny.
5. https://twitter.com/danrather/status/974852496152604677.
6. https://news.umbc.edu/usnews2019/.
7. National Science Foundation, National Center for Science and Engineering Statistics, WebCASPAR. https://ncsesdata.nsf.gov/webcaspar/.
8. https://cwit.umbc.edu/.
9. https://sherman.umbc.edu/.
10. https://careers.umbc.edu/files/2018/03/2016-2017UMBCCareerOutcomes.pdf.
11. https://news.umbc.edu/umbc-leads-nation-in-producing-african-american-undergraduates-who-pursue-m-d-ph-d-s/.
12. https://issues.org/toward-a-more-diverse-research-community-models-of-success/.
13. https://chess.umbc.edu/.
14. https://news.umbc.edu/umbc-cyber-dawgs-top-2017-national-collegiate-cyber-defense-competition/.
15. http://www.theacc.com/news/2014/12/12/548b8904e4b00463dae48aee_131480975585167515.aspx.
16. www.washingtonpost.com/news/soccer-insider/wp/2014/12/09/who-is-umbc-college-cup-semifinalists-thats-who/.
17. Freeman A. Hrabowski III, "The Secret behind the Greatest Upset in College Basketball History," *Atlantic*, March 18, 2018, www.theatlantic.com/education/archive/2018/03/the-secret-behind-the-greatest-upset-in-college-basketball-history/555872/.
18. Hrabowski, "Secret behind the Greatest Upset."
19. www.nytimes.com/2018/03/17/us/politics/umbc-basketball.html.
20. www.acenet.edu/news-room/Pages/UMBC-President-Freeman-Hrabowski-to-Receive-ACE-Lifetime-Achievement-Award.aspx.
21. www.washingtonpost.com/sports/colleges/umbc-president-is-an-activist-innovator-and-mega-nerd-his-latest-role-giddy-basketball-fan/2018/03/17/bf5b88f6-2a15-11e8-b79d-f3d931db7f68_story.html.

22. www.baltimoresun.com/news/opinion/editorial/bs-ed-0317-umbc
-virginia-ncaa-20180317-story.html.

23. www.nytimes.com/2018/03/17/us/politics/umbc-basketball.html.

24. www.washingtonpost.com/sports/colleges/umbc-president-is-an-activist
-innovator-and-mega-nerd-his-latest-role-giddy-basketball-fan/2018/03/17
/bf5b88f6-2a15-11e8-b79d-f3d931db7f68_story.html.

Chapter 2. Higher Education Matters

1. Claudia Goldin and Lawrence Katz, *The Race between Education and Technology* (Cambridge, MA: Belknap Press of Harvard University Press, 2008). Goldin and Katz note that the "reason for the secular increase in college rates is mainly due to the high returns to college" (250), and that "college costs relative to family income came down rapidly in the 1940s and 1950s as incomes soared and college tuitions rose more slowly" (278).

2. https://nces.ed.gov/programs/digest/d17/tables/dt17_104.10.asp.

3. Goldin and Katz, *Race between Education and Technology*, 1–2.

4. Jonathan R. Cole, *The Great American University: Its Rise to Preeminence, Its Indispensable National Role, Why It Must Be Protected* (New York: BBS Public Affairs, 2009); National Research Council, *Research Universities and the Future of America: Ten Breakthrough Actions Vital to Our Nation's Prosperity and Security* (Washington, DC: National Academies Press, 2012), www.nap.edu/catalog/13396/research
-universities-and-the-future-of-america-ten-breakthrough-actions.

5. Clark Kerr, *The Gold and the Blue: A Personal Memoir of the University of California, 1949–1967*, vol. 2, *Political Turmoil* (Berkeley: University of California Press, 2002), 92.

6. Center for Education and Workforce, Georgetown University, *America's Divided Recovery*, 3, https://cew.georgetown.edu/wp-content/uploads/Americas
-Divided-Recovery-web.pdf.

7. Center for Education and Workforce, *Recovery: Job Growth and Education Requirements through 2020*, 15, https://1gyhoq479ufd3yna29x7ubjn-wpengine
.netdna-ssl.com/wp-content/uploads/2014/11/Recovery2020.FR_.Web_.pdf.

8. Center for Education and Workforce, *A Decade Behind: Breaking Out of the Low-Skill Trap in the Southern Economy*, https://cew.georgetown.edu/wp-content
/uploads/MD-South.pdf.

9. Frederick M. Lawrence, "Rediscovering the Role of Public Citizen and the Art of Public Discourse," *Hill*, November 14, 2016, https://thehill.com/blogs/pundits
-blog/presidential-campaign/305794-rediscovering-the-role-of-public-citizen
-and-the-art.

10. William G. Bowen et al., *Equity and Excellence in American Higher Education* (Princeton, NJ: Princeton University Press, 2005); William G. Bowen et al., *Crossing the Finish Line: Completing College at America's Public Universities* (Princeton, NJ: Princeton University Press, 2009).

11. American Academy of Arts and Sciences, *A Primer on the College Student Journey: Facts and Figures: Getting Through and Getting Out*, www.amacad.org
/content/publications/pubContent.aspx?d=22374.

12. William G. Bowen and Michael S. McPherson, *Lesson Plan: An Agenda for Change in American Higher Education* (Princeton, NJ: Princeton University Press, 2016), 9.

13. "Gates Foundation Puts New Focus on College Completion," *Chronicle of Higher Education*, www.chronicle.com/article/Gates-Foundation-Puts-New/1331; The Lumina Foundation, *A Stronger Nation: Learning beyond High School Builds American Talent*, http://strongernation.luminafoundation.org/report/2018/#nation; The College Board, *Coming to Our Senses: Education and the American Future*, https://secure-media.collegeboard.org/digitalServices/pdf/advocacy/admissions21century/coming-to-our-senses-college-board-2008.pdf; President Barack Obama, "Address to Joint Session of Congress," February 24, 2009, https://obamawhitehouse.archives.gov/the-press-office/remarks-president-barack-obama-address-joint-session-congress.

14. NCES, IPEDS Data Center, Graduation Rate Survey.

15. American Academy of Arts and Sciences, Commission on the Future of Undergraduate Education, *The Future of Undergraduate Education: The Future of America*, 7, www.amacad.org/multimedia/pdfs/publications/researchpapers monographs/CFUE_Final-Report/Future-of-Undergraduate-Education.pdf.

16. Paul Taylor, *The Next America*, April 10, 2014, http://www.pewresearch.org/next-america/.

17. https://nces.ed.gov/programs/digest/d17/tables/dt17_104.10.asp.

18. Brit Kirwan, quoted in Bowen and McPherson, *Lesson Plan*, 46.

19. Suzanne Mettler, *Degrees of Inequality: How the Politics of Higher Education Sabotaged the American Dream* (New York: Basic Books, 2014).

20. Freeman A. Hrabowski, "Beyond the Numbers—Dreams and Values," *Public Purpose*, Spring 2011, 17–19.

21. www.washingtonpost.com/news/answer-sheet/wp/2017/12/20/the-surprising-thing-google-learned-about-its-employees-and-what-it-means-for-todays-students/.

22. www.insidehighered.com/blogs/leadership-higher-education/toughest-job-nation.

23. James Duderstadt, *A University for the 21st Century* (Ann Arbor: University of Michigan Press, 2000), 50.

24. The Aspen Institute's *Renewal and Progress: Strengthening Higher Education Leadership in a Time of Rapid Change* discusses the many challenges and opportunities facing university presidents today. See https://assets.aspeninstitute.org/content/uploads/2017/05/Renewal_and_Progress_CEP-05122017.pdf.

25. The Aspen Institute Task Force on the Future of the College Presidency, *Renewal and Progress: Strengthening Higher Education Leadership in a Time of Rapid Change*, May 2017, www.aspeninstitute.org/publications/renewal-progress-strengthening-higher-education-leadership-time-rapid-change/; American Academy of Arts and Sciences, Commission on the Future of Undergraduate Education, *The Future of Undergraduate Education, the Future of America*, www.amacad.org/content/Research/researchproject.aspx?i=21999.

Chapter 3. Culture Change Is Hard as Hell

1. White House Summit on College Opportunity, December 4, 2014.

2. James Duderstadt, *A University for the 21st Century* (Ann Arbor: University of Michigan Press, 2000), 6–7.

3. Eric Weiner, *The Geography of Bliss: One Grump's Search for the Happiest Places in the World* (New York: Twelve, 2008), 3.

4. Elliot L. Hirshman and Freeman A. Hrabowski, "Meet Societal Challenges by Changing the Culture on Campus," *Chronicle of Higher Education*, January 16, 2011, www.chronicle.com/article/Meet-Societal-Challenges-by/125937.

5. Boris Groysberg et al., "The Leader's Guide to Corporate Culture," *Harvard Business Review*, January–February 2018, https://hbr.org/2018/01/the-culture-factor.

6. Edward Warfield IV, "Baltimore's Institutional Leadership at a Crossroads," *Warfield's Business Record*, September 11, 1992, cited in George R. LaNoue, *Improbable Excellence: The Saga of UMBC* (Durham, NC: Carolina Academic Press, 2016), 115–16.

7. https://news.umbc.edu/chronicle-names-umbc-one-of-the-best-universities-to-work-for-with-honors/.

8. A thoughtful work on organizational change in higher education that has informed our thinking is Adrianna Kezar, *How Colleges Change: Understanding, Leading, and Enacting Change* (New York: Routledge, 2014).

Chapter 4. Leadership and Empowerment

1. Kenneth I. Maton et al., "Enhancing Representation, Retention, and Achievement of Minority Students in Higher Education: A Social Transformation Theory of Change," in *Toward Positive Youth Development: Transforming Schools and Community Programs*, ed. Marybeth Shinn and Hirokazu Yoshikawa (New York: Oxford University Press, 2008), 115–32.

2. William G. Bowen and Michael S. McPherson, *Lesson Plan: An Agenda for Change in American Higher Education* (Princeton, NJ: Princeton University Press, 2016), 136.

3. Aspen Institute, Task Force on the Future of the College Presidency, *Renewal and Progress: Strengthening Higher Education Leadership in a Time of Rapid Change*, May 2017, https://assets.aspeninstitute.org/content/uploads/2017/05/Renewal_and_Progress_CEP-05122017.pdf.

4. Aspen Institute, *Renewal and Progress*.

5. Aspen Institute, *Renewal and Progress*.

6. Aspen Institute, *Renewal and Progress*.

7. Aspen Institute, *Renewal and Progress*.

8. A discussion about shared governance with current and former faculty senate presidents in November 2015 informed this book. Participants in the discussion included Kathleen Carroll, Timothy Nohe, Philip Rous, Sarah Shin, Tim Topoleski, and Terry Worchesky.

9. Kenneth I. Maton et al., "The Meyerhoff Scholars Program: A Strengths-Based, Institution-Wide Approach to Increasing Diversity in Science, Technology, Engineering, and Mathematics," *Mount Sinai Journal of Medicine* 79 (5): 610–23, www.ncbi.nlm.nih.gov/pmc/articles/PMC3444508/.

Chapter 5. Grit and Greatness

1. https://president.umbc.edu/founders-day-speech/.

2. https://president.umbc.edu/founders-day-speech/.

3. Edwin Warfield III et al., *A Plan for Expanding the University of Maryland* (Annapolis: State of Maryland, 1960), cited in Albin O. Kuhn Library and Gallery, University of Maryland, Baltimore County, *UMBC at 50: Sharing the Past, Building the Future* (2016), 5.

4. George LaNoue, *Improbable Excellence: The Saga of UMBC* (Durham, NC: Carolina Academic Press, 2016), 9–14.

5. www.umbc.edu/blogs/library/A_Campus_Is_Born.pdf.

6. Michael Hooker, Installation as Chancellor, University of Maryland, Baltimore County, October 29, 1986.

7. Freeman A. Hrabowski III, Installation as President, University of Maryland, Baltimore County, September 24, 1993.

8. www.umbc.edu/blogs/umbcnews/2002/07/howard_hughes_medical _institut.html.

9. www.bestworkforce.org/sites/default/files/research/downloads/Bridge%20 for%20All%20Higher%20Ed%20report.pdf.

10. www.nytimes.com/2006/05/25/opinion/25thu4.html.

11. http://issues.org/33-3/toward-a-more-diverse-research-community -models-of-success/; https://news.aamc.org/diversity/article/how-undergraduate -programs-boost-minority-success/.

12. www.washingtonpost.com/opinions/u-md-baltimore-county-serves -its-students-well/2012/04/09/gIQAneVv6S_story.html?utm_term=.06ebe 3b247d5.

13. Carol Dweck, *Mindset: The New Psychology of Success* (New York: Ballantine Books, 2006); Angela Duckworth, *Grit: The Power of Passion and Perseverance* (New York: Scribner, 2016).

14. Jim Collins and Jerry I. Porras, *Built to Last: Successful Habits of Visionary Companies* (New York: HarperCollins, 1994).

15. A discussion in June 2015 about our research park, bwtech@UMBC, that informed this book included David Fink, David Gleason, Ellen Hemmerly, William LaCourse, and Gregory Simmons.

Chapter 6. At the Crossroads

1. Center on Education and the Workforce, Georgetown University, *America's Divided Recovery: College Haves and Have-Nots* (2016), https://cew.georgetown.edu /cew-reports/americas-divided-recovery/.

2. https://en.wikipedia.org/wiki/Majority_minority; www.census.gov/quick facts/fact/table/md/PST045217.

3. National Academy of Sciences, National Academy of Engineering, and Institute of Medicine, *Rising above the Gathering Storm: Energizing and Employing America for a Brighter Economic Future* (Washington, DC: National Academies Press, 2007), xi, www.nap.edu/catalog/11463/rising-above-the-gathering-storm -energizing-and-employing-america-for.

4. National Academy of Sciences, National Academy of Engineering, and Institute of Medicine, *Expanding Underrepresented Minority Participation: America's Science and Technology Talent at the Crossroads* (Washington, DC: National Academies Press, 2011), 1, www.nap.edu/catalog/12984/expanding-underrepresented -minority-participation-americas-science-and-technology-talent-at.

5. National Academy of Sciences et al., *Expanding Underrepresented Minority Participation*, 2.

6. Underrepresented minorities in STEM in the United States include African Americans, Hispanics and Latinos, Native Americans and Alaska Natives, and Pacific Islanders. Pacific Islanders have only been included in the category when national data sources have reported them as a category separate from Asians.

7. National Academy of Sciences et al., *Expanding Underrepresented Minority Participation*, 36; National Science Foundation, *Women, Minorities, and Persons with Disabilities in Science and Engineering* (2017), www.nsf.gov/statistics/2017/nsf17310 /digest/occupation/overall.cfm and www.nsf.gov/statistics/2017/nsf17310/digest /introduction/.

8. National Academy of Sciences et al., *Expanding Underrepresented Minority Participation*, 3.

9. Freeman A. Hrabowski III and Peter H. Henderson, "Toward a More Diverse Research Community: Models of Success," *Issues in Science and Technology* 33, no. 3 (Spring 2017), https://issues.org/toward-a-more-diverse-research -community-models-of-success/.

10. US Department of Education, National Center for Education Statistics, Digest of Education Statistics, https://nces.ed.gov/programs/digest/d15/tables /dt15_306.10.asp?current=yes; National Science Foundation, *Women, Minorities, and Persons with Disabilities in Science and Engineering* (2015), www.nsf.gov /statistics/2017/nsf17310/digest-fod-minorities/degree-share.cfm.

11. UCLA, Higher Education Research Institute, "Degrees of Success: Bachelor's Degree Completion Rates among Initial STEM Majors," www.heri .ucla.edu/nih/downloads/2010%20-%20Hurtado,%20Eagan,%20Chang%20-%20 Degrees%20of%20Success.pdf.

12. National Academy of Sciences et al., *Expanding Underrepresented Minority Participation*, 12.

13. National Academy of Sciences et al., *Expanding Underrepresented Minority Participation*; President's Council of Advisors on Science and Technology, *Engage to Excel, Producing One Million Additional College Graduates with Degrees in Science, Technology, Engineering, and Mathematics* (Washington, DC: Executive Office of the President, February 2012), https://obamawhitehouse.archives.gov/sites/default /files/microsites/ostp/pcast-engage-to-excel-final_2-25-12.pdf; Bayer Corporation, *STEM Education, Science Literacy, and the Innovation Workforce in America: 2012 Analysis and Insights from the Bayer Facts of Science Education Surveys* (Pittsburgh: Bayer Corporation, 2012), www.se.edu/dept/native-american-center/files/2012/04 /STEM-Education-Science-Literacy-and-the-Innovation-Workforce-in-America .pdf.

14. US Department of Education, National Center for Education Statistics, "Fast Facts: Historically Black Colleges and Universities," https://nces.ed.gov /fastfacts/display.asp?id=667.

15. American Institutes for Research, *The Role of Historically Black Colleges and Universities as Pathway Providers: Institutional Pathways to the STEM PhD among Black Students* (2014), www.air.org/sites/default/files/downloads/report/Role%20of%20 HBCUs%20in%20STEM%20PhDs%20for%20Black%20Students.pdf.

16. Monica Anderson, "A Look at Historically Black Colleges and Universities

as Howard Turns 150," Pew Research Center, February 28, 2017, www.pew
research.org/fact-tank/2017/02/28/a-look-at-historically-black-colleges-and
-universities-as-howard-turns-150/.

17. Protests against "Tilted Acres," a fictionalized version of the now-defunct
Gwynn Oak Amusement Park, appear in the movie *Hairspray*. The carousel is
now installed on the National Mall in Washington, DC, with a sign that notes its
historical importance.

18. A discussion in April 2016 about racial climate and faculty diversity that
informed this chapter included Mauricio Bustos, Scott Casper, Tyson King-
Meadows, Patrice McDermott, Kimberly Moffitt, Yvette Mozie-Ross, Chris
Murphy, Autumn Reed, Valerie Thomas, and Nancy Young.

19. Leah Libresco, "Here Are the Demands from Students Protesting Racism
at 51 Colleges," FiveThirtyEight, December 3, 2015, https://fivethirtyeight.com
/features/here-are-the-demands-from-students-protesting-racism-at-51-colleges/.

20. A discussion in 2015 about civic agency and community engagement that
informed this chapter, as well as discussions elsewhere in the book, included
Beverly Bickel, Lee Boot, Stephen Bradley, David Hoffman, Tyson King-Meadows,
Jason Loviglio, Kathy O'Dell, and Gregory Simmons. See also http://circa.umbc
.edu/imagining-america-2015/.

21. http://baltimoreuprising2015.org/.

22. https://retriever.umbc.edu/2015/11/bsu-marches-in-response-to-blackface
-on-campus/

23. Email from President Freeman Hrabowski and Provost Philip Rous to the
UMBC community, re: Campus Response to Offensive Social Media Posts,
November 4, 2015.

Chapter 7. Pillars of Success

1. www.umbc.edu/blogs/umbcnews/2002/07/howard_hughes_medical
_institut.html.

2. College Board, "Calculus and Community: A History of the Emerging
Scholars Program," May 2001, https://research.collegeboard.org/sites/default
/files/publications/2012/7/misc2001-1-calculus-emerging-scholars-program.pdf.

3. Kenneth I. Maton and Freeman A. Hrabowski III, "Increasing the Number
of African American PhDs in the Sciences and Engineering: A Strengths-Based
Approach," *American Psychologist* 59, no. 6 (2004): 548.

4. Willie Pearson Jr. and Freeman A. Hrabowski III, "Recruiting and Retaining Talented African American Males in College Science and Engineering," *Journal
of College Science Teaching* 22, no. 4 (1993): 234–38.

5. These studies include Pearson and Hrabowski, "Recruiting and Retaining
Talented African American Males"; Freeman A. Hrabowski III and Kenneth I.
Maton, "Enhancing the Success of African-American Students in the Sciences:
Freshman Year Outcomes," *School Science and Mathematics* 95, no. 1 (January 1995):
19–27; Freeman A. Hrabowski III et al., "The Recruitment and Retention of Talented
African Americans in Science: The Role of Mentoring," in *Diversity in Higher
Education*, ed. H. T. Frierson Jr. (Greenwich, CT: JAI, 1997), 103–14; Freeman A.
Hrabowski III et al., "Preparing the Way: A Qualitative Study of High-Achieving
African American Males and the Role of the Family," *American Journal of Commu-*

nity Psychology 26, no. 4 (August 1998): 639–68; Freeman A. Hrabowski III et al., "African-American College Students Excelling in the Sciences: College and Post-college Outcomes in the Meyerhoff Scholars Program," *Journal of Research in Science Teaching* 37, no. 7 (2000): 629–54; Maton and Hrabowski, "Increasing the Number of African American PhDs"; Freeman A. Hrabowski III, "Fostering First-Year Success of Underrepresented Minorities," in *Challenging and Supporting the First-Year Student: A Handbook for Improving the First Year of College,* ed. John Gardner et al. (San Francisco: John Wiley & Sons, 2005), 125–40; Freeman A. Hrabowski III et al., "Opening an African American STEM Program to Talented Students of All Races: Evaluation of the Meyerhoff Scholars Program, 1991–2005," in *Charting the Future of College Affirmative Action: Legal Victories, Continuing Attacks, and New Research,* ed. G. Orfield et al. (Los Angeles: Civil Rights Project at UCLA, 2007), 125–56; Freeman A. Hrabowski III et al., "Enhancing Representation, Retention and Achievement of Minority Students in Higher Education: A Social Transformation Theory of Change," in *Toward Positive Youth Development: Transforming Schools and Community Programs,* ed. M. Shinn and H. Yoshikawa (New York: Oxford University Press, 2008), 115–32; Kenneth I. Maton et al., "Enhancing the Number of African Americans Who Pursue STEM PhDs: Meyerhoff Scholarship Program Outcomes, Processes, and Individual Predictors," *Journal of Women and Minorities in Science and Engineering* 15, no. 1 (2009): 15–37; Freeman A. Hrabowski III and Kenneth Maton, "Beating the Odds: Successful Strategies to Increase African American Male Participation in Science," in *Black American Males in Higher Education: Diminishing Proportions,* ed. Henry F. Frierson et al. (Bingley, UK: Emerald Group, 2009), 207–28; Freeman A. Hrabowski III et al., "African American Males in the Meyerhoff Scholars Program: Outcomes and Processes," in *Beyond Stock Stories and Folktales: African Americans' Paths to STEM Fields,* ed. Henry Frierson and William F. Tate (Bingley, UK: Emerald Group, 2011), 47–70; and Kenneth I. Maton et al., "The Meyerhoff Scholars Program: A Strengths-Based, Institution-Wide Approach to Increasing Diversity in Science, Technology, Engineering, and Mathematics," *Mount Sinai Journal of Medicine* 79, no. 5 (September 2012): 610–23, www.ncbi.nlm.nih.gov/pmc/articles/PMC3444508/. See also Freeman A. Hrabowski III et al., *Beating the Odds: Raising Academically Successful African American Males* (New York: Oxford University Press, 1998); and Freeman A. Hrabowski III et al., *Overcoming the Odds: Raising Academically Successful African American Young Women* (New York: Oxford University Press, 2002).

6. Freeman A. Hrabowski III, *Holding Fast to Dreams: Empowering Youth from the Civil Rights Crusade to STEM Achievement* (Boston; Beacon, 2015).

7. Hrabowski, *Holding Fast to Dreams*; and Hrabowski and Maton, "Beating the Odds."

8. Maton et al., "Meyerhoff Scholars Program."

9. https://meyerhoff.umbc.edu/about/results/.

10. The data that follow were provided to the authors in custom tables by the NSF, the National Center for Science and Engineering Statistics, and the AAMC. Hrabowski and Henderson have published some of these data in an article in *AAMC News* (see https://news.aamc.org/diversity/article/how-under graduate-programs-boost-minority-success/) and two articles in *Issues in Science and Technology* (see https://issues.org/toward-a-more-diverse-research

-community-models-of-success/ and https://issues.org/challenging-us-research
-universities/).

11. A discussion in June 2015 about UMBC's scholars programs that informed
this chapter included Keith Harmon, Rehana Shafi, and Anupam Joshi.

12. https://humanitiesscholars.umbc.edu/.

13. https://linehan.umbc.edu/.

14. https://sondheim.umbc.edu/.

15. https://cwit.umbc.edu/cwitscholars/.

16. National Academy of Sciences, National Academy of Engineering, and
Institute of Medicine, *Rising above the Gathering Storm: Energizing and Employing
America for a Brighter Economic Future* (Washington, DC: National Academies Press,
2007), 5–7, www.nap.edu/catalog.php?record_id=11463.

17. Executive Office of the President, President's Council of Advisors on
Science and Technology, *Prepare and Inspire: K–12 Education in Science, Technology,
Engineering, and Mathematics (STEM) for America's Future*, September 2010, https://
obamawhitehouse.archives.gov/sites/default/files/microsites/ostp/pcast-stem-ed
-final.pdf.

18. https://sherman.umbc.edu/.

19. http://chemistry.umbc.edu/undergraduate/b-a-in-chem-edu-bioc/;
http://chemistry.umbc.edu/undergraduate/b-a-in-chemistry-education-physical
-chemistry/; http://physics.umbc.edu/undergrad/undergrad_degrees/ba/;
http://biology.umbc.edu/undergrad/undergraduate-programs/b-a-in-biology
-education/.

20. A discussion in June 2015 about our partnership with Lakeland Elemen-
tary/Middle School that informed this chapter included Rehana Shafi, Gregory
Simmons, Joby Taylor, and Michele Wolff.

21. https://sherman.umbc.edu/lakeland/.

22. https://news.umbc.edu/umbc-receives-1-3-million-grant-from-the-alfred
-p-sloan-foundation-to-diversify-economics-ph-d-s/.

23. Meyerhoff Adaptation Partnership, Mid-term Report, March 1, 2017.

24. Meyerhoff Adaptation Partnership, Mid-term Report.

Chapter 8. An Honors University

1. UMBC, Office of Institutional Research, Analysis, and Decision Support.

2. Interviews with and documents from Jack Suess, UMBC vice president for
information technology and chief information officer, have informed the history
of computing technology and services at our university that is described in this
chapter.

3. https://honors.umbc.edu/.

4. https://meyerhoff.umbc.edu/.

5. https://ur.umbc.edu/.

6. https://ur.umbc.edu/umbc-review/.

7. https://bartleby.umbc.edu/.

8. https://fye.umbc.edu/programs/dsllc/.

9. https://stemllc.umbc.edu/.

10. Jack Suess, "UMBC Retention Implementation Plan: Moving Strategy into
Action," UMBC, October 9, 2005.

11. UMBC, Division of Undergraduate Academic Affairs, Annual Reports.

12. http://stemtransfer.org/.

13. https://stembuild.umbc.edu/.

14. William LaCourse et al., "Think 500, Not 50! A Scalable Approach to Student Success in STEM," *BMC Proceedings* 11, no. S12 (2017), https://bmcproc .biomedcentral.com/articles/10.1186/s12919-017-0094-5.

15. Jack Suess provided us with the "Chronological Table of UMBC Information Technology Deployment" for the period 1982–2018. He also provided us with two important historical documents that provide details for this chapter: UMBC, "Strategic Plan for Information Technology," April 2000; and John Fritz, "Richness and Reach: A Strategic Plan for Teaching, Learning, and Technology (TLT)," UMBC, Spring 2007.

16. Freeman Hrabowski and John Suess, "Enabling Transformative Change," *EDUCAUSE Review*, November/December 2016, 8–9, https://er.educause.edu /articles/2016/10/enabling-transformative-change.

17. https://icubed.umbc.edu/.

18. A discussion in 2015 about our data warehouse and data analytics at UMBC that informed this chapter included Michael Dillon, Yvette Mozie-Ross, and Jack Suess. See also Freeman A. Hrabowski III et al., "Assessment and Analytics in Institutional Transformation," *EDUCAUSE Review*, September/ October 2011, 15–28, https://er.educause.edu/articles/2011/9/assessment-and -analytics-in-institutional-transformation.

19. Suess, "UMBC Retention Implementation Plan"; Suess, "Chronological Table."

20. https://rex.umbc.edu/.

Chapter 9. A Challenge of Quality

1. American Academy of Arts and Sciences, Commission on the Future of Undergraduate Education, *The Future of Undergraduate Education: The Future of America*, 1, www.amacad.org/multimedia/pdfs/publications/researchpapers monographs/CFUE_Final-Report/BRIEF_Future-of-Undergraduate-Education .pdf.

2. American Academy of Arts and Sciences, *Future of Undergraduate Education*, 4.

3. National Academy of Sciences, National Academy of Engineering, and Institute of Medicine, *Expanding Underrepresented Minority Participation: American's Science and Technology Talent at the Crossroads* (Washington, DC: National Academies Press, 2011), 40.

4. University of California, Los Angeles, Higher Education Research Institute, *Degrees of Success: Bachelor's Degree Completion Rates among Initial STEM Majors*, HERI Research Brief (January 2010), www.heri.ucla.edu/nih/downloads/2010 %20-%20Hurtado,%20Eagan,%20Chang%20-%20Degrees%20of%20Success.pdf.

5. Mitchell J. Chang et al., "Considering the Impact of Racial Stigmas and Science Identity: Persistence among Biomedical and Behavioral Science Aspirants," *Journal of Higher Education* 82, no. 5 (2011): 564–96; Sylvia Hurtado et al., "Priming the Pump or the Sieve: Institutional Contexts and URM STEM Degree Attainments," Presentation, Association for Institutional Research, New Orleans,

Louisiana, 2012, http://heri.ucla.edu/nih/downloads/AIR2012HurtadoPriming thePump.pdf.

6. President's Council of Advisors on Science and Technology, *Engage to Excel: Producing One Million Additional College Graduates with Degrees in Science, Technology, Engineering, and Mathematics*, Executive Office of the President, February 2012, https://obamawhitehouse.archives.gov/sites/default/files/microsites/ostp/pcast -engage-to-excel-final_2-25-12.pdf.

7. National Research Council, *Discipline-Based Education Research: Understanding and Improving Undergraduate Learning in Science and Engineering* (Washington, DC: National Academies Press, 2012), www.nap.edu/catalog/13362/discipline -based-education-research-understanding-and-improving-learning-in-under graduate.

8. We are grateful to Bill LaCourse, dean of UMBC's CNMS, for conversations that have informed the discussion of "Discovery as Learning" in this chapter. This discussion is also informed by Laura E. Ott et al., "Discovery Learning: Development of a Unique Active Learning Environment for Introductory Chemistry," *Journal of the Scholarship of Teaching and Learning* 18, no. 4 (December 2018): 161–80.

9. Melanie Cooper and Michael Klymkowsky, "Chemistry, Life, the Universe, and Everything: A New Approach to General Chemistry, and a Model for Curriculum Reform," *Journal of Chemical Education* 90 (2013): 1116–22.

10. Jeffrey Mervis, "Better Intro Courses Seen as Key to Reducing Attrition of STEM Majors," *Science*, October 15, 2010, 306, http://science.sciencemag.org /content/330/6002/306.

11. R. M. Pollack and W. R. LaCourse, "Discovery Learning in Introductory Chemistry Courses at UMBC," Files, UMBC Office of the President, January 22, 2007.

12. Ott et al., "Discovery Learning."

13. Pollack and LaCourse, "Discovery Learning in Introductory Chemistry Courses at UMBC."

14. http://chemistry.umbc.edu/overview/discovery-center/.

15. Gregory Light and Marina Micari, *Making Scientists: Six Principles for Effective College Teaching* (Cambridge, MA: Harvard University Press, 2013).

16. www.aau.edu/education-service/undergraduate-education/under graduate-stem-education-initiative.

17. www.bhef.com/publications/national-higher-education-and-workforce -initiative-forging-strategic-partnerships.

18. www.professionalsciencemasters.org/.

19. www.tpsemath.org/.

20. www.usmd.edu/usm/academicaffairs/courseredesign/.

21. https://fdc.umbc.edu/; https://fdc.umbc.edu/academic-innovation -competition/.

22. Discussions in June and July 2015 about academic innovation at UMBC that informed this chapter included many current and former colleagues, including Raji Baradwaj, Taryn Bayles, Tara Carpenter, Tiffany Gierasch, Linda Hodges, Tracy Irish, William LaCourse, Diane Lee, Jeffrey Leips, Sarah Leupen, Eileen O'Brien, Marc Olano, Timothy Phin, Ann Rubin, Sally Shivnan, Anne

Spence, and Marc Zupan. Additional resources informing this chapter included Linda C. Hodges, "Academic Transformation at UMBC," December 5, 2013; and Peter Henderson, "UMBC: Undergraduate STEM Education Programs and Initiatives," February 2015.

23. https://cnms.umbc.edu/teachinglearning/learning-centers/castle/.

24. https://biology.umbc.edu/directory/faculty/person/VB77771/.

25. www.summerinstitutes.org/about.

26. www.chronicle.com/article/Not-Your-Grandfathers-Comp/137951.

27. https://innovationfund.umbc.edu/how-to-apply/.

28. https://innovationfund.umbc.edu/projects/.

Chapter 10. The New American College

1. Ernest L. Boyer, "Creating the New American College," *Chronicle of Higher Education*, March 9, 1994.

2. We are grateful to John Martello for several interviews that have informed the discussion in this chapter. Also, a discussion in June 2015 that informed the sections in this chapter on service learning and the Shriver Center included John Martello, Michele Wolff, LaMar Davis, and Eric Ford.

3. https://shrivercenter.umbc.edu/.

4. https://shrivercenter.umbc.edu/shriver-peaceworker/.

5. University of Maryland, Baltimore County; University of Maryland, Baltimore; University of Baltimore; Towson State University; Morgan State University; Coppin State University; Johns Hopkins University; Goucher College; Notre Dame of Maryland University; and Loyola College.

6. In 1999, Deutsche Bank bought Alex. Brown & Sons, which was renamed Deutsche Bank Alex Brown.

7. A discussion in June 2015 about UMBC's entrepreneurship initiatives that informed this chapter included Gregory Simmons, Vivian Armor, Amy Froide, George Karabatis, and Gib Mason.

8. http://entrepreneurship.umbc.edu/.

9. https://entrepreneurship.umbc.edu/competitions/umbcs-idea -competition/.

10. https://entrepreneurship.umbc.edu/competitions/the-cangialosi-business -innovation-competition/.

11. https://civiclife.umbc.edu/breakingground/.

12. A discussion in 2015 about civic agency and community engagement that informed this chapter, as well as discussions elsewhere in the book, included Beverly Bickel, Lee Boot, Stephen Bradley, David Hoffman, Tyson King-Meadows, Jason Loviglio, Kathy O'Dell, and Gregory Simmons.

13. David Hoffman et al., "Democratic Agency and the Visionary's Dilemma," *Diversity and Democracy* 18, no. 1 (2015): 2, www.aacu.org/diversitydemocracy/2015 /winter/hoffman.

14. Hoffman et al., "Democratic Agency."

15. David Hoffman, "Fostering Civic Agency by Making Education (and Ourselves) 'Real,'" in *Democracy's Education: Public Work, Citizenship and the Future of Colleges and Universities*, ed. Harry C. Boyte (Nashville: Vanderbilt University Press, 2015), 154.

16. Hoffman et al., "Democratic Agency," 2.

17. Discussion with David Hoffman, June 2015.

18. Email from David Hoffman to Peter Henderson, June 17, 2015.

19. Hoffman, "Fostering Civic Agency," 158.

20. David Hoffman, "Ethos Matters: Inspiring Students as Democracy's Co-creators," NASPA, September 29, 2016, 4, www.naspa.org/about/blog/ethos-matters-inspiring-students-as-democracys-co-creators.

21. Hoffman, "Fostering Civic Agency," 158.

22. Discussion with David Hoffman, June 2015.

23. Hoffman, "Fostering Civic Agency," 156.

24. Hoffman, "Fostering Civic Agency," 159.

25. Hoffman, "Fostering Civic Agency," 156.

26. https://sga.umbc.edu/proveit/.

27. Email from David Hoffman to Peter Henderson, June 17, 2015.

28. Email from David Hoffman to Peter Henderson, June 17, 2015.

29. Email from David Hoffman to Peter Henderson, June 17, 2015.

30. Hoffman, "Fostering Civic Agency," 159.

31. https://breakingground.umbc.edu/about/history/.

32. https://africanastudies.umbc.edu/news/?id=57352.

33. We are grateful to Tyson King-Meadows for sharing insights with us about this course during one of our discussion sessions.

Chapter 11. Difficult Conversations

1. A discussion in June 2015 about women faculty in science and engineering and our ADVANCE program that informed this chapter included Kathleen Hoffman, Patrice McDermott, Autumn Reed, Phyllis Robinson, Julia Ross, and Janet Rutledge. Patrice McDermott and Autumn Reed also reviewed a draft of this chapter and provided insights and edits that were extremely helpful in finalizing the story about ADVANCE for this chapter.

2. http://web.mit.edu/fnl/women/women.pdf.

3. National Academy of Sciences, National Academy of Engineering, and Institute of Medicine, *Beyond Bias and Barriers: Fulfilling the Potential of Women in Academic Science and Engineering* (Washington, DC: National Academies Press, 2007), www.nap.edu/catalog/11741/beyond-bias-and-barriers-fulfilling-the-potential-of-women-in.

4. Carole McCann et al., "Report of the Ad Hoc Committee on Gender Equity in Science, Mathematics, Information Technology, and Engineering," June 22, 2000.

5. UMBC, Proposal to National Science Foundation, "ADVANCE Institutional Transformation Award University of Maryland, Baltimore County," September 24, 2003.

6. https://advance.umbc.edu/wise/.

7. www.nsf.gov/crssprgm/advance/.

8. UMBC, Proposal to National Science Foundation, "ADVANCE Institutional Transformation Award University of Maryland, Baltimore County," September 24, 2003. See also https://advance.umbc.edu/framing-success-for-women-faculty-in-stem/.

9. https://advance.umbc.edu/search-committee-training/.

10. https://advance.umbc.edu/faculty-development-plans/.

11. https://advance.umbc.edu/eminent-scholar/.

12. https://facultydiversity.umbc.edu/files/2013/10/Family-Support-Brochure .pdf.

13. www.usmd.edu/regents/bylaws/SectionII/II225.pdf.

14. Marc Goulden et al., *Staying Competitive: Patching America's Leaky Pipeline in the Sciences* (Berkeley, CA: Center for American Progress, 2009), www.american progress.org/issues/women/reports/2009/11/10/6979/staying-competitive/.

15. https://advance.umbc.edu/on-ramps/.

16. https://careerlifebalance.umbc.edu/.

17. https://advance.umbc.edu/leadership-cohorts/.

18. https://advance.umbc.edu/tenuredtenure-track-data/.

Chapter 12. Looking in the Mirror

1. A discussion in April 2016 about racial climate and faculty diversity that informed this chapter included Mauricio Bustos, Scott Casper, Tyson King-Meadows, Patrice McDermott, Kimberly Moffitt, Yvette Mozie-Ross, Chris Murphy, Autumn Reed, Valerie Thomas, and Nancy Young. Autumn Reed reviewed a draft of this chapter and provided insights and edits that were extremely helpful in finalizing the story about our work in diversifying UMBC's faculty.

2. Summary (Meeting Minutes and Action Items), CAHSS Black Faculty Committee Meeting with Provost Elliot Hirshman, April 2, 2010.

3. https://facultydiversity.umbc.edu/diversity-initiatives/underrepresented -minority-faculty-executive-committee/.

4. Ben Myers, "Where Are the Minority Professors?," *Chronicle of Higher Education*, February 14, 2016, www.chronicle.com/interactives/where-are-the -minority-professors; www.amacad.org/sites/default/files/academy/multimedia /pdfs/publications/researchpapersmonographs/PRIMER-cfue/Primer-on-the -College-Student-Journey.pdf (see fig. K).

5. www.brookings.edu/blog/brown-center-chalkboard/2017/10/05/ examining-faculty-diversity-at-americas-top-public-universities.

6. National Academy of Sciences, National Academy of Engineering, and Institute of Medicine, *Expanding Underrepresented Minority Participation: America's Science and Technology Talent at the Crossroads* (Washington, DC: National Academies Press, 2011), www.nap.edu/catalog/12984/expanding-underrepresented -minority-participation-americas-science-and-technology-talent-at.

7. Myers, "Where Are the Minority Professors?"

8. https://facultydiversity.umbc.edu/.

9. https://facultydiversity.umbc.edu/postdocs/.

10. https://facultydiversity.umbc.edu/faculty-groups-2/.

11. https://facultydiversity.umbc.edu/diversity-initiatives/umbc-outlist/.

12. https://president.umbc.edu/state-of-the-university-2015/.

13. Email from Philip Rous and Tyson King-Meadows to UMBC Community, November 25, 2015.

14. https://facultydiversity.umbc.edu/stride/background/.

15. https://cahss.umbc.edu/events/?id=39451.

16. https://facultydiversity.umbc.edu/natural-sciences-pre-professoriate
-fellowship-chemistry-and-biochemistry/.

17. https://facultydiversity.umbc.edu/faculty-groups-2/.

18. www.facultydiversity.org/fsp-bootcamp.

19. Susan Sturm cited in UMBC, Proposal to National Science Foundation, "ADVANCE Institutional Transformation Award University of Maryland, Baltimore County," September 24, 2003.

Chapter 13. Success Is Never Final

1. The Trump administration has rescinded the 2011 guidance, and as of this writing (fall 2018), we are awaiting new regulations.

Index

Page numbers in *italics* indicate tables.

teaching and learning (*continued*)
projects, 68; "weed-out" culture in, 163, 164, 166. *See also* learning
team-based learning (TBL), 77–78, 174–76
technology, harnessing for learning, 167
Title IX, 15, 265–66, 271–72, 273–74
transfer student seminars, 147
Transforming Postsecondary Education in Mathematics, 172
Treisman, Uri, 57, 115
True Grit (mascot), 7, 67

University of Illinois at Urbana-Champaign, 95
University of Maryland, Baltimore County (UMBC): basketball victory over UVA, 3–4, 5–6; challenges faced by, 58–59; chancellors of, xvi; culture of, x–xi; fiftieth anniversary of, 58; history of, xiii–xiv, 60–62; overview of, 4–5; President's Council, 53–54, 113; as research university, 63–64; strategic questions for, 59–60; strengths of, 27–28. *See also specific colleges and divisions*
University of Maryland, College Park (UMCP), 39, 60, 123, 183–84
University of Michigan: Center for Research on Learning and Teaching Players, 221, 254; STRIDE program of, 252–53
University of Missouri, protest at, 97–98
University of North Carolina, 137–38

University of Virginia, 3–4, 5–6, 8, 26
University System of Maryland (USM): Board of Regents, 182; Course Redesign Initiative, 45, 164–65, 172–73, 177–80; Family Support Plan, 228
US News & World Report rankings, 4, 64

values, shared, 38, 53–54, 60, 185, 248–49
Vest, Chuck, 212
vision: articulation of, and culture change, 37, 38–39; of inclusive excellence, x, 57, 62–63, 65

Washington Post, 10, 11, 66
We Believe You, 268
Weidemann, Craig, 195
Weiner, Eric, x, 36
Wieman, Carl, 171
Wi-Fi deployment and course engagement, 166–67
women: as faculty, advancement of, 210–11; MIT report on status of, 45, 211–12; on-ramps to full professor for, 261–62; in science and engineering, 211–14. *See also* ADVANCE Institutional Transformation Grant
Women in Science and Engineering (WISE) group, 214, 221–22, 226
Women's Faculty Network, 259

Yarmolinsky, Adam, 189–90, 192

Zimmerman, Lynn, 217